ORIGINARY VIOLATIONS

ORIGINARY VIOLATIONS

DISCURSIVE CONSTRUCTIONS OF CARIBBEAN MOTHERHOOD AND MOTHERLANDS

PAULA MORGAN AND **HANNAH REGIS**

UWI PRESS
The University of the West Indies Press
Mona • St Augustine • Cave Hill • Global • Five Islands

The University of the West Indies Press
7A Gibraltar Hall Road
Mona, Kingston 7, Jamaica
www.uwipress.com

A catalogue record of this book is available from the
National Library of Jamaica.

ISBN: 978-976-658-068-1 (paper)
978-976-658-069-8 (ePub)

Cover image: *Volcano Triptych 1* by Kwynn Johnson; From the Exhibition – Quiet as Drawings, March 2021, based on Marie Vieux Chauvet's *Dance on the Volcano.*
© Kwynn Johnson. Used with permission of the artist.

The authors express their sincere gratitude to Kwynn Johnson for granting permission to use this work as the cover image and for allowing her drawings to be included as a case study in chapter 1. The drawings featured in chapter 1 originate from her practice-based PhD in Cultural Studies at The University of the West Indies, entitled *How the Light Enters: Visualizing Absence and Continuity in the Jacmelian Ruinscape.*

Cover and book design by Robert Harris

Set in Minion Pro 11.2/15 x 24.

Printed in the United States of America

For my mothers and other mothers –
Leain, Yolande, Bernice, Vilma, Marlene, Hermia,
Gemma and Beverly;

my sisters – Jessy, Margot and Jill;

my daughters – Sasha, Kerri-Ann and Whitney,

and to my granddaughters – Sinae, Leanne and those yet unborn

In recognition of the unsung value of matrilineage
to contemporary Caribbean families and nations.

PAULA MORGAN

For my mother, Martha, who has shepherded me through
life's many turns, and to my daughter, Heidi, who changed
not only the story but the language of my life forever.

HANNAH REGIS

Contents

Introduction

> To reconnect our thinking and speaking with the body of this particular living human individual, a woman. Begin, we said with the material, with matter, mma, madre, mutter, moeder, modder.
>
> —*Adrienne Rich, Notes Towards A Politics of Location*

HUMAN BEINGS ARE CRAFTED WITHIN FAMILIES, communities, nations and nation families of the Global South or North, all of which are embedded in complex and overlapping networks of social relations. These social relations, based on race, class, gender and nationality, are invariably structured around axes of dominance. Arguably, the foundational relationship for each human person is embedded in maternal more so than paternal nurturance or lack thereof. This book explores the potentialities of societies and individuals who have suffered violence from inception/birth to create viable individual, familial and societal orders. It explores correlations between motherhood and symbolic appropriations of violating historical experiences; the narrativized tropes of racialized sexual violence against women in dynamics of national and diasporic identity formation; correlations between collective and personal histories, cultural dispossession, loss and mourning; haunted and suppressed ontologies from birth; and potentialities for recuperation and new beginnings. The pattern of association between the frames of reference as it pertains to 'motherhood', 'matrifocality' and 'matrilineal' persists throughout this work, but in some cases, the crises and issues they provoke are quite distinct. 'Motherhood' should, therefore, not be read as a homogenous entity since the term serves different functions in the contexts within which it appears in the narratives.

Andrea O'Reilly defines matrifocality as "mother-focused" and "characteristic of a cultural cosmology that radically differs from the exaltation of the nuclear family as the most central building block of a society". She suggests that "[cultures] which allow for matrifocality tend to be much more communal in nature" (O'Reilly 2010, 736). An evolving ethnographic study of matrifocality, both in the Caribbean and globally, reflects shifting attitudes towards the term, with more recent research emphasizing its cultural significance and the central role of women in these family structures. The growing body of work seeks to challenge reductive or pathologizing narratives, instead recognizing matrifocality as a distinctive and integral aspect of specific communities. Leighan Renaud's doctoral thesis, *Representations of Matrifocality in Contemporary Anglophone Caribbean Fiction*, offers one such contribution and is situated within the broader framework of feminist literary scholarship that aims to underscore women's contributions to male-centred literary histories. This significant scholarship on Caribbean women writers and their representations of mother characters is undeniably invaluable. *Originary Violations* diverges from Renaud's research by encompassing the psychological and sociological dimensions of parenting, attachment and care. Unlike Renaud's more narrowly focused thesis, this work adopts an interdisciplinary lens to zoom in on the circuits of movement between the personal and the collective. Furthermore, we engage with a wider array of texts and authors (including male writers) and draw on connections between trauma theory and literary analysis, thus situating itself as a distinct contribution to the discourse.

Veronique Maisier's book, *Violence in Caribbean Literature: Stories of Stones and Blood*, similarly zeroes in on the theme of gendered violence and offers analyses of literary works by acclaimed anglophone and francophone authors, covering fiction by Gisèle Pineau, Patrick Chamoiseau, Michelle Cliff, Merle Hodge and others. Maisier identifies a range of poetics employed by various francophone Caribbean writers to explore the theme of gendered violence. These include the use of the child protagonist; symbolic deployment of colour to evoke innocence; a hesitancy to name perpetrators or explicitly ascribe blame for acts and violence; and nuanced portrayals of Caribbean women as "trapped in cycles of fear, resignation, and violence" even when they project outward strength (Maisier 2015, 71). She notes that while families in these narratives may exhibit matrifocality, they are not matriarchal, thus reflecting the entrenched social disempowerment of women. In her analysis of anglophone Caribbean texts, Maisier engages works such as Harold Sonny Ladoo's *No Pain Like This Body*, M. NourbeSe Philip's *Harriet's Daughter* and V.S. Naipaul's *Miguel Street*. According to Maisier, the writers employ the narrative voice of the child to heighten the emotional resonance of domestic violence writ large in every vernacular community, while emphasizing the limitations imposed on women's agency within these familial systems. *Originary Violations* diverges from Maisier's work by shifting its focus exclusively from gendered violence to the concept of mothering as a central thematical and analytical concern. While Maisier's text examines how gendered violence is depicted across a range of francophone and anglophone Caribbean texts, our analysis attends to the ways in which mothering and motherlands interface with inherited legacies of colonial violence, displacement and economic precarity, while simultaneously serving as a conduit for care and survival. Thus, our analysis broadens the discussion of gendered violence by showing how mothering is not only affected by trauma, but also operates as a response to it, shaping intergenerational narratives of survival, resistance and care in Caribbean literature.

Supriya Nair's *Pathologies of Paradise: Caribbean Detours* (2013) also comes to mind as it provides a nuanced examination of trauma narratives, situating texts like V.S. Naipaul's *The Enigma of Arrival*, Jamaica Kincaid's *My Garden* and Shani Mootoo's *Cereus Blooms at Night* within the context of the region's colonial history. Unlike *Originary Violations*, Nair does not employ the trope of the mother as a structuring or organizing principle, and her critical framework is less interdisciplinary in scope. Similarly, Sabrina Brancato's *Motherhood and Motherland in Jamaica Kincaid* (2005) explores the depiction of mother-daughter relationships in Kincaid's works and illuminates how this theme connects to the concern with colonizer/colonized power dynamics in the texts. While Brancato's work shares this study's thematic focus on motherhood and motherlands, her exclusive emphasis on a single author stands in contrast to the broader range of writers and creative workers examined in this book. Our project thus aims to establish new connections and create a dialogue between the fields of literature, ethnography, cultural studies and social science.

This multidisciplinary approach resonates with Jane Flax's arguments in *Disputed Subjects*. Drawing on her background as a psychoanalyst, Flax contends that many social practices and theoretical claims are shaped by the evasion, denial or repression of the significance of human attachment in the constitution of the subject. She contends that for psychical reasons, human beings need the sense of grounding that the concept of core, pre-discursive notions of selfhood provide. Flax contends, "the *first experience* of such attachments and their power occurs in *early childhood, especially in mother-child relations*" (Flax 2013, 105; emphasis added). This idea may be further complicated in mother-daughter relations, which are challenged by personal issues such as separation, ambivalence and rejection. In "The Conflict between Nurturance and Autonomy in Mother-Daughter Relationships and Within Feminism", Flax concludes that mothers and daughters struggle significantly with attachment and detachment in their relationship. She proposes that women generally crave nurturance and independence in adult relationships, which is indicative of their own relationships with their mothers. Conflict is inevitable in the mother-daughter relationship as the mother seeks to provide her daughter with nurturance and autonomy, which are often contradictory goals. Flax notes that mothers tend to relate more strongly to their daughters than their sons, and those daughters have more difficulty determining clear physical boundaries between themselves and their mothers. Women in therapy admit that they are uncertain about "where they end and their mothers begin" (Flax 2013, 174). This apparent closeness causes a dilemma in defining and transitioning from 'closeness' to 'independence'. Significantly, in male-dominant cultures, the importance of such relations is simultaneously romanticized, devalued, denied, repressed and placed firmly outside the public realm (Flax 2013, 118). This complicated scenario of independence, closeness, intimacy, attachment and detachment was further problematized in colonial plantation societies in the Caribbean, where the enslaved woman's womb was defined solely as a reproductive chamber that belonged to the master.

Legally, a black woman could not be raped because rape implies the capacity to give or to withhold consent to sexual intercourse. In the same manner, marriage was disallowed with its implicit capacity to give one's self within a legal bond to another. Indeed, the black woman belonged to the private enterprises of the master, wherein she served as a generating chamber to produce labour to support the plantation economy. When the slave trade was abolished in the British colonies in 1807, slave owners sought to encourage the natural reproduction of their workforce. Perceptions of women's fertility as it relates to profit were reflected in the prices demanded for African women in terms such as "breeding women" in advertisements. Hilary Beckles tells us that the commonplace mention of rape, murder and general humiliation of African Caribbean women suggests that the exploitation of female sexuality was closely enmeshed with the exploitation of their labour (Beckles 1989, 122). In other words, an enslaved woman was only a part of the exchange of objects; feelings of intimacy and bonding had no place in the equation. Even with changes in the centuries after emancipation, most Caribbean women emerging from peasant and working classes have been economic actors since the inception of modern Caribbean society.

European slave owners were also unconcerned by the paradox that arose from their denial of paternity. The enslaved mother was recognized as the only parent. In fact, fathers and grandfathers were rarely mentioned in plantation records dealing with slave families, not because colonial record-keepers acknowledged slave families as matrifocal or even matriarchal, but because managers and owners were deeply invested in the reproduction of property. The failure by white enslavers to recognize the existence of biracial children perpetuated the stereotype of the deviant black families. T.S. Simey's book, *Welfare and Planning in the West Indies,* offers insight into how Eurocentric approaches towards non-nuclear families in the Caribbean were expressed through the language used to categorize different household structures. In his research, Simey describes four distinct types of households: "The Christian Family, based on marriage and a patriarchal order . . . Faithful Concubinage, again based on a patriarchal order, possessing no legal status . . . The Companionate Family, in which the members live together for pleasure and convenience . . . The Disintegrate Family, consisting of women and children only" (Simey 1946, 82–83). What's interesting is Simey's lack of nuance and understanding about the region, which becomes clear in his suggestion that the "symptoms of serious disease in the body of modern society are only too obvious in the colonies in general, and the West Indies in particular" (Simey 1946, 8). This statement, made in the introduction, signifies that Simey means to problematize the Caribbean family as a symptom of a wider disease, rather than consider any merits of a non-nuclear family structure. Our study responds to these constructions of originary violence and traumas,[1] suppressed ontologies and epistemologies, and opens up the conversation to explore the ideological significance of intensely beautiful, numinous, yet ravaged landscapes and cityscapes in the Caribbean, and their correlation with the polyvalent trope of mothering. We probe the violations embedded within the origins of familial and societal systems, and the potentialities of individuals, island habitations and societies who have suffered violence from birth or inception to create viable individual, familial and societal orders.

Additionally, we look to a cross-section of fictional and personal discourses to explore symbolic appropriations of violating historical experiences; images of sexual violence and particularly racialized violence against women in dynamics of national and diasporic identity formation; cultural dispossession, loss and mourning; potentialities for recuperation and new beginnings. We are therefore concerned with formulating an ethical and productive stance in relation to complex and enmeshed personal and communal, national, regional and transnational histories. Caribbean nation states have been founded on migration, loss, displacement and trauma. The evolving challenges of migration, homecoming and the politics of relation to motherlands remain fluid and highly contested. Part of our aim is to apply literary and discourse analysis of interviews to the pressing social issues of alienation, abandonment and estrangement to shed light on these thorny issues and thereby diversify the research foci as bases for interventions.

FRAMEWORKS

Originary Violations analyses discursive representations of criminogenic communities, race and class relations, migration, environmental degradation and disaster preparedness. We focus on problematic intimate relations such as incest, motherhood in childhood, statutory rape, domestic servitude, gendered subjectivities and embodiments of subjugation as spatialized in images of despoiled landscapes. This contribution, rooted in the humanities, which is not the traditional port of call for scholarship on social issues, adds a valuable facet to the multi-disciplinarity of our engagements. To extrapolate on Homi Bhabha's formulation in "The World and the Home" (1992), if imperial conquest has generated a scenario in which the discombobulating impact of global movement has touched down in private domains, thus eroding the barrier between the world and the home, this becomes even more disconcerting for Caribbean women, for whom this touchdown is not simply within their homes, but within their bodies, which have been a site of invasion for imperialism's monetizing impulse. The visceral nature of this invasion has been highlighted repeatedly as an invasion associated with female embodiment, sexuality and mothering. It is reflected in the insistence that African diasporic women have felt social movements, migrations and wars within the bloodstream of their inheritance. Overseas migration from the Caribbean was male-biased until the 1970s, when women began to be much more common as overseas labour migrants, largely as a result of changing international labour markets. Since 1970, there has also been an increase in women migrating independently. These social forces have shaped the obstacles and barriers to opportunities that their children face.

In their introduction to *Reclaiming Home, Remaking Motherhood, Rewriting History*, Thiele and Drews argue that black women's narratives cannot be confined to geographical spaces; it must necessarily "include considerations of home as domestic, social and political realms" (Thiele and Drews 2009, xiv), in which women not only learn to preserve stories that narrate a people's heritage, but occupy spaces in which they can navigate and embrace kinship bonds that are tied to historical and political structures. It recalls a reclamation of the home space as an extension of national and cultural movements. Angelita Reyes avers that as early as the 1980s, Caribbean women writers have deployed the trope of marronage to engage with the themes of language, identity, race, movement and ethnicity within the context of transnational migrations (Reyes 2002, 84). This perception of an alternative community structure, rebellion, alternate homes, motherland, motherhood and communal history, illustrates the extent to which coming to know a woman's home – whether that home is articulated as a community of individuals, as a distinct and private place, or as an abstract imagining of homeland – is contingent upon conversations about mother figures in general.

Giselle Anatol's PhD thesis, "Mother Countries, Motherlands, and Mother Love: Representations of Motherhood in Twentieth-Century

Caribbean Women's Literature" (1998), is a useful and sophisticated work on the correlations between Afro-Caribbean diasporic constructions of motherhood and a fraught colonial history. For Anatol, motherland and mother country in women's writings are depicted as divergent elements, where the mother in motherland is symbolic of the land and the body, while 'mother country' is defined by its unknown vastness and unattainable nature. Anatol mines the memories of original relationships which exist between empire, continental homelands and the diaspora to illustrate, in part, the impact of fierce global, political and capitalistic machinations on familial relationships. Anatol then links both historical and metaphorical representations of the fragmented relationships between mothers and their children, and troubles the romanticized bonds to continental Africa. While a careful reading of works by women writers such as Maryse Condé, Jamaica Kincaid and Paule Marshall challenge inherited European and middle-class social norms that limit women's mobility, there is room for the important discursive appropriation and interrogation of the praxes of Caribbean *Indigenous* and *black* women's oppression which, as we demonstrate in this project, can be subverted and overcome through concerted, creative writing strategies. The aim is, therefore, to extend established tenets of critical thought that encourage us to rethink long-held notions of chattel slavery, Indigenous genocide, race and gendered structures.

To further shed light on how constructions of homelands, being and becoming are intricately tied to both the communal and private domains, and the ways that a personal and visceral memory of a torturous past reverberates across bodies, spaces and times, the opening lines of Marlon James' *The Book of Night Women* presents a particularly evocative case in point. It grants access into a strange world with shattered meaning systems and unique atmospheric tincture generated by excesses of violence:

> People think blood red. But blood don't got no colour. Not when blood wash the floor she lying on as she scream for that son of a bitch to come, the lone baby of 1785. Not when the baby wash in crimson and squealing like it just depart heaven to come to hell, another place of red. Not when the midwife know that the mother shed too much blood, and she who don't reach fourteenth birthday yet speak curse 'pon the chile and the papa, and then she drop down dead like old horse. Not when blood spurt from the skin, or spring from the

> axe, the ca-o'-nine, the whip, the cane and the blackjack every day in slave life is a day that colour red. It soon come to pass when red no different from white or black or blue or black or nothing (James 2009, 3).

In this economy, ordinary associations which shape the way we know the world are ruptured to produce contrary modalities of knowing and being. The most visceral and universal of symbolic associations are emptied of meaning. The unknowable and unspeakable are reflected in graphic obscenities and the loss of commonsensical associations, which defy human impulses to make meaning. Blood is robbed of its colour because it is spilt so fulsomely that it washes the floor; because a newborn baby with preternatural senses squeals as if it has been let down into bloody hell; because an underdeveloped child loses life blood to bring an infant to birth; because rapacious white men daily pillage and torture the bodies of women and children and men; because time and life cycles are compressed as excessive pain and blood loss transform a child into a cursing woman and precipitates her death like an old horse. The mouth expressing curses and the vagina expulsing the accursed child are conjoined. The association of the mother with processes of being, both of them oppressive and threatening at the same time, resonates in David Dabydeen's *Turner*, in which the vulnerabilities of female embodiment, rape, unwilling wombs, and enforced motherhood prove endemic to slavery's terrorist systems, yet remain imbricated in our contemporary regional and national histories.

Within the confines of this project, mother-child relationships are not limited to biological mothers and children, since maternal absenteeism, whether due to diasporic dispersion, abandonment or death (as in James' *The Book of Night Women*), is a common feature in Caribbean literature. As a result, the mother's absence often entails that the maternal role be adopted by a surrogate, who may be a grandmother, an aunt, a godmother, or a woman who has a close or intimate connection to the family. This practice is prevalent in Caribbean society as maternity is not always regarded as an individual responsibility. Merle Hodge in "Caribbean Family Values and *Beka Lamb*" explains that "a very important Caribbean family value is a collective responsibility for children. We do not consider children to be only the concern of their biological parents" (Hodge 1997, 193). Thus, in this book, we fundamentally engage varied conceptualizations of maternity in the Caribbean imaginary. Hence, historical, political and environmental constructs such as the motherland, mother country, Mother Nature, and traditional expectations of maternity are all deployed to examine the ways in which Caribbean authors assert and affirm motherhood. The significance of maternity in Caribbean society cannot be disputed since Caribbean mothers, as in other cultures, have historically been tasked with the perpetuation of cultural traditions, values and sensibilities. Nathalie Elvire Gaillot, in her PhD dissertation, "Mothering Nation: Caribbean Women Writers Interrogating National Identity through Works of Fiction", writes: "In West Indian societies, cultural history has been transmitted and preserved by passing traditional tales, personal narratives and cultural artefacts from one generation to another, typically through the matriarchal line: from mother to daughter. Mothers do not just reproduce in a biological systematic order in postcolonial feminine literature, they nurture social and historical memory of the nation, the land and the people that they represent" (Gaillot 2007, 112).

The interconnections between contemporary and historical maternal constructs complicate expressions of nation, subjectivities, belonging and facets of marronage and transcendence. Thus, foremost on the agenda is the creative exploration of issues regarding what exactly constitutes historical futures. Are they submerged, originary and unarticulated histories which thrust their rhizomes inexorably into our personal, communal and national futures? Are they unpropitiated vengeful duppies of our histories who lurk in our present, seeking pathways for bizarre materialization? More importantly, how do we negotiate the inescapable cycles of uncanny repetition which ensure that our futures relive our past? Our task is to probe the connection between violated motherlands, motherhood birth in trauma, and envisioning potentialities for empowering and ennobling futures. Trauma, with its inherent qualities of dislocation of temporalities, conflation and confusion of past, present and future, belatedness and uncanny repetition, invites interrogation of the Janus-faced concept of historical futures – transgenerational hauntology that mocks efforts towards transcendence. Caribbean artists and cultural practitioners have had a long history of grappling with meaning-making and the manner in which the violations of our traumatic origins are materializing contemporaneously in myriad troubling incarnations. It can come as no surprise that the violent origins of modern Caribbean societies have created legacies of societal restlessness and dis-ease, as well as eruptive violence which beg for therapeutic intervention to interrupt their intergenerational continuity. Increasingly, our creative writers are reaching beyond the material, social, legal and political domains to probe the interface between the psychological condition of having been colonized and contemporary cultural and material practices. They are probing societal woundedness, grappling with an ethical stance to memorialization of trauma, imaginatively pursuing modes of spatializing woundedness, as well as generating spaces in which trauma can be alleviated. We contend that these modalities are inscribed in discursive constructions of motherhood and motherlands, which are inextricably associated with dynamics of violence and violations embedded within the origins of Caribbean familial and societal systems.

Caribbean writers are thus delineating agendas which are alternative to Eurocentric paradigms, illuminating previously unexplored areas of Caribbean experience and bringing to the foreground the nexus of history, gender and cultural positioning. Susheila Nasta, in *Motherlands: Black Women's Writing from Africa, the Caribbean and South Asia,* probes the complicated connection that exists between the maternal and the nation in literature since the nation, whose values and ideology are nurtured and perpetuated predominantly by the mother, is not only viewed as a place of belonging but has also been perceived by some as a vehicle of ideological conflict rather than as fully realized individuals. The stereotypes that have prevailed in male-authored fictions position the mother as a rural folk matriarch figure, representing the doer and repository of oral traditions, the perpetuator of myths and stories, the communicator of fibres and feeling. Alternatively, women were identified as sexy mulattos or a luscious fruit living on or off the edges of urban communities, belonging to no settled culture or tradition, an object who can be scorned precisely because she epitomized rootlessness and cultural confusion (Nasta 1994, 214). She further asserts that the employment of the mothers-motherland themes in Caribbean fiction is to demythologize the glorification and illusion of these narrow categories, while moving towards a rediscovery, recreation and genesis of new forms and languages of expression. These self-assertive acts illuminate the real, personal and political relationships attendant to the realities of Caribbean women, which are intensified through ideas of alienation, displacement and methods of adaptation.

In their chapter, "The Bloodstream of Our Inheritance: Female Identity and The Caribbean Mother's Land", Ann R. Morris and Margaret M. Dunn similarly argue that, for the Caribbean woman, the notion of the motherland is especially complex, encompassing in its connotations the idea of an island home, as well as its maternal bonds that have been passed down through generations of women from continental homelands, thus shaping both individual and communal identities (Nasta 1994, 219). According to Morris and Dunn, the motherland should feel like a woman's home, a site of their heritage, but given the turbulent colonial history of the region, Caribbean women in particular find themselves at odds with their island motherland. As such, writers often symbolize their relationship to the motherland through a strained mother-daughter dyad, in order to articulate the ambivalent and precarious relationship between African Caribbean people and the land they inhabit. Morris and Dunn posit that connections to both mother and land are essential to the self-development of Caribbean women in fiction, and if a woman is denied a "developmental bond with her own mother, then the 'mother's land' itself may provide a surrogate" (Nasta 1994, 219). Thus, the relationship between the daughter and the mother, and the relationship between daughter and motherland, become symbiotic and interchangeable in Caribbean women's writing.

Offering another dimension and reading of mother, mother cultures, mother tongues and motherhood is Jamaica Kincaid, who, in her interview with Allan Vorda, points to the correlation between mother and imperial motherland. Kincaid positions both as simultaneously nurturing and progressive, threatening and desirable. Both maternal power and imperial power are narcissistic since they demand acquiescence and imitation, and in both cases, conflict arises at the first signs of emerging maturity. Commenting on Kincaid's works, Moira Ferguson observes, "the relationships between Kincaid's female protagonists and their biological mothers are crucially formative yet always mediated by intimations of life as colonized subjects" (Ferguson 1994, 1). Unquestionably, the mother-daughter relationship is formative; however, this relationship is not just simply a matter of mediation by intimations of life as colonized subjects. Instead, this relationship can be classified as a colonized relationship between the colonizer and the colonized, where the (powerful) mother fits the profile of a colonizer and the (powerless) daughter is the colonized. Kincaid confirms this in an interview with Ferguson herself, "In my first two books, I used to think I was writing about my mother and myself. Later I began to see that I was writing about the relationship between the powerful and the powerless" (Ferguson 1994, 164). Here, mothering seems to be a process of othering which produces alienation and as the child has to negotiate a separation from the mother to become an autonomous individual, so the colony has to break free from the oppressive power of the mother country. Like Nasta, who asserts that "in countries with a history of colonialism, women's quest for emancipation, self-identity and fulfilment can be seen to represent a traitorous act, a betrayal not simply of traditional codes of practices and belief but of the wider struggle for liberation and nationalism" (Nasta 1994, xv), we examine the ramifications of colonization on the female psyches, and the betrayal that self-assertion engenders. Given that these understandings of self-assertion are articulated in terms of primal paradigms of life, whereby a politics of resistance and self-autonomy is envisaged on the basis of freedom at multiple levels, we also seek to uncover the symbolic constructions of the landscape through the mother/motherland metaphor.

Jocelyn Fenton Stitt, in "Gendered Legacies of Romantic Nationalism in the Works of Michelle Cliff", points to the evocation of tropes of national landscape – wild, exotic, rapacious and fecund; valorization of the folk as vital and loving as opposed to the emaciated upper strata; and the centrality of the Afro-Caribbean mother figure. Schiff argues, however, that referencing the (black) mother in Caribbean postcolonial discourse as the point of origin displaces more complex notions of national identity, which considers racial, sexual and cultural hybridity. She credits Cliff as offering an alternative formulation:

> *No Telephone* offers a paradigm of national identity based on shared experiences rather than on essentialist notions of race or landscape. This novel suggests something more risky, more threatening to the traditional boundaries of

> nationalism than earlier West Indian formulations: that all of us in the Americas are hybrid, creole subjects and that very hybridity can be the basis for a politics of nation which is neither racially exclusionary nor complicit in the maintenance of essentialist gendered identities (Stitt 2007, 72).

Here, Stitt is clear that the trope of the mother, which is often engaged to symbolize essential qualities of the land, is displaced, as epitomized in Cliff's *No Telephone to Heaven*, which enables a radical political re-positioning of female figures as undeniable to the nationalistic agency and rooting of cultural and environmental identity. Like race or gender, land has also been a site of much conflict in the Caribbean because it represents a continuous struggle to maintain control of both the socio-economic and political power that accompanied colonial occupation. Several ecocritical scholars (many of whom were already advocates of environmental awareness and protection) found their voices within postcolonial debates and connect the struggle against sexism to the struggle to preserve and maintain the environment.

In "The Power and the Promise of Ecological Feminism", Karen J. Warren delineates this gap between environmental activism, literary scholarship and feminist values:

> Ecological feminism is the position that there are important connections – historical, experimental, symbolic, theoretical – between the domination of women and the domination of nature, an understanding which is crucial to both feminism *and* environmental ethics . . . [A]ny feminist theory and any environmental ethic which fails to take seriously the twin and interconnected dominations of women and nature is at best incomplete and at worst simply inadequate (Warren 1996, 19).

Responding to the interface between Caribbean environmental activism and woman-centred thought, chapters eight and nine in this study are devoted to underscoring the complex connections between nature, landscape and mothering as it has traditionally been conceived in the Caribbean literary imagination. This relationship between the land and maternal figures is by no means a re-inscription of the exoticizing or romanticizing that Stitt condemns, but is rather grounded in Edouard Glissant's notion of relation, that is "not made up of things that are foreign *but of shared knowledge*" (Glissant 1997, 18; emphasis added). With this symbiotic Caribbean relationality in hand, we hope to be able to take the element of intellectual and cultural exchange to pluck knowledge from alternative knowledge systems.

One of the primary themes that emerges in our investigation is the recurrence of earth-based and stratospheric motifs that are utilized to extrapolate on both the physical and spiritual dislocation and domination that happens to a people as a result of the gleaning of resources – both in a historic and contemporary sense. Nature – the earth, the sea, the wind and elements – emerges in contemporary Caribbean literature through the extended metaphor of maternal figures, not only as a source of pain and displacement, but also as a symbol and a physical site of aesthetic connection with the elements, spiritual transcendence and political empowerment. It is but one far-reaching example of how much of the work being done by Caribbean writers simultaneously considers both the socio-political and the spiritual/communal source of power in reclaiming the role of the mother to cultivate sustainable relationships with the gods, communities, and the sea and landscapes that surround them.

Similarly significant is that no exploration of Caribbean motherhood and motherlands can exclude the issue of paternity. While acknowledging the efficacy of the project of female-authored representations of motherhood, our enquiry diverges in that we explore cross-ethnic and cross-gender studies of mothering. The currency and the tight focus, for a season, on female-authored constructions of mothering has certainly been useful; however, we contend that this strand of critical exploration has matured and it is time to reinsert the myriad voices and perspectives of men into parenting and motherland discourses. The creative works of Jason Allen-Paisant, Wilson Harris, Lawrence Scott, Paul Keens-Douglas and Derek Walcott, which were selected for this project, are invested in both Afro-Caribbean and Indigenous archetypes and syncretic religious systems. That other rich Caribbean ancestral faiths and spiritualities are not included is acknowledged as a limitation of this work. The prospect of such a scope invokes exciting possibilities, but it would certainly require a more extensive investigation and space than this project permits.

Indeed, Caribbean fiction on the polyvalent trope of mother/mother cultures/mother tongues/motherhood and motherlands traffic at bewitched crossroads, where survival has usually required an enabling cooperation between impossible forces, whether that be drawing sustenance from ancestral mother countries or bonding with river deities to imagine means of defining a viable sense of self. In her essay, "Something Ancestral Recaptured: Spirit Possession Trope in Selected Feminist Fictions of the African Diaspora", Carolyn Cooper draws on what Toni Morrison has spoken of as "discredited knowledge": "that body of subterranean knowledge that is often associated with the silenced language of women and the 'primitiveness' of [the] orally transmitted" (Cooper 1991, 65). The works of Dionne Brand, Erna Brodber, Olive Senior and Grace Nichols certainly demonstrate how womenfolk from every vernacular community repossess themselves through divine embrace. The authors employ appropriate oral strategies to parallel the collective cultural context. At the centre of Dionne Brand's *A Map to the Door of No Return* and Erna Brodber's *Nothing's Mat* is an understanding of ancestral figures who represent the dimension of spirituality that is so central to women's characterizations within their texts. Aquatic spaces, memory and history are embedded and embodied refrains in these works. Remembering a time of the womb comes to the fore when breathing in submerged fluid becomes linked to concepts of migration, survival, existing in multiple worlds and the function of water as a portal to matrilineal links.

In keeping with the broad characteristics of Caribbean mothering activity and the wide-angled approach that the selection of texts allows, one is therefore able to discern trends and patterns. To this extent, each chapter focuses on multiple texts which display evolving concerns about ontological formations, originary violations, and the polyvalence of mothering in the Caribbean world. It is a method that provides a nuanced understanding on the ways that the self has been envisioned in order to open a space for more informed choices and decisions in the future. This research technique is also used to orchestrate the arrangement of the chapters. While the selection of texts can be seen as providing ten different perspectives on motherhood/mothering/mother cultures, they can be grouped in terms of their relation to particular socio-cultural, geographical and historical contexts. This divides the book into eight interrelated sections. As the subsequent chapter overview demonstrates, the texts thrive on the similarities and echoes as well as their counterpoints and distinctions.

Chapter 1, "When Ancestral Cosmologies Meet Global Modernities in Caribbean Culture in Johnson's Jacmelian Ruinscape and Miller's *The Last Warner Woman*", is a critical starting point as it underscores the ways in which Caribbean fictions are replete with yearnings for mothers, mother cultures, ancestral cosmologies and motherlands. These represent more than an imperative to demythologize an illusory colonial culture and motherland. We argue that these yearnings, invariably steeped in nostalgic sepia-toned memories, become the sustaining ground and groundation, an umbilical connection for the emergence of modes of being, vigorous and vital enough to withstand the impact of postcolonial anxieties, disillusionment and multiple secondary migrations. In this chapter, we look to Kei Miller's *The Last Warner Woman* and a body of art created by Kwynn Johnson for the practice-based PhD in Cultural Studies at the University of the West Indies entitled *How the Light Enters: Visualizing Absence and Continuity in the Jacmelian Ruinscape* as exemplary of this quest for mother cultures. For Johnson, the process of archiving Caribbean realities moves away from simply gathering fragments of the past, to the articulation of the unspeakable; probing of the unknowable; grasping after the imperceptible. And these tasks emerge as fundamental to weaving a patchwork social fabric which is sturdy and resilient enough to bear a viable future. We argue that while we cannot productively look into our impoverishing and ideologically skewed state-sponsored archives for the key to our historical futures, we can look to our creative voices who have been persistent in their identification of the myriad ways in which the region's traumas have been archived. Kei Miller's evocation of the warner women is a radical conception of not only a way of life, but a compelling mode of self-making. The primary character's 'speaking out' transgresses the edicts that had forbidden enslaved communities from speaking their native/ancestral tongue. Miller's narrative implicitly raises questions about authority which inheres within the expressive modes of gendered texts. We interrogate the impact of discrete spaces on subject formation and the traumas involved in entering, negotiating and leaving communal, national and diasporic spaces. With a particular emphasis on the mother figure as an embodiment and locus of national and individual desire, identity and affiliation, this reading argues that these creative works foreground notions of belonging as sustaining to the subject in formation, while simultaneously entrenching homelessness and loss.

The second chapter, "Black Countermapping: Brodber's and Brand's Re-conceptualizing of Loss, Belonging and Resistance", broadens the application of plumbing submerged repositories of black memory as a basis for empowering cartographies of self and society. The underwater archive is interrogated as a meeting ground of spatialization and temporalization, through which traces and hauntings, undead spectral entities, restless and wondering ghostly presences intrude unbidden and unwelcome into the present. We examine the specific enunciative strategies deployed by Brand in *A Map to the Door of No Return* and Brodber in *Nothing's Mat* to illuminate submerged networks of relations and the embrace of a mythic universe, which yield therapeutic interventions to contemporary in/visible wounding generated by oppressive, neo-fascist systems in the black diaspora and the tacit acceptance of this evil. The search for self is arguably complete when one has a sense of home, and has made peace with the motherlands. However, we contend that this acquisition of "wholeness" is achieved and defined by spiritual anchoring. The invocation and retention of past experiences are aided by the imagination, a main constituent of memory. Through close textual analysis and an engagement with Tiffany King's geologic metaphors, we interrogate the quest for ontological freedom and wholeness amidst a new world order that thrives on oppressive systems of cultural, social and racial alienation. In their respective fictions, Brand and Brodber provide fictional cartographic tools and strategies, which are rooted in multivalent ancestral, cosmic and cultural forms with the power to revitalize, heal and instruct on empowering ways to be human.

In chapter 3, "Servant Mothering, Memory Work and Empathy in Senior's 'The Pain Tree' and Scott's 'The Wedding Photograph'", the trope of the more-mythic-than-real maternal figure is explored. Both Senior and Scott are equally invested in acts of recovery and representations of haunted memories. Their discourses lend credence to the correlation between trauma and ageing, and particularly the resurgence of traumatic memories when ageing persons forget to forget. An analysis of ancestral veneration, generational transmission and postmemory (Marianne Hirsch) ensues through the construction of cultural memory as a ceremonial practice.

Moreover, we engage the psychological phenomena of dreams and trauma, which come with their own haunting and menacing forces. The analysis is framed in relation to a historical sensibility, which posits that each writer's self-conscious use of surrogate mothers dovetails with the main character's personal journeys.

Cycles of abuse and violence are spatialized in chapter 4, "Incest, Violation and Trauma in Caribbean Narratives". This chapter explores Scott's representation of intergenerational incest and sexual violation as endemic to the plantation economy, its grim outworking in Shani Mootoo's post-indentureship family narrative and Nalo Hopkinson's complex deployment of the fantasy genre, which locates incest within a social order that straddles folklore and technologically determined future worlds. This chapter analyses the cultural norms that create an enabling environment for abusive acts and the recourse to cultural expression as therapeutic intervention. Locating incest at the extreme end of a continuum of child abuse, it posits that literary representation can be instrumental in probing the cultures of violence that facilitate sensitizing readers to the nuanced manner in which this domestic crime ravages families and generates troubled futures.

Shifting from the fictional to real-life narratives, the fifth chapter analyses the narrative of a mature woman who contemplates the grim circumstances which led her into co-habitation in her mid-teens and the birth of her first child before the age of seventeen. According to the United Nations' regional offices for Latin America and the Caribbean, this is the only region in which the teenage pregnancy rate is either stagnant or increasing. "Baby Mama Talks: Motherhood in Childhood Caribbean Style" presents a case study with a focus on self-perception and lived experience. It analyses an interview to probe the experience of early motherhood with a focus on the interface between gender prescriptions, cultural norms and the myriad vulnerabilities attendant upon teenage pregnancy. We contend that research of this nature can enhance bottom-up understanding and provide useful qualitative data as a basis for interventions.

The balance of the study from chapter 6 onwards shifts attention to traumatized, violated and vulnerable urban societies and ravaged motherlands of the Caribbean. In chapter 6, "'Killing don't need no reason': Trauma and Criminality in *A Brief History of Seven Killings*", we explore the issue of how writers attempt to alleviate another type of violence which, when imbricated with political processes, devastates individuals, families, communities and nations, and spreads its tentacles transnationally and transgenerationally. This chapter unearths connections between criminality and silenced, submerged, unresolved traumas on multiple levels in Marlon James' award-winning novel. In the process, it argues for an understanding of individual, collective and apparently random criminal behaviours as eruptions of the out-workings of historical, natural and transnational insidious traumas that seep into the lives of individuals, families and communities. We argue that effective intervention must therefore excavate and address these rhizomes, while acknowledging more immediate invidious societal conditions.

In chapter 7, "A Chorus of Resistance: Hurricane Narratives of Loss and Resilience", we also contend that a major facet of vulnerability confronting the small island states of the Caribbean comes from the risk of natural disasters, specifically the looming annual threat of hurricanes. Hurricanes bring profound physical and social vulnerabilities. As effectively as they kill and maim people, they topple buildings, damage infrastructure and devastate agricultural and tourist-based economies in a day. They possess the imminent potential of undermining restoration efforts, come next hurricane season. The focus of disaster risk reduction efforts has been on assessing resilience and the capacity of a people to anticipate, prepare for and recover from the battering meted out by natural hazards. This chapter reads a cross-section of hurricane narratives by David Dabydeen (*Turner*), Olive Senior ("Hurricane Story, 1903" [1944/1951/1988]), Derek Walcott (*Omeros*), Erna Brodber (*The Rainmaker's Mistake*) and Paul Keens-Douglas ("Story of a Storm – Ivan") to probe the trail of devastation and mindsets, coping and resilience of peoples for whom to possess their island homelands is to be poised for the threat of annual devastation. What becomes particularly salient in these texts is the return, in part, to maternal figures and instincts as vital conduits of endurance. Amid the debris of ruined homes and fractured futures, it is often maternal care – embodied in literal mothers, grandmothers and metaphorical motherlands – that anchors the collective will to survive. In other words, these narratives remind us that resilience in the Caribbean is not merely a bureaucratic metric, but a deeply affective and historically sedimented practice – often grounded in ideas of the maternal – that continues to shape the trajectories of individuals, communities and nations long after the winds have calmed down. It also explores the factors which alter anticipation and resilience over time.

Chapter 8, "Harrisian Narratives of Environmental Degradations and Indigenous Healing", based on Wilson Harris' short stories, "The Laughter of the Wapishanas" and "The Age of Kaie", grapples with articulations of Caribbean ontological beginnings. It focuses on the myriad vulnerabilities of ecological degradation, starvation and extinction, which confront Indigenous communities. In "The Laughter of the Wapishanas", Harris spatializes a new method of artistic creation to encapsulate the visionary journey of the Wapishana woman who ruminates an inchoate universe to search out the elixir of life (laughter) for her community. Harris explores the most intimate regions of the psyche and the body, and a searching for pre-oedipal and pre-colonial innocence – a primal space where the self is indistinct in form and embraced by maternal images. Similarly, in "The Age of Kaie", fragments of Indigenous lore intersect with present communities in the wake of environmental and human devastation to inform modalities of cultural affirmation. An imaginative participation in the cosmovisions of the Caribbean's first communities demonstrates how the idea of intergenerational transfer operates on several levels.

The final chapter, "Whispers from the Roots: Reclaiming Nature through Spirit in the Poetry of Allen-Paisant and Nichols", is devoted to probing the creative relationship between Jason Allen-Paisant and Grace Nichols, whose respective texts illustrate the deeply felt ideology that the land is a physical and psychic sanctuary, a complex repertoire of values and a nexus of ancestral, maternal power relations amidst accelerating forms of neocapitalism and dispossession in modern times. Allen-Paisant's poetry in *Thinking with Trees* recalls Edouard Glissant's relational poetics through his emphasis on womb-like images to exude ideas of rebirth, nurturance, potential and newness, while Nichols, in *Passport to Here and There,* carefully affirms transgenerational connections that emerge from the landscape to invoke a psychic connection that is necessary for working out the centuries-long collective struggle for emancipation.

Originary Violations posits that in the sequence of fourteen creative workers, there is a compact experimentation with the philosophical and ideological theorization of Caribbean motherhood, the signifying relationship between biological or surrogate mothers and ancestral motherlands, which complicates ideas of selfhood, the intricate mother-child dyad and the repossession of narrative space to underscore trajectories of accommodation, negotiation, invention, creativity, resistance and healing.

The underlying ethical foundation of the enquiry counters the narrative which was pivotal to the foundational historical trauma of modern Caribbean societies – the enterprise of the Indies. Unfortunately, this is also the hegemonic narrative of our present, as we gaze with incredulity upon the nightmarish reconfiguration of the global order of the mid-2020s. We base this enquiry on the assumption of the value and significance of all human beings. In our economy there are no futile, throwaway people. We assert that historical traumas do not simply disappear with time. Their submerged tentacles lurk beneath the surface, waiting to emerge the moment a fissure opens, in even the most civilized and advanced social orders. This eruption begins most often within the socially and psychically dis-eased body of the silenced, impoverished and dispossessed. Scholars and cultural knowledge workers face an urgent imperative to unearth and expose these tentacles so as to contain, shed light on, and perchance even predict their future eruption. Diligent and respectful attention must be placed on the trajectories of the very impoverished, marginalized and dispossessed.

The despised of the earth and the interface of oppressor and oppressed are the major focus of this work. The centrality of this collectivity to the onward march of man must be acknowledged. As analysts, we also adopt the ethical stance of exploring the origins and continuities of violation and violence without erasing the responsibility of all to seek a higher order. We articulate our stance respectfully, keenly aware of the long-term, multivalent, collective nature of this process of discovery. The enquiry argues that hacking through thorny issues while seeking a better and more humane way has been the trajectory of numerous Caribbean authors as, together, we seek a productive, life-generating way into a viable future.

chapter 1

Collisions

Ancestral Cosmologies and Global Modernities in Johnson's Jacmelian Ruinscape and Miller's *The Last Warner Woman*

> It is because this New World is constituted for us as place, a narrative of displacement, that it gives rise so profoundly to a certain imaginary plenitude, recreating the endless desire to return to 'lost origins', to be one once again with the mother, to go back to the beginning. Who can forget, when once again seen rising up out of that blue-green Caribbean, those islands of enchantment. Who has not known, at this moment, the surge of overwhelming nostalgia for lost origins, for 'times past'?
>
> —*Stuart Hall, Cultural Identity and the Diaspora*

WHEN THE WORLDS OF AFRICA, ASIA, EUROPE AND THE AMERICAS collided on the island archipelago and coastal settlements of the Caribbean, it triggered violent and violating clashes of peoples and cultures, languages and ideologies, cosmologies and faiths. Explorations of the resultant crises of being and becoming, which have occupied the attention of architects and knowledge workers of the emerging new world order, have not given primacy to matters of faith. Yet, the cosmologies of the First Peoples and that of every ethnic migrant group that has come to the region have been pivotal to the processes of subject formation and to the evolving social order. It is our view that modern Caribbean nation states that have emerged out of these historical crucibles, generated by early experiments of capitalism, have endured what cultural scholar Stuart Hall calls 'double displacement'. This encompasses ontological dislocation and a radical decentring of the subject from self and from their place in the social and cultural world. In this chapter, we look to visual art as a way to approach questions of precarious, uprooted, fragile and moving identities, which pose a challenge to the matrix of Enlightenment orthodoxies and the deeply held values of Western civilization, as they relate to time, the self and the mind.

The Enlightenment subject is configured around rationality, consciousness and high individualism. This notion, which is rooted in liberalism, holds individual responsibility, autonomy and self-sufficiency to be sacrosanct. As an alternative to the monolithic and imperialistic order of Enlightenment discourses, we adopt an analytic approach – a mode of reading and writing where we mine the vibrant historical and cultural realities of the Caribbean to glean new understandings from the region's lands, seas, peoples and resources as forms vital to contest Western world orders, which have turned Caribbean space and communities into commodities. The social subject is thus mediated via cultural symbols, values and constructions of meaning. This interactional notion posits that the subject is formed in interactions between self and society, and the goal is to arrive at harmony and balance between subjective value systems and meaning construction and objective being in the social and cultural worlds.

While recognizing the fluid and contested nature of subjectivity and social identities, we aim to illuminate the interconnectedness and complexity of Caribbean ontologies. Stuart Hall's notion of identity as constructed within plays of "power inclusions and exclusions" is useful at this conjuncture for as he notes: "Identities are never unified and in late modern times, increasingly fragmented and fractured; never singular but multiply constructed across different, often intersected and antagonistic discourses, practices and positions. They are subject to a radical historicization and constantly in the process of change and transformation" (Hall 2012, 4). Where he highlights fracture, fragmentation and fluidity, Wilson Harris privileges submerged networks of relations which transcend space and time. He points to the subjectivity of the West Indian as a person in the world who is imbued with vast potentialities for subtle interconnection and linkages: "What in my view is remarkable about the West Indian in depth is a sense of subtle links . . . the series of subtle and nebulous links which are latent within him, the latent ground of old and new personalities" (Harris 1967, 28). Harris, ever aware of ancestral pathways and presences, and the need to envision a reality beyond deterministic cycles of conquest and disempowerment, points to the existence of unplumbed depths of inarticulate feeling and unrealized wells of emotion (Harris 1967, 28). Cultural critic Gordon Rohlehr, unafraid of allegations of essentialism, references the efforts of writers such as George Lamming and Edward Brathwaite to illuminate a hidden interior dimension of Caribbean peoples which may yet prove to be accessible to creative imaginations:

> These are writers who constantly recognize a sort of interior dimension of the Caribbean people. We are really not what we seem to be on the surface. They speak about descending beneath the surface to some more genuine aspect of self, of identity, of consciousness. I think they try to find ways of depicting what happens and takes shape; what arrangements of words capture how we feel when we move beneath the surface to what is locked up inside of us (Interview with Morgan 2013, 15).

Against these varied notions, and drawing reference to examples from visual and scribal culture, we address the paradoxical nature of the collision of cosmologies with attendant implication for evolving ontologies and epistemologies. Zeroing in on one facet of the region's complex and divergent modes of being, we probe the manner in which an African-derived Indigenous cosmology in particular, with its notions of a numinous, spirit-infused universe, has permeated the world view and perceptions of Caribbean peoples of all ethnicities and has been pivotal to acts of resistance and recuperation.

The first example is drawn from a body of art created by Kwynn Johnson for the practice-based PhD in cultural studies at the University of the West Indies entitled "How the Light Enters: Visualizing Absence and Continuity in the Jacmelian Ruinscape". The drawings were created over a three-year period as an act of secondary witnessing to trauma generated by the Haitian earthquake in 2010. Johnson produced these drawings in open air on location in Jacmel, Haiti, where she immersed herself in the banalities of survival and transcendence within a lived ruinscape. During eight field visits, she lived among and interacted with people in the street, and shared their difficulties of accessing services and their requirements to creatively implement practical strategies for overcoming basic life challenges. One of the energies that drives Johnson's art is the urge to transform traumatic fragmentation and dissolution into a connected life – a life where the essential human connection to ancestral presences is restored.

Figure 1.1: "How the Light Enters": Kwynn Johnson's dissertation exhibition, "How the Light Enters", which comprises twenty 2ft by 3ft graphite drawings on vellum, mounted between sheets of Perspex, suspended from free-standing wooden door frames and lit by spotlights with yellow gels. The display/installation included intermittent spurts of "fog" from machines in the gallery space.

Figure 1.2: *Marché en fer* by Kwynn Johnson

Figure 1.3: *Place de Toussaint L'Ouverture* by Kwynn Johnson

In figures 1.2 and 1.3 the drawings represent persons balancing themselves and objects on their heads as if daily life becomes a tightrope walk that can be negotiated only with extreme skill and at extreme risk. Resolutely engaged in moving on with the business of life, the majority of the figures are in motion, often moving away from the viewer as if escaping representational fixity, escaping the gaze of the other and the attendant essentialisms, embracing agency and mobility, despite the paralysing impact of the trauma. This work is in dialogue with the plethora of post-earthquake images, the majority of which cast Haitians in a negative, mendicant light as passive victims. Johnson sought a visual grammar for capturing energies that flow beneath the surface of the reality; the illumination which penetrates the darkness. She looks beyond mountains of rubble, the despair, hopelessness, loss and grief to grapple with the life force of the survivors, while probing the potentialities for transcendence and the ghostly absent presence of those who lost their lives. What is interesting is the choice to envision and represent the interface of the living and the dead who have recently joined the ancestors. African cosmologies define community as comprising the unborn, the living and the dead. In this domain, we cease to think about community and genealogy through the prism of the individual, but through the lens of all those with whom we share space, including ancestral communities and the unborn. Communal well-being depends on the maintenance of balance and harmony between all three groups. The awareness of this interrelatedness and porosity of time leads us into a different relationship and understanding; it is one that emphasizes our status as co-dwellers in a world of communicative life. To experience the Haitian universe as aware and agential (as Johnson has), is to be intertwined with a deep, ancestral and primordial sense of time. It is noteworthy that ancestors are perceived as possessing the power to safeguard and benefit families and communities and, conversely to perpetrate mischief which may be deleterious to the communal well-being. Ancestral veneration is predicated on the notion that the ancestors spatially coexist with the living and are influential in daily affairs.

Spectrality becomes a key element of Johnson's work. The issue was how best to represent the interface between the built, human and spectral elements which cohabit the same landscape. The selection of graphite on vellum reflects fragility, the entrance of light, the haunting sense of otherworldliness and rite of communication with parent cosmologies, which Johnson represents as integral to daily life in this lived ruinscape. The absence of colour within the context of brilliantly coloured traditional Haitian art and aesthetics generates defamiliarization, which constrains closer scrutiny and a nudge towards a different vision. Art as metaphysical participation and enmeshment lead us into this state of mind – one that is attuned to an original vitality and ancestral/spiritual temporality. This emphasis on the incorporeal world hinges on recoveries of Indigenous knowledge systems, with its instructive capacity to bring realignment and preservation. The sense of the spectral is also enhanced by locational choices that blur the distinction between the living and the dead. Persons figured in unlikely places and positions could just as readily be actual or spectral presences. Their domains seamlessly coexist within a crumbling, imbricated and intricately built landscape, rendered faithfully and in minute detail – from filigreed wrought iron railings to stone enclosures, which lend a sense of situatedness. The drawings point to the precious heritage

Figure 1.4: *Rue du Commerce* by Kwynn Johnson

that was threatened or lost, in this city which has been designated a World Heritage Site.

Johnson also grapples with how to convey the subtlety of trauma and loss as imbibed and carried within the living. The coexistence of absence and continuity is represented in people carrying out their routine and ordinary activities in the ruinscape. Persistent shadowy presences impinge gradually from representation to representation, conveying the sense that they are all still here. Moreover, the expanses of white spaces in the collages create a sense of void and emptiness.

In producing this body of work, the artist was sensitive to the ethics of secondary witnessing and modalities of entering respectfully into another person's direct trauma – Johnson's artistry invites participation in an empowering and transcendent world view and cosmology. The result of this conceptualizing entails an attempt to affirm a related spiritual lineage and the ancestral ties that bind communities. In the process, Johnson argues effectively against notions of Haitian exceptionalism by framing the Haitian disaster and artistic responses to it within the broader framework of visual memorializing of contemporary disasters. Additionally, she represents the working persons in the street as energized survivors who are backing the viewer and resolutely engaging the exigencies of everyday life. This she identifies as the locus of recovery in the post-earthquake ruinscape.

In his essay, "The Trope of the Ancestor", Okunoye Oyeniyi lists the ways in which ancestral consciousness permeates contemporary poetry in the black world. He indicates that this sacred praxis has been redeployed to reflect a longing for "spiritual reunion with a lost spiritual essence" in exilic scenarios (Oyeniyi 2007, 3). It also follows the conventions of praise poetry which banishes evildoers from ancestral space and in the African diaspora. In this related endeavour, Johnson, in seeking an empowering representation and hope for the restoration of community, presents the spectral presences of those who perished as transcendent, coexistent and collaborating with the living in the act of restoration. When asked to explain this choice, she stated simply that in post-earthquake Jacmel, the spirits of the dead had not departed; their absent presences were everywhere. This standpoint resonates with the Myalist framework erected by Erna Brodber, whose notion that spirits walk among the living shows us quite simply how living may be co-constituted, implicating not just other humans, but other manifested and non-manifested beings.

The valorization of the secular and the scientific in modernist discourses were vital facets of the Western orthodoxies – beliefs, knowledge, values, social enactments and practices which relegated emerging New World societies, along with the entire so-called Third World, to the backwaters of time and margins of history. Ideological war was waged against peoples for whom spiritual cosmologies were integral to every aspect of their lives. Their notions of the existence and operation of spirit beings, the existence and nature of life after death, the destiny of humans beyond the grave, the interface between the living and the dead were seen as particularly backward and retrogressive, and in large part responsible for the incapacity of the people groups and their societies to flourish and progress. Indeed, explanations for their inability to join the merry march of progress foregrounded cosmological matters and obscured the impact of social and economic injustices engineered and imposed by imperial and neo-imperial strategies. It was preferable to perceive of non-Western societies, including the new nations of the Caribbean, as mired in superstition and irrationality, poverty and underdevelopment, savagery, and most of all, severely retarded in terms of negotiating pathways toward global capitalism.

Parallel to this denigration was the promotion of modernity discourses designed to buttress Euro-American ideological hegemony over the future by the imposition of its ideologies, hegemonies and socio-cultural practices, all of which valorize capitalist paradigms as its holy grail. Adopting a temporal paradigm which has now come under scrutiny, Third World societies were seen as migrating towards enviable First World status. In "Spectres of the Third World: Global Modernity and the End of the Three Worlds", Arif Dirlik argues that the shift from modernity to globalization discourses has spatialized temporal notions and teleologies of the technological, scientific and rational realm unfettered by religion and ideology (Dirlik 2004, 131–48).

Even as First World nations continue to expand, their ideological underpinnings and spatial borders are under threat from the enemy outside and within. The second – that is, the communist and socialist worlds – were perceived as rational and sophisticated, but contaminated by ideological allegiance. This world is now effectively dissolved, leaving no substantial obstacle to the political manoeuvres and sociocultural paradigms that promoted the globalization of capitalist modernity. The Third World, comprising non-Western societies, was envisioned as mired in superstition and irrationality, poverty and underdevelopment, savagery and ungovernability. Most of all, this entity was perceived as severely retarded in terms of negotiating pathways towards capitalist modernity and First World status. The boundaries of the Third World have now shifted, with some of its citizens functioning as members of a global class that facilitates First World intrusions into their societies. Also, mass migration of its citizens into metropolitan cities, which the Jamaican poet Louise Bennett-Coverley (Miss Lou) referred to as "colonization in reverse" (Bennett-Coverley 1966), has also introduced Third World enclaves to the metropoles.

We also look to the literary evocation of grim outcomes of migrations when cosmological confrontations erupt within alien and alienating metropolitan centres. Kei Miller indicates that the seeds which grew into *The Last Warner Woman* dated back to the period of his study in Manchester, where he heard a Jamaican woman crying hell and damnation on the streets. This incident stirred thoughts of home, where she would have been clearly recognized as a warner woman. In the British context, his classmates interpreted her as a crazy menace. This dovetails with his recall that the highest incidence of schizophrenia in England is recorded among West Indian immigrant women. So, Miller muses, were these women really insane or were they misunderstood in England? Or were they really crazy and did Jamaicans mask their craziness? The seed of the narrative encapsulates issues of pathological racialized identity, conflicting cosmologies, fluid subjectivities, and travelling ontologies, as they interface with a quest for mother and motherland.

In relation to spatiality, what happens to the subject unaccommodated at home, where legacies of colonialism, including persistent interlocking strictures of racism and classism, condemn one to lifelong poverty and denigration? What is the fate of the subject in motion when migration takes one to a physically, culturally and spiritually cold and alien space? Can evolving cosmologies and ontologies rooted in African retentions, mediated through the body, and grounded experientially in mystical spirituality and social responsibility, survive in metropolitan, sceptical, materialist environments? For the protagonist, the world at home, despite its familiarity, warmth and comfort, is also replete with peril. The text, which resonates with numerous female-authored evocations of this psychosocial terrain, figures women as made vulnerable in domestic and national contexts by their sexual and reproductive capacities. This includes women widely recognized as fearsome spiritual mothers empowered because of their ritual practices and divine connections. Adamine Portious is called away from her home in a leprosarium to become a powerful prophetess known as a Warner Woman in a revivalist movement. She loves powerful revival leader Captain Lucas, who initiates the sexual contact which takes her virginity, but, intimidated by the fulsome passion of her response, beats her in the revival meeting for her sluttish behaviour. Frustrated at ongoing poverty, which no amount of hard work would alleviate, she decides to enter an arranged marriage with a man she has never met in order to migrate to England.

Her husband subsequently beats her regularly because his "soft man parts" give him a heavy hand. Finally, in solitary confinement, incarcerated in the mental hospital for which the listed cause of incarceration is West Indian, she is subject to brutal rape by a man she calls "Satan" – the father of her child, whose mother-loss drives the plot of the novel. Miller's respected and feared warner women, who channel divine power to warn and to call judgement on a nation, tolerate sexual abuse and violence because it seems normative and because they do not believe that the divinities they serve are vested in freeing them from domestic oppressions. The women bear in their bodies the psychic laceration of diseased men in a dysfunctional social order. This conundrum of female spiritual and ideological empowerment, alongside financial poverty, vulnerability, disempowerment and abuse, has engaged Caribbean feminists from as early as 1977, when Lucille Mathurin penned the essay "Reluctant Matriarchs". The notion of Caribbean matriarchy, which describes a sociopolitical system where women hold primary power, leadership and authority, has since been replaced by matrifocality. In a matrifocal system, women in predominantly female-headed households carry the lion's share of responsibility for childcare. This is invariably combined with laborious wage-earning at low-paid jobs, often within exploitative circumstances. The resultant affective ties position the mother as the core of the home, generating a substantial debt of gratitude, eventually earning the economic support of her adult children. As a result of paternal male absenteeism within the home, women in matrifocal households, even women who endure abuse from their partners, tend to have wide-ranging decision-making and disciplinary power. All of this is to say that within lower strata African-Caribbean households, indices of maternal positioning need to be placed on a matrix – a sliding scale of diverse markers in relation to which mothers score differently at various life stages.

The empowerment of women within the revivalist movement is unquestionable. The movement is gendered in significant ways. As powerful a healer and leader as Captain Lucas may be, warning is woman's work within the narrative and within the Caribbean imaginary. Mounted by Legba, the androgynous god of the crossroads, Adamine is subjected to terrible compulsion to give warning. In "Something Ancestral Recaptured", Carolyn Cooper indicates "as a metaphor of spirit possession double signifies both the dislocation and rearticulation of Afro-centric culture in the Americas; divine possession mirrors its submissive other – zombification – than diabolical owning of the enslaved in the material world" (Cooper 1994,

64). She argues in favour of a validation of identity, which is accomplished through "reappropriating devalued folk wisdom" – that body of subterranean knowledge openly associated with the silenced language of woman and the primitiveness of orally transmuted knowledge (Cooper 1994, 65).

The visceral energies of danced religions provide a modality for negotiating other worlds in which the human is not devalued based on externalities. The whirling disturbs spatial environments; the wailing and crying alters sound waves; together, these disruptions create fissures and then pathways through which spirits impart alternative knowledge that is then channelled through the bodily enactments and ritualized speech of the warner women, known as spiritual mothers. Yet the evocation of the Revival is paradoxical and contradictory and, at times, seasoned with dashes of scepticism. Stylized representations, as symbolized by writer man's print of ritual dancing, are bright and beautiful; eroticized and idealized, as opposed to being reflective of far more grim and mundane realities. In keeping with the narrative insistence on multiplicity of ways of viewing any reality, the evocation of the Revival is subject to statements which are quickly undermined by alternatives to faith. The famed incident of the warner woman's speaking a warrant on the driver, who promptly proceeds to drive a bus full of schoolchildren over a bridge, is followed in Ada's explanations of why "it never need God to make people know the bus was going to crash" (Miller 2010, 140). Indeed, the title of the text and thrust of the narrative is on the supplanting of ritual practice by the act of warning.

The Warner Woman, whose naming and identity hinges first and foremost on her powerful spiritual and societal purpose, is balanced by that of Writer Man. His task is to seek out and present a cross-gendered construction of submerged women's history of their role in the Revival movement, its interface with the national project, their migratory pathways and the discontents of their exile to Britain. Writer Man is in pursuit of submerged lost personal and social histories as avidly as he is seeking connectivity to his mother. Indeed, the text is an explication of methodologies and challenges of constructing such a project. Secondary to the roles of warner woman and writer man are the roles of mother and son grappling with their positionality in relation to the ancestral motherland and to the land of their actual or symbolic exile.

Writer man becomes a redemption forced on multiple levels. Indeed, Adamine paradoxically questions whether this white-skinned, green-eyed man could perchance be the Christ. As a mulatto who rejects Eurocentric prescriptions, seeks and restores his lost mother and claims his African ancestry, he is a deliverer and a foil to the mulatto son, hater and rapist who reacts to self-denigration by raping his half-sister in the cane field. As son of a brutal rapist, Writer Man offers pure generous love to his mother, thus ameliorating the conditions of his birth. He redeems his mother's calling by successful therapeutic intervention. As the son of a rejected warner woman, he becomes her healer, lifting her out of her private hell into peace. The piecing together of the narrative empowers her to recognize the good that she has done. She alleviates the mother/child loss. By calling to life her child, born blue and beautiful, but quite dead, she ameliorates the curses of the enslaved and their progeny who, by word and deed, delivered their children into infanticide and social death. The polyvocal narrative becomes a collaborative work of reconstructing personal, societal and subcultural group history, which lends individual and collective meaning and healing.

Miller joins a host of other creative writers who locate migration of the therapeutic dimension of African ritual practices to other avenues and activities. Ella O' Grady of Erna Brodber's *Myal* becomes a teacher in her quest to liberate children from mental slavery. Brodber deploys numerous works of fiction intended to teach the progeny of those who awoke from a nightmarish journey on the shore of the New World to enter into "the free". At the end of Lovelace's *The Wine of Astonishment*, the visceral energies of the Spiritual Baptist migrate to the steel drum. The Writer Man declared in a statement which ruptures spatial, linguistic and gender boundaries:

> The Warner People is still here, Mama. We is still here. Seers. Prophets. Forecasters of Earthquakes. We is here. But things is different now. We been writing a hole heap of books . . . they buy the things we write . . . And plenty times they don't know that all these things they been reading was not no novel, was not no poem, was not no history book. It was a simple warning. Mama, plenty people in this world have ears but they don't know how to hear. And plenty of them have eyes, but they don't know how to see (Miller 2010, 272).

In conclusion, cosmologies are pivotal to human societies. They encapsulate norms; craft group identities; and shape interface between the individual, the community and broader human society. They locate persons within natural and supernatural universes. This chapter contends that Caribbean writers and thinkers, while grappling with the legacies of the traumatic collision of worlds, are throwing out a challenge. Their creative works are drawing from a fluid repertoire of Indigenous reconfigurations of African-derived cosmologies.

In concert, these works are indicating that nascent Caribbean social orders, as well as modern and post-industrial ones, cannot continue to practise erasure and amnesia; the impact of the reduction and commoditization of racialized human persons to units of production and consumption cannot create a just, viable, prosperous and harmonious global order. The natural world groans under rampant disregard for ecological responsibility and balance. It erupts in chaos and upheaval, and it threatens extinction. And ancestral spirits, who believers insist travel in and manifest in the bodies and souls of their companionate humans, threaten hell and damnation – indeed, they arguably manifest within contemporary social orders as malignant, vengeful duppies of history that are wreaking havoc worldwide. Western world views slowly migrate away from notions of an assimilated modern global civilization dedicated to secular progressivism, as understanding dawns that fundamental reconfiguration of its ideologies and hierarchies is required to support the pursuit of conviviality and sociality across cultures and the quest for ground and groundation of a common humanity.

This stance prompts a broader application of plumbing submerged repositories of black memory as a basis for empowering cartographies of self and society, and to envision liberatory patterns of interaction, which the discourses of Dionne Brand and Erna Brodber commemorate. Foundational to the illumination and mobilization of the more-than-human networks of relations and embrace of a spirit-infused universe are *A Map to the Door of No Return* (2001) and *Nothing's Mat* (2014) in which Brand and Brodber probe correlations between forms of originary violations and their effects on the modern socio-political order. The conceptual framing and significance of maps as talismanic tools and stitchwork which represent the layering of several narratives of history and myth that have gone into the making of the black diaspora is the focus of the next chapter.

chapter 2

Black Countermapping

Brodber's and Brand's Re-conceptualizing of Loss, Belonging and Resistance

> The land remembers and the sea does, too.
>
> —*Victoria Adukwei Bulley, On Water*

MATRIFOCAL AND KINSHIP NETWORKS ON CARIBBEAN plantations formed communities forged on both fictive and blood ties that provided critical social and emotional support to the enslaved community. Erna Brodber, in *Nothing's Mat,* explores and dramatizes this argument, while Dionne Brand, in *A Map to the Door of No Return*, explores the importance of local history and uses Indigenous oral and archaeological stories to create a cohesive narrative about the networks and genealogies that span the circum-Afro diaspora, and the recursions of violence that haunt secondary diasporas. Antonio Benitez Rojo reads the Caribbean as a "chaos that returns, a detour without purpose, a continual flow of paradoxes; it is a feedback machine with asymmetrical workings" (Benitez-Rojo 1996, 314). By defining the Caribbean as an iterative space, he is drawing on ideas of fragmentation, instability, reciprocal isolation, and uprootedness. He argues that in the Caribbean, within the "historiographic turbulence and its ethnological clamour [. . .] one can sense the features of an island that 'repeats' itself, unfolding and bifurcating" (Benitez-Rojo 1996, 314). The ideas of repetition with a difference resonate in both Brand's and Brodber's texts with contemporary immediacy. When one thinks about the blood on the hands of neo-fascist nations and the incessant objectification and vilification of subaltern communities in the contemporary world, one senses that a spectre is indeed haunting the post-colonies. The specific relationship between black bodies and the catalogue of police-involved killings, as well as the relentless repetition of anti-black violence in the modern world, underpin the terrorism and semiotics of the transatlantic slave trade. Brand and Brodber, in *Map* and *Nothing's Mat* respectively, have provided a poetics of black haunting in which the terms of black death, survival and transcendence of new crises in contemporary times are negotiated through the intersection of memory, nurturing and homecoming. This is achieved through experimental textual strategies that are mapped outside the paradigmatic ordering of conquistador discourses.

Using white imperial cartography as a framework for questioning Western modernity, Tiffany King notes that eighteenth-century map-making conceived a geometry of the human that violently wrote man/woman into being through modern imaginings – Indigenous genocide, white settlement and black enslavement (King 2019, 78). She shines a retrospective light on Western cartography, noting that "the map was created in the midst of the scientific revolutions and epistemic shifts of the Enlightenment, prompted by the planetary migration and exchange of objects, people and ideas in the era of colonization. The map reflects the White human as a possessor of things" (King 2019, 88). In principle, it is between the lines of imperial cartography and power that representations of the human are made. Empire's articulations of the empirical verities of territorial sightings are part of a larger discourse on the relationship between predatory forms of rule and the specific ways to be human. In probing this interface between Western cartography and conceptions of the human, John Harley asserts, "As much as guns and warships, maps have been the weapons of imperialism. Insofar as maps were used in colonial promotion, and lands claimed on paper before they were effectively occupied, maps anticipated empire. Maps were [therefore] used to legitimatize the reality of conquest and empire" (Harley 2002, 282).

If mapwork is a poesis of self-making, the burden to develop new cartographies in the black Atlantic world outside of monolithic and hegemonic ways of reading takes on a new level of intensity. As a capacious metaphor for shaping and signposting both human and social change, literary cartography embraces lines of inquiry that are substrate with the realities of black life. Brand's and Brodber's fictions, which are symptomatic of erasure, gaps, connections and portals, accrue alternative forms of consciousness that effectively challenge the linearity of Western discourses. By way of implication, their polyphonic narratives are stripped of binaries and normative modes of the human. Evidenced in the framework of Brand's memoir are the narrative strategies of embodiment, intermediality, ancestral cosmologies and geo-psychic maps within the broader context of black haunting. The aim is, in part, to plot principles of self-articulation that dismantle and transcend the sins of the white neo-colonizer who attempts to re-impose systems of ontological elision in North American diasporic communities. Similarly, Brodber assembles an intimate cacophony of voices (material and immaterial) to procure the transgressive grounds of understanding black Atlantic 'livingness' outside of the colonial structures that seek to frustrate sites of black futurity.

The terrain of haunting is thus critical to the inquiry at hand since it addresses how the black body is uncannily linked to ecologies of subjugation, disproportionate labour, nationalist chauvinism and supremacist bias. Jacques Derrida defines haunting as that which is made to reside or inhabit the present (Derrida 1994, 3). The body, according to Derrida, is "inhabited in its inside, that is, haunted by a foreign guest [ghost or spectre]". Haunting is a "sense of obsession, a constant fear, a fixed idea or a nagging memory" that operates within the body (Derrida 1994, 3). To be haunted is to "live with ghosts [. . .]. This being with specters would also be . . . a politics of memory, of inheritance, and of generations" (Derrida 1994, xviii). In this sense, spectres are part of the undetectable genealogies of black life and custom. What empire has rendered invisible and disposable, Brand and Brodber reconfigure into incisive narrative strategies that not only contest such erasures, but also carve out spaces for the articulation and healing of wounds.

Their discursive ritual of plotting new narrative lines on the atlas of world literature invokes Edouard Glissant's theorem of rhizomatic unpredictability and openness. He posits:

> [T]he rhizome [is] an enmeshed root system, a network spreading either in the ground or in the air, with no predatory rootstock taking over permanently. The notion of the rhizome maintains, therefore, the idea of rootedness but challenges that of a totalitarian root. Rhizomatic thought is the principle

behind what I call the Poetics of Relation, in which each and every identity is extended through a relationship with the Other (Glissant 1997, 11).

His rhizomatic effect materializes in both writers' disruption of normative notions of time, space, dimensionality and narrative form to produce a self and a community that are in intimate concert with the presences of history. This malleable, fictional arrangement disrupts authoritative regimes that lock black futures into stasis and stone. Speculative work thus enables a tangible mapping of a heterogeneous history that could be truly coalesced and fertilized to produce creative syncretism, which permeates the worldview and perceptions of the black diaspora.

BRAND AS BLACK MAPMAKER

We turn attention to Dionne Brand's interrogation of black global haunting, the conundrums of 'home' and ontological erasure in the wake of a violent colonial history. Brand narrates how she became victim and witness. She begins her memoir by recalling her childhood desire for a homeland. When the thirteen-year-old writer-protagonist asks her grandfather to divulge from which part of Africa they originated, he finds he "could not summon . . . a people which would add up to a name" (Brand 2001, 5). It is this sense of a vanishing history and a yearning for ancestral motherlands that are nurturing and sustaining enough to support ontologies adrift in hostile metropolitan landscapes that enable Brand to travel the world "with a will" (Brand 2001, 92) and survey the undocumented parts of her past that she deems necessary to cultivate a narrative praxis. Her approaches to negotiating black identity are anchored in her search for origins. By starting at the entrances of ancient slave forts in Senegal circa 1600 and tracing continuous moments of black death four centuries later, she deconstructs the colonial archive, with its neat ledgers that produce what Glissant calls the "non-history" of the diaspora (Brand 1992, 62). Her meditation at length on the Door of No Return (a historical holding area in Africa used by slave traders, which endures and erupts as a haunting consciousness in the modern world) allows her to investigate the created legacies of societal dis-ease and restlessness in the diaspora, which call for therapeutic interventions to interrupt their intergenerational continuity. Paul Gilroy's configuration of roots and routes points to the possibilities embedded in her quest (Gilroy 1993). Roots (or origins) can become mobile, forked, branching and rhizomatic, while routes offer strategies for cultivating rootedness in new geographies.

This complex process of tracking a highly fragmented and submerged history is congruent with Edward Kamau Brathwaite's theoretical debates. In *Roots*, he observes:

> [Africa] is a permanent part of our heritage. It comes in a way, as an almost physical inheritance . . . where in nature, drought and lushness, the flower and the desert, lie side by side. It is a spiritual inheritance from slavery and the long story before that of the migrant African moving from the lower Nile across the desert to the Western Ocean only to meet the Portuguese and a History that was to mean the middle passage, America, and a rootless sojourn in the New World (Brathwaite 1986, 29–30).

Transposing this historical psychic and physical uprooting with mutated passages of dispossession, Brathwaite reflects on the pattern of the indeterminate tide, which is difficult to record. In *Missile and Capsule*, he provides the principle of the tidalectic to craft a new narrative form, which dovetails with the processes of Caribbean/black becoming, since the wave hits many points of origins in its travelling and gathering of materials from the seabed (Brathwaite 1983). The process of becoming is then, accumulative, and meaning is constantly sought from various encounters outside of time and space (Brathwaite 1983, 9–54). The logic of his tidalectics acquires new significance when paired with the embodied rhythms and manifold crossings of African-descended people in Canada whom Brand encounters. The ripple of the ocean is symbolically delineated in *Maps*, demonstrated in the traffic between the historical transatlantic voyage and contemporary forms of warfare on the black body in North America.

Apart from the echoes of the sea routes thematically embedded in the text, Brand's narrative range also involves the role of the intuitive mind and journal format, which enable the authority of personal experience and the cumulative effect of representing speculative voices across the diaspora. To begin her confrontation with colonial history, she locates the ghostly presences whose voices remain resident within contemporary bodies. The ability to engage in the imperishable dimensions of black existence without the obstruction of an imperial or authoritative idea is supported by both Glissant's process of relation and Brathwaite's tidalectic arrangements (Brathwaite 1983), through which literature and the creative imagination operate. Literature facilitates a form of associative and metaphoric thinking whereby one concept erupts into the next.

Fittingly, Brand employs sea and aquatic imagery: storm-surge, breakers and the sensation of life as she used to know it on the beaches of her Trinidadian childhood, now torn from its moorings. This ultimate violation of the concept of home signals uprooting and rupture. This is the daunting task that Brand sets herself: the task of journeying through and then beyond catastrophe – the essential journey of diasporan Africans. It seems apt that she announces herself as a "drifter" and asserts, "My body feels always in the middle of a journey" (Brand 2001, 87). Her posture of threshold figure allows her to simultaneously intercept voices from across space and time, and record the uncanny ways in which other black migrants are "wrapped in the crypto-fascist romances of . . . dominant nations" (Brand 2001, 67). For example, in Canada, she inspects the "body [that is] pushing a grocery cart through the city housing [. . .]. Young, perhaps a mother, the cart trundling further away from the supermarket than it ought to go" (Brand 2001, 27). The spatial emplacement of the young mother within the toxicity of the city, and her hands pushing the timeworn trolley cast the inner city as a dystopian setting for the dissolution of the black family. The social hierarchy, erasure and muted potentiality of the plantation are sustained in this evocative image and recall the postulations of Antonio Benítez-Rojo, who describes the grim aftermath of the plantation as "the womb of my otherness – and of my globality" (Benítez-Rojo 1998, 54). The social construction of blackness as otherness is documented as lived experience in Brand's memoir. The felt materializing of the outsider/insider logic plausibly catalyses her intent of disrupting the geometrics of white power and exclusion, which disavow inequality and new forms of conquistador humanism.

Continuing to inspect the fabric of routine in the diaspora, Brand interrogates the culpability of corporate practices that devour migrant workers. More particularly, as she inspects the circulation of labour in the "market-place in Montevideo" and in Chicago (Brand 2001, 49), she unveils the cadence of such spaces as a treadmill of accumulation that is managed by capital-intensive extraction. She observes, "The black body is situated as a sign of particular cultural and political meanings in the Diaspora. All of these meanings return to the Door of No Return as if those . . . bodies made to dance and then to work, those bodies curdling under the . . . whips [and] those bodies cursed [. . .] remain curved in these attitudes" (Brand 2001, 35). Operating within the broadest geopolitical framework, the setting replicates the shadow of migrant cargo embedded in the legally sanctioned violence of the slave trade. It is as if the North American metropoles are historicized in and through the writer's imagination, where layers of economic ejection and abjection cast a haunting spell on individual and communal consciousness. The trade and exchange of black flesh makes it a never-ending raw material, which stands in for machineries and other utilities of labour. This is an important touchstone because of how the writer is able to elaborate on how the body is steeped in economic and industrial contingencies. It also invokes the ruthless technologies of European cartography that were wedded to the imperial projections of desire, which have fixated the European 'other' into categories of raced inferiority and labour.

The overarching logic of objectification as a mode of black subjectification again surfaces in the images of athletes such as Shaquille O'Neal and Ben Johnson. Hazel Carby delineates how Hollywood's multimillion-dollar international trade in black male bodies continues to hold in place the monstrosity of racial marketization by re-positioning colonialism as entertainment (Carby 1998, 1). This monetization and cultural appropriation of the human emphasizes the point that despite its thrusting for transformative power, black flesh continues to be symbolically detained and consumed by forms of market power. History, with its prevailing structural inequities, serves as an agent influencing and, at times, even dictating the spaces in which the body is re-colonized. The fundamental issue hinges on the imperial conventions of maintaining the illusion that the black body is, after all, not human but chattel, and bespeaks the expressive and affective capacities of fantasies, enjoyment and desire. Fred D'Aguiar argues that it is this terror which precisely preys upon the flesh, heart and the soul of black life (D'Aguiar 2015, 5). With recourse to deconstructing the enterprises predicated on the sub-humanity of the African athlete, Brand gives authority, via the creative imagination, to rephrase the present according to its own priorities. The projection and co-existence of the past with the present allows her as a new historian, who is inscribing, to chronicle continuances and diversions. Her artistic agenda encompasses a resistance of the systems that subjugate and dictate the terms of black existence.

The violence of colonialism is also re-inscribed in the apparatus of policing. This is immanent in the graphic sodomy of Haitian immigrant Abner Louima by New York police officers (Brand 2001, 47). Brand subsequently draws attention to Amadou Diallo's horrific death (shot forty-one times by four white police officers) in 2000 (Brand 2001, 47). Oppression is ingrained in a system in which the humanity of the African American is so easily denied. The exploitative technique of policing plausibly follows a direct line of power from the overseer/slave dynamic. The continuity of violence is disturbingly evident in the physical stance of former officer Derek Chauvin, who, on 25 May 2020, knelt on George Floyd's neck for more than nine minutes – hands in his pockets, sunglasses on his head, unmoved – as Floyd pleaded for his life. According to data and analysis from the Black Lives Matter movement and other advocacy organizations,[1] US police brutality remains alarmingly prevalent in the year 2023, disproportionately impacting black communities and continuing patterns of systemic abuse rooted in racial injustice. For example, Black Lives Matter reported that, despite public outcry and reform promises, police killings in 2023 exceeded twelve hundred, with black persons nearly three times more likely to be racially profiled and killed than white individuals. Saidiya Hartman contends that the disproportionate number of deaths in the black diaspora reflects "the racial [and . . .] political arithmetic that was entrenched centuries ago" (Hartman 2007, 17). She declares, "This is the afterlife of slavery – skewed life chances . . . premature death, incarceration [and] impoverishment" (Hartman 2007, 17). By quoting and dating these modern accounts of disempowered positions alongside extracts from colonial materials – as in the abduction and imprisonment of black bodies at Fort King George, "baking in the iron prison atop [the] highest of peaks" (Hartman 2001, 197) – Brand illuminates how judicial conventions and their violence continue to discount and punish black lives. Imprisonment at forts and military prisons was an early spatial formation and modality of conquest. Far from describing a passage of progress, the writer relocates similar crimes in the present. Taken together, these pieces of information comprise a fluid and coherent narrative of historical cruelty that is enjambed in modern occasions. The effect is a chilling and ghostly visitation of colonial history – a portent of subaltern futurism.

To redefine the evaluative status of black life, Brand sets out to provide resuscitative interventions by plotting alterable codes that will recuperate black ontology. In her telling of multiple stories, the logic of black being engenders new personal and historic truths. Her concerns are with inventing alternative conceptual ways of seeing that will, in effect, empower African-diasporic communities to become their own creators and subsequently break out of the prison house of conquistadorial history. This is the resourcefulness of the creative imagination, and the creative artist can indeed be viewed as carrying the incipient seed of social transformation. Brand's attempt to show how a particular kind of art born of a people who suffer and endure is signalled in her contact with Yemaja, an archetypal mother of submerged African traditions who functions as a cultural repository, despite the fragmentation and calamity in the black diaspora. As the writer stands on the St Lucian coastline, a space where she encounters Yemaja, she begins to imitate the tide's ebb-like consciousness and places the guidance to begin her artistic experimentation squarely at the deity's feet (Brand 2001, 171). Yemaja is the Yoruba goddess of the ocean who exemplifies all women crossing the Atlantic. Her presence lures the writer to re-vision the lives she has missed. Yemaja, in this sense, manifests as Sycorax – uncremated and unburied. Her appearance equally signals separation and serves as a paradigm of the recurrent historical situation of severance, loss and anguish that is reborn during seasons of intense despair.

Folded into a process of journeying, Brand becomes immersed in a series of cycles, time zones and temporalities. In her own situation, she spends months searching for a form that is only found when she enters into a world of bridges and connections. While the water refers to the catastrophe of the Middle Passage, it is also a transitory space that provides artistic reflections and ancestral kinship. Brand's encounter with the water deity facilitates an imaginative re-evaluation of continental African cosmology and history. By implication, the legends of the diaspora's original peoples are legitimized, and Brand entertains the possibility that these are the true nexuses of self-affirmation, power and healing. As she moves across this new frontier, she incorporates and updates the past, while probing the undiscovered darkness of uncertain futures. The text can thus be read as a rendition of ritual reconnection with submerged feminine energies that provide the essential inspiration that a still alienated offspring needs. Recognition of these buried energies can thus be viewed as the beginning of cultural reclamation and building. In fact, this encounter facilitates an immediate need to rewrite histories and relocate identities in the postcolonial spaces.

Spurred by Yemaja to invent a narrative form that will model the shape of the Door of No Return and foreground the humanity of those victims whose existence has been flouted by racial terror, Brand's discursive representation takes on a fluid process of diasporic map-making that encompasses the vicissitudes of acquiescence, reaction and a movement away from stereotype to archetype. The effect lends to the comfort of belonging. The frame of simultaneous journeys, migrations, Middle Passages and crossings formulates a potentiating praxis in the quest for self-definition, agency and the capacity to chart a viable future and destiny outside of the fixities of absolute colonial representations and power. Black map-work is thus a destination deed and radical renewal of intellectual and civic order.

Brand's emphasis on and balance of ethnographic material embodies what Gilroy calls a "dramaturgy, enunciation, and gesture – the pre- and anti-discursive constituents of black metacommunication" (Brand 1993, 75). By formulating a conversation with the submerged and concealed presences of history, she designs liberating networks across a wide spiritual continent. This radical interweaving of the past with the present reflects a need to restore equality between thought and intuitive knowledge systems. Her fluid narrative technique recalls the contraction that underpins Brathwaite's tidal expansion, and which abandons the narrative linear advancement for the pulsion of cross currents. Brand's radical transhistorical aesthetic certainly makes the ghosts of history felt as they intervene in the modern world. Speaking back to the frontier of white colonial cartography, in which the price demanded was silent surrender and an abandonment of potentially subversive ideas, she evades the grip of metropolitan stagnation/sterility.

This is foregrounded in the manner in which she activates the life that is beneath the surface of things: the ghostly histories of forced and voluntary migration; the forces and agencies – human and divine – that work together to terminate neocolonial stagnation; and the persistence of alternative cultural modalities that offer the potential for creative transformation. Her focus is on activism and the ushering in of change through artistic invention. This modality of knowledge production is overtly affirmed when Brand states, "'It is 4:45 am' and grips a compass that appears before her" (Brand 2001, 52). In this theatre of ritual and performance, she encounters the spirit of Gabriel Garcia Marquez whose "fountain pen with peacock blue ink" (Brand 2001, 72) she borrows to produce coordinates that lead to new maps. This extra-terrestrial and psychic connection with New World writers makes the point that the diaspora's maps are, in part, psychic. What is apparent is a constant pull of 'home' (the Caribbean) –which becomes mythologized in her memoir. The leitmotifs of the page and pen, as epitomized at the point in which she "bow[s] to a page [and where] the pen moves in scars" (Brand 2001, 39) concretize the cultural sites from which she retrieves liberatory tactics. Her experimental techniques may be usefully applied to how a radically decentred subject can respond to history. Moreover, her circling back to foundational experiences enables a transgressive mental landscape.

By tracing the debut violence of conquest and the scene of making the sub-human through the dominant frame of the Door of No Return, she stirs a necessary dialogue about the ways in which black life and its interface with the butchery of white privilege can be rethought so that it is given an alternative political and social force. Her acute representation of the always-felt ghosts, vicissitudes of capital and embodied stereotypes in the modern world serves as a small but potent redress for the belated haunting of colonial trauma. Her memoir creates critical occasions to reimagine black entanglement through the frameworks of spectrality and literary cartography. Although largely edgeless in its form, Brand's text invites the reader to partake in a process of what listening for justice sounds like.

Her literary cartography nudges towards a different vision as illustrated in the images of fluidity and alterability that are apropos to the processes of movement and journeying. Her statement at the end of the text gestures towards this analytical leap: "A map, then, is . . . a life of conversations about a forgotten list of irretrievable selves" (Brand 2001, 224). The "life of conversations" signposts the framing mechanisms of deities who become guides, the implicit deployment of cultural memory that bonds ideology to language, and the encircling movements between real and imagined spaces, which generate their own creative energy. Central to this framework is the recognition that maps are not solely physical or geographical, but extend into generational, metaphysical and imaginative spaces that create a multidimensional sense of place, which defy colonial binaries and hierarchies. The reflective apparatus of memoir-writing, therefore, becomes a new cartographic template that is associated with self-knowledge, revolution and indeed a rise to new interventions that interrupt violent present outworkings of old and new empires. In other words, this reimagined map disrupts the epistemic violence of imperial cartographies that erase and distort Indigenous and diasporic knowledge systems. It subsists on the power of autobiography and the communities that the self is rooted in. Wholeness, unity, stability and linearity are rejected in favour of a more fragmentary approach to piece together the details of a life. Doing so allows for multiple factors to overlap and crosscut each other; as the text itself demonstrates, there are multiple issues present in any given moment.

STITCHWORK AS HEALING

Erna Brodber, in *Nothing's Mat,* similarly approaches the issues of ontological erasure, the contestation for equal rights to space and the advocacy for cultural memory, albeit by paying close attention to the concepts of home and community. While Brand trades the home space for constant passages through the Door of No Return, Brodber makes creative use of communal spaces to find alliances that would facilitate the channelling of black self-interest and recovery. The novella spans the post-slavery era through to contemporary times and chronicles the struggles of the formerly enslaved population to achieve physical and psychic reconstitution. The events unfold from Princess' A-Level project assignment of crafting a family tree. Alongside Brodber's reimagining of the family tree, the text engages with the themes of marronage, the landscape as nurturing presence, orality, and diaspora. The turn towards the intimate archive of the family provides a methodological foray into how the colonial past needs to be understood through its traces of memory (or lack thereof) deep within the individual, familial and communal realities.

Born in England to Jamaican parents, Princess is energized by revitalizing trips to Jamaica. These journeys are impelled by her mother, who suggests that a study of her father's complex West Indian lineage would necessitate a radical revision of received European ideas of the nuclear family. Princess' father is asked, "Where are you going to put Conut, your mother's sister who isn't your mother's sister?" (Brodber 2014, 5). It prompts Princess to unravel the enigma of her intricate lineage. Her voyage to the "odd places [where] . . . wisdom reside" (Brodber 2014, 36) speaks to her criteria for a template that rejects her British classmates' seemingly stable and linear assemblage of the family tree. The text thus carries references to the earliest perspectives of the Caribbean family wherein non-nuclear family structures were described as disintegrated families. Princess grapples with moments of self-doubt as she garners fragments of a submerged past to assemble her project. She remembers being in a dismal place of emptiness, dehumanized by the barrenness of her family's archive and must "pull forward [her] memory to console [her]self" (Brodber 2014, 3). Like the thirteen-year-old Brand, who longs to know her ancestor's names, Princess is a cultural orphan who is cut off from her community. This sense of alienation is buttressed by the point that she is educated out of her skin and is subjected to a curriculum that pivots itself on classed vantage points. Her desire for answers finds remedy in Cousin Nothing's statement: "[We] have an anchor" (Brodber 2014, 5). It is a cryptic declaration that offers the young protagonist a series of cardinal points available through memory, which, if harnessed, will point the way out of un-belonging.

When Princess first arrives in Jamaica, Conut begins her revelation of the family's heritage. Her storytelling, with its dedicated focus on female representations of abuse and survival, begins with her mother's (Clarise) first sexual encounter with a much older neighbour called Maas Eustace. Clarise, who is too young to grasp the significance of her rape and the reality of pregnancy, gave birth on her own in a latrine to a premature baby girl. Upon hearing unusual noises, Clarise's adoptive mother, Aunt Maud, inquired what was wrong. Clarise responded with, "Nothing" (Brodber 2014, 17).

Maud retrieves the child from her and responds, "So dis ya something wid two legs, ten toes and ten fingers, and a head is 'nothing'?" (Brodber 2014, 17). Although the child is named June, she is consistently called Nothing. However, in this character, Brodber enacts a paradoxical manoeuvre that negates the larger purported history-less-ness of the family – an amnesia that resonates in Brand's discourse. Despite her inauspicious beginnings, Nothing becomes, in effect, a conduit of redemption since her memories and emblematic tapestries are essential to repairing the lost narratives in her family's lineage. Her storytelling enterprises convey the importance of cycles through which Princess recognizes the necessity of spontaneity, cooperation and creative agency.

The mat that Conut weaves carries important communal associations with cultural preservation as it curves back into the family's history. It also brings forth into the present moment ancestral, earth-based resources that provide empowerment. For example, the fronds from which the mat is made require chopping from the macca plant; then they have to be cut, beaten and washed to ensure the strings of the sisal are sturdy. Subsequently, the sisal is dried, combed and coordinated into strong cords, which are finally sewn into circles. Princess is taught this symbolic process by Conut. It is through this shared activity of mapping textiles and storytelling that both women form a mutually enriching relationship. Interestingly, Conut's meditative exercise in braiding together the vines from the sisal plants in honour of those pre-slavery communities invokes a creative connection with the Egyptian goddess, Ma'at, who is the personification of truth and communal balance. Paul Johnson recognizes Ma'at as the cultural ideal of social harmony and connective justice. He notes, "Ma'at was . . . the form of justice dispensed when a man [or woman] died and appeared at the last judgement: his [or her] soul was then weighed in a pair of scales against Ma'at. There was, in short, a very close association in the Egyptian's mind between moral goodness, mundane justice, and artistic order" (Johnson 1999, 50).

Taking a lead from Johnson, one can discern that in Conut's technical weighing of fibre and cloth, which she spins to organize and synthesize the disparate parts of her heritage, the principle of Ma'at prevails. Furthermore, Conut's position as artisan, which involves the regulation of the relationship among cords and strands that ply around one another, resonates with the ethical principles of the goddess as in her perpetuation of harmony and cosmological balance. When Princess is unable to fit the stories that Conut tells her into her English lesson plan, she decides to create a suitable template of "never ending circles that . . . seemed like a mat of family" (Brodber 2014, 14). These circles, which carry the imprint of history (facts) and story (mythical truths), become a platform for the performance of psychic revelations that lead to further illumination. Princess says, "In my mind I called this [circle] Miss Maud. Smaller ones in descending order were crafted" (Brodber 2014, 18).

Melvin Rahming assesses the syncretic and shamanic nature of Brodber's fiction and observes that she presents her readership with "a pre-existing and transhistorical order . . . where the operations of deceased characters allow for the delimitation of time, space, and history" (Rahming 2001, 11). According to him, these transhistorical and cross-cultural intersections "affirm the imaginative process by which [black diasporic] history can be probed beyond its materialist, and into its cosmospiritual [. . .] terrain. This recognition makes clear an important aspect of [Brodber's] contribution to the discourse of Caribbean hybridity: the world of cross-cultural fertilization turns on the axis of cosmic integrity" (Rahming 2001, 7). One can see how Conut's textiles operate as an interwoven metaphor that fits into Rahming's spiritual-critical evaluations. More particularly, her mat combines cross-cultural threads of conversations and reflects the deep capacity of literature to produce new ways of seeing. The strings tied into its fabric represent several narratives of history and myth, which reinforce the layering of belief systems that have gone into the making of the black diaspora. In its progression of tracing a history of atrocity, the novel moves towards the discovery of what is hidden between lines of sight and legend.

Of equal significance is that Conut identifies the anatomy of the ping wing macca plant with a growth progression that follows the natural path (Brodber 2014, 13). Her description of the shape of the leaves as fractals (as opposed to fractured) is noteworthy: "one leaf would emerge, then another, then two – the sum of one and one – then three – the sum of two and one, then five would emerge [. . .] the number of leaves continuing to determine the next number of leaves to infinity" (Brodber 2014, 3). The interlaced progression of the plant articulates the intricate spiritual, artistic and ideological interconnectedness across African communities. Through these intersections, Brodber is in fact producing patterns of self-similarity and is curating alternative epistemological frames for envisioning ideas of communal identity and value systems. Her deployment of a critical human geography that reaches out from one body to another has deep echoes with Brand's discursive enterprise of new cartographies that she wields to interrogate a history of brutality that goes back at least five hundred years. To this extent, Conut's mat functions as a talismanic mirror, which is emblematic of self-reflection and life review.

As an agent of life, the mat carries not only one's immediate reflection but also images of the self which are stored in memory. In *The Continent of Black Consciousness*, Brodber elaborates on the need to locate metaphors, tools and tropes that will give centrality to the submerged history and nature of black communities globally – the knowledge of which will serve to authorize subalternized identities worldwide (Brodber 2003, xi). Princess becomes a self-seer with the aid of the talismanic tapestry and Conut's hypnotizing storytelling initiatives. She is able to psychically travel deep into Maud's history (Conut's grandmother) and learn of the suffering and remarkable survival of the womenfolk in her lineage. Her contact with the mat's spiral stitchwork transports her to the year 1865, during the Morant Bay rebellion. Similar to the historical labour uprising, which facilitated a greater degree of equitable wages, food security, ethical working conditions and articulations of self-agency for the newly emancipated black working class, Brodber polemically raises questions about the force and power of communal consciousness in the diaspora.

Embedded in the context of the revolution are the smaller stories of sexual violence and how the black female body is held as commodity. This is evident in Maud's brutal gang-rape by seven Maroons who seek revenge for her part in the labour riots.[2] Thus, amidst the transformative action of the rebellion, there is also the specific banality of human violence that exists prior to any context of social unrest. The struggle for personal emancipation is therefore eminently grounded in the erstwhile efforts of individual perseverance and sacrifice. This is revealed in Maud's immediate action to protect young Clarise, the sister of her slain betrothed, Modibe.

To safeguard her health, Maud travels on foot from Stony Gut to Kingston, and in that time, looks after Clarise, whom she barely knows. So violent is Maud's rape that she has to self-medicate using a blend of local herbs and rely on psychic connections with spirits (as instructed by Ma Lou, a ceremony woman) to address the wounding and infection that set in. On a micro level, Maud's fleeing of the parish stimulates a recall of black bodies on the move – or transitional bodies – who have the capacity for unexpected and unanticipated movements that overturn their proprietors' or slave owners' claims to them as property. Accordingly, some of the most intense connections between the past and the present operate during transitional moments and a palimpsest collapse of time and space.

As Princess listens in on the conversation between Ma Lou and Maud, she learns about the value of community and healing rituals. Maud's statement to Clarise, "Good spirit . . . will show me things . . . Modibe would be with [us,] so [we] press on" (Brodber 2014, 49) as they trod the off-beaten path brings illumination to Princess about the reliance on a pre-existent cosmic-spiritual order that is engaged to exert guidance and healing influences on the lives of specific individuals. Brodber, it seems, is illuminating the hidden springs of exterior reality, revealing a complex tapestry comprised of the mundane workings of the physical world and its deep connection with a spiritually complex reality. Princess is established as an initiate who must discover the metaphysical keys that have been buried deep within her consciousness. Another of Maud's silent strategies in the looming threat of violence is to seek cover at nights in a cave near the ocean. The shape of the cave suggests a maternal womb within which the women fleeing rape and despoliation find safety and rest. Both Clarise and Maud would perform the ritual of sleeping on the bunka skin – a sacred quilt handed over by Ma Lou – to ensure their safe passage to Kingston. The signifying protection of the quilt creatively connects with Conut's mat that she crafts nearly a century later. Cultural artefacts are therefore to be perceived as a communicative network that engenders attitudes of resilience and perseverance.

Also couched within the narrative of Maud's violation and subsequent movement is the observation that violence may be perceived as a haunting, inter-generational presence. Despite Maud's excessive vigilance over Clarise's well-being, the girl is molested by Maas Eustace at an obscenely young age.

Conut, too, is brutally beaten by Everard Turnbury. The son of a white father and a black mother, Everard marries Cousin Nothing and they move into the house which belonged to the Turnbury family before his father drank away the family estate. Fractal repetition sees Everard's return to his family estate, but Everard observes that he is shunned because of his inter-racial marriage: "My father once made a comment which suggested that he felt my mother was forced on him because she could bring to Turnbury some material things it needed. If this was my father's psychological pain, his path to drunkenness, then my projected relationship with the girl was just a reliving of my father's relationship" (Brodber 2014, 69). In this sense, he recognizes how easy it would be to repeat generational patterns, which would render him a lonely alcoholic like his father. However, the novel reveals a variety of incarnations of matrifocal strength amidst cycles of domestic abuse, violence and abandonment. Repetition with a difference thus allows for potentiality, which is symbolized in the gift of interiority and strength. Brodber's approach of breaking the silence around their suffering, and re-inventing their crises as "fractals" rather than "fractures" (Brodber 2014, 14) informs an empowering, grassroots and communal activity of weaving the diversely powerful and texturized cords into the mat to communicate the stories that can no longer haunt. The immersive and interactive installation of personalized patterns in Conut's quilt-work provides a nurturing activity where participants joined in the craftwork, weaving the shreds of their histories together in a unique shape.

The circuit of histories, which the fractals represent, also breaks secret narratives of abuse. Silence is challenged through the enterprise of fashioning more open communities every day within the diaspora. Brodber instructs that such work is likely to ensure that the region will not be "lost in a recursion" of gendered violence (Brodber 2014, 39). Ron Eglash states that the binding components of a diasporan grid of points include an affinity with ancestors, the effective reliance on transnational, collective memories and the augmenting of material history to the spiritual, artistic and everyday work across African diasporic communities (Eglash 1999, 4). After taking her backward glance, Princess returns to the present with an irreversible wealth of knowledge. The ramifications of her time-travel are profound as she begins to articulate the influence of the fractals. She declares that the fractals are connections made from generation to generation, often simply because her ancestors were devoted to safeguarding the power of their memories. Brodber's text does not gaze back nostalgically for a provincial, rural past, but rather operates as a material after-image of history. These after-images are imaginatively pursued as generating spaces in which trauma can be alleviated.

Embedded in the utility of Conut's mat is the concept of the Golden Mean, which suggests a way back to connectedness with that which is larger than one's self and offers the possibility of redemption (Brodber 2003, 36). Arithmetically, the concept of the Golden Mean encompasses both the notions median and mean. The median is defined as the middle number in a distribution of numbers while the mean is the average of the numbers. Both concepts combine to illustrate the necessity of procuring balance between opposites in a spectrum. The mean or median finds representation in the terrain of the mat that operates between two extreme spaces – the past and present, the immaterial and the material, inertia and agency. The mat's position as intermediary or conduit is enhanced by its inherent power of being formed from the sisal plant, which is rumoured to carry imperishable prophetic resources. Through its integration and arrangement in the level of the observable or material world, Princess is furnished with revelation and spiritual transformation. When she returns to England, her teacher informs her that her research might prove that the West Indian family is "fractal" rather than "fractured" (Brodber 2014, 36). In effect, the teacher means that the complex connections which comprise her family lineage exhibit Princess' family structure as defiant of Western mono-linear traditions. Conut's mat, with its woven terrains and range of scales, becomes a powerful tool which empowers those who encounter it to think about the subject-making violence of slavery (and its afterlife) as a unique and irreducible process of social relation, without producing neat borders around them. Her stitchwork re-arranges normative modes of feeling, thinking and understanding blackness.

The climax of the novel coincides with Princess' recognition that her destiny is wrapped in the responsibility of continuing to fashion strings of circles into recursions and iterations. That she returns to Jamaica at the age of thirty to further probe and weave together stories about her community underscores Brodber's ethos of continual acts of self-fashioning. This unceasing process of cultivating knowledge is a style that is rooted in diligent spadework which are spatialized in the three narratives that Princess bridges together (the history of Maud's rape, set in 1865; the tradition of Conut's mat, which she sews to represent the transmigration of souls to Jamaica across the Atlantic; and the narrative of Conut's marriage to Everand). Like a vast net with looping patterns that are filled with far-flung relatives, with *Nothing's Mat*, there is multiplicity, heterogeneity and a network of coordinates that resist linear progression. Not unlike Brand's *Map*, Brodber's narrative design works as a treatise on the quest for a new form and vocabulary that will continuously transgress and push the boundaries of homogenizing and imperialist logic towards a re-evaluation of ideas, such as family, community, ancestor, identity and culture. The fractal, however, is not necessarily always a redemptive move, especially when combined with the kind of trauma that attends to sexual abuse repeated over generations. The point that repetition can be a condemnation is recognized in Nothing's instructions to Princess: "Your end is your beginning" (Brodber 2014, 14). Conut is equally cautioning on the imperative of constant creative labour, where every person in the diaspora is bound to the task of self-authoring enterprises, despite the differences in nationality and culture. The type of recursion Brodber describes is an iteration, a loop whereby each time the process creates an output, it uses this result as an input for the next iteration. This modality of repetition is laden with dual potential: it may facilitate transformative regeneration and may offer a means of revisiting and reshaping inherited legacies; yet it also risks perpetuating patterns of unaltered intergenerational hurt. This duality thus compels an active negotiation embedded in the symbol of the recursive loop, where repetition becomes not merely an echo of the past but a site of potential re-creation and even rebirth.

After her death, Conut's memory is kept alive in patterns of voicing and storytelling. The same can be said of the structure of the novel through which each chapter leaves a strand that is developed in the next section. The novel,[3] in this sense, symbolically becomes an extension of the mat that Conut weaves in its circular format as Princess assumes the role of storyteller and transmitter to her adopted children who are symbolically named Clarise and Modibe. This imbibes the creative practice of the fractal. At the heart of the concept is Benoit Mandelbrot's observation that natural shapes, such as clouds, coastlines and mountains, which seem completely irregular, often resolve themselves into repeated patterns of recursions (Mandelbrot 1967, 636). Epitomized in the self-repeated acts of migration, return and child-shifting practices, the fractals may also be engaged to reimagine Caribbean communities as a variegated patchwork of polymorphous connections. These are not nuclear or linear family trees but communities in which people make complex connections with one another in repeating patterns of ad hoc affinity and adoption, often simply because they care for each other: "We feel for each other and carry each other's pain and blessing so much so that if the designated one cannot or will not perform, we take on the task" (Brodber 2014, 103). The underlying patterns of multiple stories and histories that weave into and through each other produce a strong but flexible representation of community that is always recursively produced. Such communities cannot be assumed, but are the products of everyday labour, shared activity, mutually enriching relationships and the capacity to recognize each of its members, despite barriers caused by ongoing legacies of oppression, forced migration and violence.

The mat, with its representative network of cultural and transhistorical connections across time and space, is paradoxical to the idea of 'nothing-ness' in Caribbean historiography and with regional critics such as V.S. Naipaul, who declared, "The history of the islands can never be satisfactorily told [. . .]. History is built around achievement and creation; and nothing was created in the West Indies" (Naipaul 1996, 39). His articulation of a Caribbean void is certainly counteracted by Brodber's novel, which embodies an impulse to retrieve, craft and procure the movement of progress, maturation and development by placing Princess within the shifting networks of increased connectivity and juxtaposition of time-spaces, rather than within linear progression and colonial power relations. Contrary to her name, it is Nothing who becomes a respected elder in the black community – a prosperous entrepreneur of a large estate in Kingston and a living repository of untold knowledge that dispels the social dislocation of her decedents.

Across both Brand's and Brodber's fictions, the entrance of ancestors creates the sense of otherworldliness which is integral to daily life. The preeminence of polyvocality, multiple journeying and the collapse of traditional time generate defamiliarization, which constrains closer scrutiny of the present. The sense of the spectral is also enhanced by locational choices which blur the divide between the living and the dead. As illustrated in Johnson's images in chapter 1, persons figured in unlikely positions could just as easily be actual or spirit presences. Territories which seamlessly coexist suggest the need for greater attention to the nature of the diasporic consciousness through which an unsilencing of the unspeakable provides immense healing worth and liberatory praxis. Interestingly, the trope of the more-mythic-than-real maternal figures is rehearsed in Olive Senior's and Lawrence Scott's creative works. We contend that both books by Senior and Scott, which evoke memory work in relation to black othermothers, who are enslaved or yoked to domestic servitude, are equally invested in acts of recovery and representations of haunted memories. Their discourses lend credence to the correlation between trauma and ageing, and particularly the resurgence of traumatic memories when ageing persons forget to forget.

chapter 3

Servant Mothering, Memory Work and Empathy in Senior's "The Pain Tree" and Scott's "The Wedding Photograph"

> Over the shining mud the moon is blood
> falling on ocean at the fence of lights-
> My course I set, I give my sail the wind
> to navigate the islands of the stars
> till I collect my scattered skeleton
> till I collect . . .
>
> —*Martin Carter, "Till I Collect" (2006)*

DEEP INTENSITIES OF FEELING AND PASSION have been expended by live-in domestic workers who have served as caregivers to their masters' children, invariably at the expense of fostering intimacies with their own. The resultant corporeal and emotional links within the children are thereafter disciplined by stringent ethnic and class prescriptions, and relationship laws which determine who should love and maintain intimacy with whom, and how such connections should be negotiated and expressed. Privileged children raised in this paradoxical framework are constrained to reject the racialized caregivers and other mothers as part of their maturation process and to adopt the prejudicial, denigrating values of the ruling elite. This chapter reads Olive Senior's "The Pain Tree" (2017) and Lawrence Scott's, "The Wedding Photograph" (2015) as acts of re-memory through which the protagonists recognize their existential void, reclaim a mythical (more so than real) affective connection with their childhood comforters and caregivers, and find ontological grounding through empathetic identification with the absent othermothers' passion and pain.

The dynamics of contemporary master-servant relations in the Caribbean carry the stamp of its colonial antecedent. Racialized embodiment of the impoverished, lower-strata, Afro-Caribbean caregivers marks them as destined for servitude, whereas embodiment of the upper-strata, white or light-skinned employers demarcates them as destined to be served. This conundrum is made more complex by the necessity within many of the high-brown descendants of the planter class to distance themselves from the enemy within, the invariably erased black ancestress who is perceived as having violated white bloodlines. The compulsion of masters to casually bed these live-in domestic servants who are serving within their homes, is compellingly evoked by Senior in "Moonlight" (2017), which is exemplary of the competition between white mistresses and their black servants for the patriarch's sexual favours. This similarly has implications for the emotional adjustment of children, who particularly in infancy, stand to develop stronger affective linkages with servant other mothers than with blood mothers.

This chapter reads servant mothering as reflecting the troubled interface of trauma and individual, communal and ancestral memory. The challenge is to dredge up the absent and erased other mother in order to interrogate and reconstruct submerged childhood moorings. Within the Caribbean framework, the raced and despised other mother is invariably associated with the natal land. Senior's "The Pain Tree" traces the inner journey of the protagonist and focalizer, Lorraine, who is a child of the wealthy planter class in Jamaica (2017). The narrative is set in the period between emancipation and independence in which the formerly enslaved were contending with the ruling elite over the parameters of emancipation and the configuration of the emerging social order. Arguably, as significant as broad-based political, economic and legal issues were, the complex forces that shaped the lives of peoples in transition were just as fiercely negotiated in the domestic and affective domains. According to Brereton and Yelvington in *The Colonial Caribbean in Transition*, grappling with this complex cause and effect dynamic which determines "the lives of people largely hidden from history, depends on an understanding of cultural stances, linguistic modes and states of mind" (Brereton and Yelvington 1999, 3). Fierce battles with high stakes raged because "Colonial power in many cases became more entrenched *after* emancipation. At the same time, the dispossessed and disenfranchised masses worked within severe constraints to create structures and situations that would guarantee autonomy, dignity and advancement" (Brereton and Yelvington 1999, 2). This narrative focuses on the affective dimension of domestic labour relations, in relation to care work and particularly the battle for heart share.

The protagonist, sent to boarding school in England at age ten, leaving behind both her parents and her servant caregiver, Larissa, returns a decade and a half later after her father dies. Her mother delights in the daughter's return as a qualified archaeologist to the plantation house, with its seventeenth-century foundations, hoping that the daughter would claim her inheritance and restore the great house and estate to its former glory. A pivotal issue in "The Pain Tree" is the inheritance of the post-colonial kingdom: What is its fruitful legacy? Who is qualified to lay claim to it? What is the basis for determining the legitimacy of the inheritance? And more specific to the concern of this enquiry, what inheritance, passed through which matrilineage, would prove most sustaining and nurturing for the descendent of the planter class? Significantly, the text charts an act of re-memory of a returning daughter whose need for ontological groundings requires her to come to terms with the individual and collective past. Given the history of ignominious beginnings, the violations, lies, erasures, shady antecedents and infamous acts which characterize colonial histories, the protagonist muses: "For us, the past was a condensed version" (Senior 2017, 2). In her quest for the source of the waste and emptiness of her inner being, she recovers the history of her erased othermother, the domestic caregiver, Larissa. Mother is associated here with home/motherland, route and rooting, ground and groundation.

In choosing the metaphor of archaeology to delineate the costly and painstaking task of unearthing erased and silenced ancestors, vestigial umbilical cords and modes of being, Senior joins numerous Caribbean writers whose works have engaged this project. Martin Carter's act of re-membering requires exhuming and collecting scattered skeletons (Carter 2006, 95). Similarly, Wilson Harris' cycles of death and rebirth are aimed at unearthing lost and submerged selves as the latent ground of new potentialities and being and becoming, which have shaken free of official histories of conquest and subjugation (Harris 1988, 111–14). These theoretical postulations are not unlike Brodber's reconstruction of the collective trauma of enslavement, which requires a quest for knowledge lost to conscious memories but entombed in the bodies reduced to cryptological archives (Brodber 2007, 29). For the protagonist in "The Pain Tree", the task is to unearth personal affective ties with her surrogate mother which is her minute subset of global patterns of master/servant relations. It is at this point that the unjust and inequitable past interfaces with post-emancipation ethnic, class and labour relations.

Lorraine, who is suffering from a vague dis/ease, disconnection, alienation and shame, all of which are associated with her complicities with the unjust imperial order, alongside her growing sense of being orphaned, must take a series of discrete steps. The first is to shake loose from the high stakes involved in her subject location as a member of the dominant class, including disavowal of the values and emotional connectivity attached to privileged group membership. To do so, she must loosen ties with her birth/blood mother, renounce the condensed, exclusionary version and seek the fuller narrative of the past. The journey is, from inception, a visionary, internal one, triggered by her arrival home: "The moment I arrived home, I had a vision of her instead of my mother, it startled me it seemed so real" (Senior 2017, 1). The implication is that for the progeny of the planter class, it would be impossible to arrive home without confronting the erased and submerged othermother. Symbolically, she must undermine the first level of preservation. Her mother is herself a relic of a past that is swiftly losing ground. As representative of the hegemonic order and the planter class, she is facing a world in which she and her kind are swiftly losing currency, all the while cherishing the hope that their offspring would resuscitate past grandeur. Described by her daughter as well preserved, her hope for everlastingness is reflected in externalities and trappings of her race and class status. Armed with impeccable grooming into hard shiny surfaces – hair, nails, dress – she appears ossified and is associated with death.

The text juxtaposes life purpose as defined in hegemonic narrative with an alternative intent and positionality which is emerging: "Mother loved to say I was coming home to possess my inheritance. She told people I had chosen to study archaeology because I had been born in a house with seventeenth-century foundations" (Senior 2017). The submerged, underlying narrative plays out in the inner musing of the protagonist: "Yes I would say to myself, built of the finest cut stone, the mortar hard as iron because it was sweetened with molasses and slave blood" (Senior 2017). The second step is to move beyond an intellectual acknowledgement of kinship and to embrace instead, emotional and affective linkages with the lost othermother. And this, the protagonist accomplishes through an act of rememory. In a generic sense, memory is evoked in order to refine and generate meaning out of life events. Indeed, it works hardest when the life experiences have been chaotic and inchoate. Moreover, the absence, erasure or repression of memories, which may be submerged beneath the level of consciousness, have the power to reshape behaviours, attitudes, aspirations and feelings. The process is embedded in the affective domain not only insofar as it induced strong memories, but also because it awakens emotions and feelings of the maternal collective of childhood.

If soul sickness and collective trauma have emerged out of denigration and loss of ancestral and cultural moorings, it stands to reason that healing intervention would rest on recuperation of this connection. In Caribbean fictions, return to revisionary African cultural mooring has sparked the literary imaginations of generations of writers of diverse ancestries and class positionalities. In a bid to recover denigrated and erased subjectivities and to recover cultural continuity with precolonial worlds, epistemologies and ontologies, these thinkers enter into what Theo D'haen, in "Cultural Memory and the Postcolonial", terms the therapeutic use of post-colonial counter-memory in discourse involving a protracted process of negotiation with the legacy of European colonialism (D'haen 2015, 3).

Marianne Hirsch, exploring the imperative faced by the progeny of holocaust survivors to become the keepers of the previous generation's often unarticulated and suppressed memories, speaks to the problematics involved in even defining them as memories (Hirsch 2008). Mentioning formulations such as belated memory, absent memory, inherited memory and vicarious witnessing, she settles on the concept of post memory, defined as the "structure of inter- and trans-generational transmission of traumatic knowledge and experience" which, though connected to the past, is not "actually mediated by recall but by imaginative investment, projections and creation" (Hirsch 2008, 107). With skilful use of narrative, Senior sketches an absent, haunting, voiceless, pervasive, mothering presence who becomes the quest object of the protagonist and the pivot of the story. The task is to materialize her from the invisibility and erasure of the past, despite her absence from the present time of the narrative. The avenue is through memory-work by the protagonist whose brisk act of rejection of her servant-mother in childhood becomes a repressed site of pain and disconnection: "I was suddenly flooded with the shame of a memory that I had long hidden from myself: when I was going off to England, I had left without saying goodbye to Larissa, closest companion for my first ten years . . . My parents were already seated in the car. I was about to get in when Larissa said, 'Wait! I forget. I have something for you.' And she rushed off" (Senior 2017, 18). The ten-year-old child who rejects the caregiver's paltry gift at parting has evolved into a tentative, fragile, unrooted, decentred adult, who gradually comes to see herself as scarred by mother loss. The protagonist finds herself mourning the loss of the gift from Larissa that she ignored in her childhood. Since Larissa is a poor woman in a plantation economy which values only the material, the protagonist muses that any benefit or wealth that Larissa represents must be in terms of emotion and connectivity.

Senior evokes a process by which personal memory fuses with cultural memory. The message is delivered through a powerful evocation of the manner in which the past becomes a palimpsest imprinted on the lives of the poor and disempowered. This is epitomized in the tapestry of newspaper clippings that both Larissa and Lorraine compiled in the past. Here, personal recollection fuses with broader communal representations that are showcased via the mass media and embodied in images of a sprawling empire, of war and mass migration:

> the walls . . . were completely covered with pages and pictures cut out of newspapers and magazines and pasted down, all now faded and peeling . . . I recognized many of the pictures as those I had helped Larissa to cut out [. . .]. I liked scenes of far-off lands and old buildings best while her favourites were the Holy Family, the British Royal Family and beautiful clothes. But, as time went on, headlines, scenes, whole pages about the War in Europe took over (Senior 2017, 3).

This process of spending hours papering the walls of the quarters is a signifier of how little the material condition of labourers' lives has changed with the abolition. The wallpaper, derived from old newspapers and magazines, is reflective of life circumstances over which Larissa and her slave ancestors have no agency. Operating as disempowered inhabitants of small island states, they are steeped in daily existence determined by the impingement of global geopolitical economy, including its warmongering manoeuvres. Complex layering of the wallpaper is the only choice afforded and the only viable option for enhancing and enlarging one's space and positioning oneself within a bigger framework. Larissa's search for significance takes the form of love for beautiful clothes that she will never wear. This she assuages by pasting fashion pictures on walls until global events take prominence. She represents an instantiation of Homi Bhabha's unhomely, in which the act of reconstruction requires retrieval of collective memory, which generates, in turn, social attitude changes and narrative reconstructions (Bhabha 1992). As Lorraine stands in a dusty, empty barrack yard – a repository of unspoken anguish – she finally understands the need to confront her own grief. Where, then, is Larissa to be found? The servant mother becomes a ghostly presence, a haunting apparition that lives in the rememory of the needy woman who parted company with her as a ten year old. This is epitomized in the vision that Lorraine has of Larissa with a gift in her hand, waiting to greet her as she arrives home.

In terms of mothering, Larissa loses her sons twice to interrelated economic forces. In order to work to provide for them, she must leave them in the care of her mother and transfer her love and mothering impulses to the child of her mistress. She loses her sons a second time when they eagerly respond to the call of the careless and oppressive imperial mother to join the Second World War. Here, Larissa suffers the tragic loss of her favoured son, Zebedee Breeze, to conflict at sea. The missive from the authorities reflects the impersonality and exploitative abuse of these soldiers from the colonies who, after all, are only highly expendable, functional parts of a formidable war machinery.

The third step is to own the histories laid down within our inner beings, which hamper or hinder our capacity to successfully negotiate life journeys. As Lorraine stands in Larissa's room – a space where memory becomes layered and textured – she begins to:

> feel almost faint, as if the walls were crawling towards me, the layers of fractured images thickening, shrinking the space, absorbing the light coming through the window and from the open door until I felt I was in a tomb surrounded by hieroglyphics; images of war and the crucified Christ; princesses and movie stars; cowboys and curly haired children, pampered cats and dogs, lions and zebras in the zoos, long haired girls strutting the latest fashions, beauty creams, toothpaste and motor cars. Images of people who were never like the people who had occupied this room (Senior 2017, 7).

Larissa's room constrains a recognition of complicity with the death-dealing machinery of the hegemonic order. It becomes a tomb surrounded by hieroglyphics – a death chamber whose walls of pulsating signs speak of violence and violation; social and physical death, administered through war and exclusionary belief systems; mass-mediated erasure of personhood through images of beauty, which denigrate the physique of the other; and life-denying location of human beings, objectified, reduced to consumers. But the quest to find her othermother under the images, icons and other paraphernalia of built civilization bears no fruit. Although these images may be used as a panacea for the grimness of the circumscribed space, they fail to lend meaning and structure to their impoverished lives; fail to generate a significant inheritance for Larissa, her predecessors, and ultimately, for the protagonist, her returning daughter. The archaeological work of stripping away this palimpsest of the past in a terrible rage generates no sense of ruptured peace and displaced haunting presences.

The story culminates in a cryptic statement which affirms the 'them' and 'us' binary that survives the most painful and passionate attempts at redirection. The text speaks to a measured rapprochement based on a recognition of shared pain and loss. Lorraine discovers the capacity to drive her own nail into the pain tree. The second portion of the binary alludes to Jesus' statement: "Blessed are the meek for they shall inherit the earth." Notwithstanding her newfound empathetic identification, the protagonist asserts, "people like me would always inherit the land, but they were the ones that would possess the earth" (Senior 2017, 11). The land in this formulation refers to built environments located in time, like the great house, with its seventeen-century foundations of finest cut stones. As massive and indestructible as the physical and symbolic great house may appear, the imperial structures and their exploitative order are being undermined and supplanted by a denigrated people struggling to emerge into freedom. Even the countless palimpsestic layers of global events, represented in words, imagery and iconography pasted on the walls of slave huts, evoke a memory of contestations over the land. The inheritance of the earth is reflected in the depth and height of the pain tree, whose roots penetrate deep into the earth and whose branches reach the heaven.

The essence of Larissa and her ancestors is to be found not in the decaying manmade structures of the built environment, but in the majestic, growing, rooted structures of the natural environment. Senior evokes a mystic, affective connection with the living landscape, in which trees can nurture, sustain and exist in symbiosis with the wretched of the earth, who would alleviate pain and transcend adversity by nailing them to a tree. The roots that delve into the earth offer stability and rootedness; the branches soar to the heavens to offer hope and transcendence over pain suffering and adversity.

FORGETTING TO FORGET

Similarly, Lawrence Scott, in "The Wedding Photograph", explores the representations of racialized identities, cross-ethnic allegiances and the role of memory (Scott 2015). Focus is given to the discomfort of the close to one-hundred-year-old protagonist, Elspeth, a descendent of the West Indian planter class who returned to England as a child, losing in the process foundational memories of her childhood spent in a plantation great house on a cocoa estate in south Trinidad. As she nears her centenary and grapples with Alzheimer's disease, her cousin seeks to trigger her memory through a family photograph of his parents' marriage, which was taken in front of the estate great house. In the photograph, Elspeth appears as a girl whose "large staring eyes did not tell us what she was seeing. She appeared to be in mourning for someone who eluded her" (Scott 2015, 69). Seeking an explanation for why Elspeth, both in her childhood and near centenarian incarnations, seems to be focused on outside the frame of the photograph, the narrator surmises: "Elspeth's recent panic and fear had originated in this terrible estrangement and abandonment as a small child who would have experienced her mother's absence from Trinidad as abandonment and as a form of death" (Scott 2015, 78). This is yet another highly credible though inaccurate speculation in relation to the catalyst of anxiety and attachment traumas. The narrative strategy warns against seeking too facile an explanation for the complex social relations of the place and season.

Physiological changes wrought by the disease throw up fragments of hitherto erased childhood memories, generating agitation and anxiety in the process. Vague presences who haunt Elspeth's consciousness beg to be admitted; their story awaits the reconstruction of fragments of memory of a near hundred-year-old mind grappling with vascular impairment. Marianne Hirsch, in "The Generation of Postmemory", argues that photographs, and especially those which survive cataclysmic events, function as "ghostly revenants from an irretrievable past world" (Hirsch 2008, 115). The viewer in the present can, through the image, arguably "see and touch the past" and also try to "reanimate it by undoing the finality of the photographic take". Thus, the photograph lends veracity, both as an "indexical or contiguous object" due to its proximity to the target in front of its lens, and is also "iconic, exhibiting a mimetic similarity to that object" (Hirsch 2008, 115). She argues that it has the power to draw from a storehouse of familiar and unexamined cultural images and assumptions that thereby intervene between thought and the "deepest emotional impulses" (Hirsch 2008, 115). At the crisis of the encounter, one is faced with the visage of the enigma in the image.

In Scott's story, the family photograph intended as a trigger for recall for the cognitively compromised elder works differently, presumably because Elspeth has lost hold on the repository of "pre-established expressive forms" (Scott 2015, 108). The photograph works to evoke what it hides, thus haunting the narrative with spectral potentialities: a shattered family, the enigmatic mother, the surrogate mother/s and the psychically abandoned daughter. Elspeth's contact with the familiar image inspires both her senses and the scene of the observed – the large plantation manor and the grounds that sit behind it. The setting is telling. Power relations were highly spatialized on plantations. The great house, constructed to display the grandeur and wealth of the estate, stood at the centre of a network of inclusions and exclusions in a symbolic economy, in which prestige and influence were accorded based on proximity to the master. The mystery which evades retrieval and resolution is also embodied in the great house, which is personified as an autonomous being, closed, shuttered, jealously guarding its secrets: "The house, with its lowered jalousies, eyelid closed, the white curtains drawn across the glass windowpanes, pulled in tightly shut, was its own self, its own veiled face, as if the photographer had not wanted his composition to be distracted by any stray detail which might have emanated from the interior of a bedroom or a dining room; *perhaps an unwanted face or the shadow of a moving figure at his or her tasks within*" (Scott 2015, 67–68; emphasis added).

Scott's elaborate descriptions of the house and its architectural design on the macro (structural) and micro (interior design, including furniture and finishes) levels, work to create not only a sense of mystery but an aesthetic that superimposes within the clear hierarchy of the estate, its boundaries and suppression of the abject. The narrator conveys the shifting ground of unreliable memory by proffering numerous inaccurate explanations for the mystery of what the photograph hides and thereby ushers the readers into the shadowy, shape-shifting mental terrain of the protagonist.

Despite collective impulses towards erasure and masking, the photograph reactivates affective responses, which direct Elspeth's focus to the world beyond its frame. It generates the recall of suppressed memories of an enslaved workforce rendered invisible in the family portrait, but lurking behind the closed visage of the house. These workers are the erased and denigrated energizers of the elegant and graceful plantation lifestyle. The house reads as a metaphor for the inescapability from coerced modes of domesticity and female servitude – an imprisoning reality still prevalent in the postcolonial world, enabled by systems of bonded or debt labour. In Scott's narrative, these domesticated women folk provide not only the productive, sexual and reproductive labour that drives the economic and psychosexual dynamics of the plantation, but also the affective labour, which is pivotal to the servant mother/child relationship. Elspeth muses: "Yes, she comes to comfort me at night, carrying me, a baby in a basket" (Scott 2015, 80).

The recall of her enslaved other mother is again triggered by the sepia-toned photograph that discloses another narrative of wilderness spaces, "barrack yards where the drumming came from at night", "women in white, with turbans of white cotton" (Scott 2015) and shadows that operate as figures behind the manor, which intersect to produce meaning and cultural values. With the recovery of Old Nurse, who was herself a repository of suppressed remembrance, the aged protagonist exhumes the presences of generations of the enslaved who lived and died without records of their names: "There were no names like there would be names on graves, or in a family Bible" (Scott 2015). Elspeth's befuddling experience of forgetting to forget is amplified into a collective requirement to restore to remembrance (non)persons erased from official and family records. Meandering through time, she recalls her youthful adherence to the strategies imposed by her enslaved other mother to override the depersonalization of the enslaved as labouring conveniences: "I repeated after Old Nurse those names: names, tasks, punishments and the number of lashes, which were noted in the earliest of ledgers, she told me" (Scott 2015, 79). They who died bereft of official and family records are admitted into personhood when this aged and incapacitated carrier of memories forgets to forget. Not unlike Senior's engagement, the house operates as a ubiquitous monument and s ymbolic space of socially conditioned relations, exploitation, oppression, empathetic kinship and cultural memory. What seems to have been excluded by the photographer re-infiltrates the place of its origin and inscribes its own force.

The near-inchoate past returns to the impaired mind of the aged protagonist at two levels. The first level deals with her personal existential mystery: "Who am I? Where did I come from?" (Scott 2015, 74). This is extrapolated into: What is my place? And who are my people? Secondly, in terms of communal histories: to what extent am I required to acknowledge culpability for the shrouded history of the plantation house? For Elspeth, this means retrieving her emotional connection to Old Nurse, who is representative of a cadre of house slaves who performed care labour, granting heart share and affective connection to the progeny of the planter class, while invariably living away from their own children. Only then does she grasp the significance of the spectres which emerge decades later to haunt her London flat.

Elspeth comes to welcome the other faces of denigrated and dishonoured workers whom Old Nurse showed her – the private faces and lives of living, breathing, social beings, graceful dancing men and women who existed beyond the limits of the photograph, out of sightlines of the great house and beyond the pastures. Ironically, Lawrence Scott, of French Creole ancestry, and his protagonist, both descendants of the planter class, point to the same terror generated by the absence of the black ancestors, which Toni Morrison identifies as a thread running through African-American fictions. Based on her reading of a cross-section of contemporary African-American fictions, Morrison identifies an overwhelmingly female cast of aged characters and maternal ancestresses in African diasporic fictions. They function as a "sort of timeless people", whose relationships to the characters are "benevolent, instructive and protective and they provide a kind of wisdom" (Morrison 1984, 343). These timeless people are culturally rooted in ancient cosmologies and practices. They transcend time, ageing, physical decay and even death to serve as pointers and guides to progeny negotiating hostile social orders and uncertain futures.[1] Morrison concludes: "Whether the novel took place in the city or in the country, the presence or absence of that figure determined the success or happiness of the character. *It was the absence of an ancestor that was frightening, that was threatening, and it caused huge destruction and disarray in the work itself*" (Morrison 1984, 339; emphasis added).[2]

She locates this process of recuperation and recovery of the timeless people in the concept of rememory, which is connected to her pique at epistemic violence that has traditionally censored and whitewashed testimonies of the enslaved, and denied expression of interiority for African Americans in slave narratives and autobiographies. In "The Site of Memory", Morrison describes an inventive process triggered by attending to the close of life of her father and grandmother (Morrison 1995). Commenting on the impulse which thereafter led her to imaginatively capture their interior lives, she notes:

> These people are my access to me; they are my entrance into my own interior life. Which is why the images that float around them – the remains, so to speak, at the archaeological site – surface first, and they surface so vividly and so compelling that I acknowledge them as my route to a reconstruction

> of a world, to an exploration of an interior life that was not written and to revelation of a kind of truth (Morrison 1995, 95).

Scott's cognitively impaired protagonist undergoes an identical process. Elspeth muses: "These memories crowded her London flat and came to live with her. These were the people she had not been able to remember. *Their absence had frightened her.* Old Nurse was that relative she was trying to recall, who *had returned now* to comfort her in the absence of her mother's protection" (Scott 2015, 80; emphasis added). The shift in temporality to the present time of the narrative is reflective of both the impaired cognition of the centenarian and of potential temporal and spatial continuities, which allow for the intrusion of the past into the present in ways which are alien to Western, secular world views. Scott moves away from essentialist notions of reclaiming memory and towards a coalition of forces across space, time and domains to assemble the interior lives and value of a people group often ignored, removed or erased from historical and personal records. In this idyllic narrative of reconciliation, Elspeth reclaims the enslaved as natives of her person, spectral ancestors who return from the other side of a troubled collective history to impart moorings, care, interventions in the wake of failing memory, groundedness and belonging.

This terrain, explored by both Scott and Senior, points to the question raised by Derek Walcott in "The Muse of History": "But who in the New World does not have a horror of the past, whether his ancestor was torturer or victim? Who in the depth of his conscience is not screaming for pardon or for revenge?" (Walcott 1996, 39). Our perspective is that these narratives of the planter class go beyond this binary to evoke latent cross-ethnic connections, affective linkages and nurturing duties of care rooted in childhood. They also declare that the alleviation of psychic disease spawned by imperialism and nurtured in contemporary systemic injustices is to be found in an admission of guilt and complicities, alongside an embrace of shared vulnerabilities. Scott's and Senior's narratives of ancestry are exemplary of a cross-section of Caribbean fictions that appeal for a way to be human, for a process which honours the humanity of the person beyond a season of social usefulness, and for a deeper understanding of the frailty, vulnerability and interconnectivity of humankind.

The narratives demonstrate the high ideological stakes negotiated within Antillean social frameworks, through representations of servant mothering, overdetermined racialized identities, cross-ethnic allegiances and ancestry. They produce a complex interface of space-time interactions, peoples, nations and narrations – some told, some submerged, some unspeakable and unrepresentable, some silenced but carried and enacted in the flesh. Violating histories act as rhizomes with unwelcome present-day eruptions. Histories ripen in individual lifespans; ageing brings harvest. Indeed, the representative narratives explored in this chapter traverse the symbologies of historic traumatic memories. They belie the Western focus on linearity and logic of expressive and healing interventions. They indicate that Caribbean knowledge workers of diverse ethnicities are weaving a collective web of memorials, informed by their diverse ethnic positionalities and vantage points in relation to shared memory.

The expressions of male and female authors alike are deeply rooted both in the domestic terrain and in tropes of motherhood. Their message extends beyond the power of narrative to resolve communal and historical traumas. In addition, and at times in substitution, they point to the declarations communicated through grim and messy corporeality; identification with incorporeal beings that testify when words fail; affirmation of cosmologies and faith systems which would nail debilitating psychic distress to pain trees. Memories are embodied in defiled and wounded women who represent the violated island body. Traumas are encapsulated in houses, recorded in family portraits; transmitted intergenerationally through blood or cross-ethnic affective lineages to do their work of discombobulation for successive generations. Marianne Hirsch points to the danger of the domestic orientation of such a project:

> Familial structures of mediation and representation facilitate the *affiliative*: acts of the postgeneration. The idiom of family can become an accessible lingua franca, easing identification and projection across distance and difference: This explains the pervasiveness of family pictures and family narratives as artistic media in the aftermath of trauma. Still, the very accessibility of familial idioms needs also to engender suspicion on our part: does not locating trauma in the space of family personalize and individualize it too much? Does it not risk occluding a public historical context and responsibility, blurring

> significant differences – national difference, for example, of differences among the descendants of victims, perpetrators, and bystanders? (Hirsch 2008, 115).

Caribbean writers have collectively avoided the pitfalls identified by Hirsch. The charge of blurring the differences between perpetrator and victim, which can be perceived as dishonest and untenable, can also be read as a literary genuflection on the part of the writerly descendants of the planter class, reflective of a conciliatory stance. Representations of intimate familial pleasures and nightmares; of horrific life circumstances and childhood traumas have been imbued in the hands of these master storytellers with complex layers of societal, transnational, transgenerational meaning.

The writers are fierce in their commitment never to occlude the moral imperative to bear witness to injustice and to chart the manner in which it drills down into individual lives. Their thrust remains transformational. Their deployment of tropes of ageing calls attention to a duty of care for those whose tumultuous journeys through more oppressive times have delivered to their progeny the opportunities and insights which must not be taken for granted today. By asserting that black and all other subjugated lives – past, present and future – matter, the narratives effectively articulate and make visible political, cultural and ethical imperatives to acknowledge and bear witness to the psychic impact of societal traumas and thereby enhance the potential for communality, and the value and dignity of all human societies.

chapter 4

Incest, Violation and Trauma in Caribbean Narratives

> Anything dead coming back to life hurts.
>
> —*Toni Morrison, Beloved*

ALTHOUGH INCEST TABOOS ARE UNIVERSAL, THERE are wide variances in related cultural norms and incest laws, and the challenges involved in policing perpetrators and recuperating victims speak to the enormity of this societal scourge. Incestuous relations, which invariably comprise both rape and child abuse, traumatize those with underdeveloped physical and psychic resources. Its most blatant consequences – motherhood in childhood and diminished life chances – do not necessarily have the most profound impact. The invisible wounding of the child's fledging psyche, generated by attachment and betrayal traumas, is particularly resistant to healing because of the cultural norms of social silencing governing the exercise of male authority, female subordination and even tacit acceptance of this evil, which has become increasingly prevalent within segments of Caribbean societies. This chapter probes fictional explorations of plausible interpersonal dynamics that culminate in incest; analyses the cultural norms that create an enabling environment for abusive acts; and the recourse to cultural expression as therapeutic intervention. Locating incest at the extreme end of a continuum of child abuse, it posits that literary representation can be instrumental in probing the cultures of violence that facilitate incest, and sensitizing readers to the nuanced manner in which this domestic crime ravages families and generates troubled futures.

TRAJECTORIES OF VIOLATION

Child sexual abuse (CSA) is universal. It is a multi-contextual violation of the human rights of the child, which has engaged the attention of scholars in a multiplicity of disciplines. Global child protection agencies usually categorize CSA as a form of gender-based violence involving "contacts or interactions between a child and an older or more knowledgeable child or adult (a stranger, sibling, or person in a position of authority, such as a parent or caretaker) when the child is being used as an object of gratification for an older child's or adult's sexual needs" (UNICEF 2012, 16). Incest is defined as sexual relations between persons related by blood who would not normally be permitted to marry.[1] Letnie Rock, in "Research on Child Sexual Abuse: Caribbean and International Perspectives", indicates that globally, millions of cases of maltreatment are reported annually. She argues: "Potentially all children are at risk for abuse and neglect." Sexual abuse, in particular, which takes place within the home is under-reported. Considered "the ultimate betrayal" and the "ultimate frontier in child abuse" (Qagnuson 1983, 28; Sgroi 1975, 19, quoted in Rock 146), CSA has come to be viewed as the "most silent form of abuse and a hidden epidemic" (United Nations 2006). A 2007 UNICEF report indicated that instances of sexual abuse against girls only marginally outnumber that meted out to boys.[2]

The persistence of CSA in the Caribbean has been attributed to numerous factors. These include but are not limited to fear of disclosure; stigma and silencing among victims and their families; the smallness, insularity and pseudo-respectability of the island societies leading to priority being given to the reputation and dignity of the perpetrator and the family; an inadequate social security net which makes it difficult for families to cope with loss of income if the perpetrator/breadwinner is removed from the home; the harshness and insensitivity of law enforcement officials in dealing with sexual crimes; generalized distrust of law enforcement agencies and practices; and unwillingness of victims and their families to deal with lengthy and complex judicial procedures (Joseph 2013, 3; UNICEF 2012). As noted in the *2012 UNICEF Report on Sexual Abuse Against Children in the Caribbean:* "In most, if not all countries there is acknowledgement among policy makers of child sexual abuse as a socio-economic and human rights issue, as well as a public health challenge linked to various forms of sexual and reproductive health challenges, the spread of sexually transmitted diseases and various mental health concerns" (UNICEF 2012, 8). This report acknowledges the substantial gains made in the past two decades in terms of criminalization of CSA and commends the region's governments for becoming signatories to the UN Convention on the Rights of the Child, which enshrines the imperative to protect children from all forms of sexual exposure and sexual abuse. Governments have also ratified related conventions and established policy initiatives and programmes to address CSA.

This notwithstanding, legislation has had less of an impact than was projected. Pointing to the limited preventative impact of legal measures and related public awareness campaigns, Lambert Petersen, in "A Legal Perspective on Child Abuse in the Caribbean", draws attention to the significance of cultural constructions. She argues that notions of CSA and, indeed, even notions of who is a child are socially constructed and reflective of deeply embedded norms, which vary with place, time, and religion (Petersen 2013, 52–53).[3] At least in principle, CSA in institutional quarters and among certain segments of society receives lip service as a heinous aberration perpetrated by a select sick or evil few, from whom the society recoils in horror. Significantly, fictional and scholarly discourses are inviting an alternative perspective, which locates CSA at the extreme end of a continuum of banal violence (Morgan and Youssef 2006; Morgan 2014).

The prevalence and normative nature of violence against children in the Caribbean has been well documented in literary, historical and sociological studies. Historian Bridget Brereton, in "The Culture of Violence in Trinidad and Tobago", suggests a connection between slavery's violent legacies of severe corporal punishment and an all-too-common contemporary overzealous application of the biblical prescription to "spare the rod and spoil the child". Brereton also attributes historical patterns of routine and even theatrical brutalization of very young children by parents and relatives to other causes: "Men and women were, no doubt, venting their frustrations on small, defenseless, easily accessible victims. But it was also probably an unconscious or conscious process of initiating the child into a harsh world, teaching him or her to suppress individuality and aggression, to know his or her place" (Brereton 2010, 5–6; 11). Scholar and activist Merle Hodge, in her seminal essay, "The Shadow of the Whip", points to correlations between the contemporary enthusiasm for corporal punishment and the deep and profound brutalities of the imperial enterprise, which spawned societies whose very existence was predicated on the gun, the whip and the authority of force. Hodge contends that while this has not manifested in mass organized violence, it has been internalized to manifest in verbal violence and in race and domestic dominance relations: ". . . the most important manifestation of the internalized violence is our profound commitment to the use of physical and verbal violence in the socialization of children" (Hodge 1974, 2). V.S. Naipaul inscribes the terrorizing potential of a good domestic cut tail and its capacity to keep the mass of children under control in *A House for Mr. Biswas* (2001) and *Miguel Street* (2002). The brutal beatings were not only perceived as crucial to address overt and latent childhood wickedness, but also as a vital stimulus for good academic performance, and as exemplifying love and commitment to child rearing. Even more extreme is Harold Sonny Ladoo's haunting evocation of the loss of cultural and ontological moorings of East Indians in post-indentureship Trinidad (Ladoo 1972). Meandering through a nightmarish landscape of unending rain and hostile biting creatures, women and children are constrained to bear the psychic lacerations of dislocated men, absorbing their irrational outbursts of murderous verbal and physical violence. As in literature so in life. The right of Caribbean parents to discipline their children, through even extreme acts of violence, is held sacrosanct across diverse ethnic groups in Caribbean societies.[4]

The cultural underpinnings of societal attitudes, as exemplified in a cross-section of literary texts, also point to a continuum between dominance relations based on ethnicity and gender, and physical and sexual abuse in what is arguably its most repugnant form – incest. In other words, we contend that the search for corrective and preventive interventions may require nuanced study of the entire continuum of violent power relations and socialization practices, and not the isolation of sexual abuse and incest as unique aberrations. In the next segment of this chapter, we mine literary texts for insights on the interface between incest and historical violations, which lie at the bedrock of New World Caribbean societies and the resultant national, communal and familial social orders. Incest, defined as sexual relations between close relatives which are socially condemned and which trade on inequitable power relations, secret seductions and myriad oppressions, induces guilt, shame as well as attachment and betrayal traumas. These are intensified when incest is accompanied by physical violence and escalate even further when the abused are driven to murder their abusers.

HISTORICAL VIOLATIONS

Numerous Caribbean writers have written on the correlations between sexuality and conquest (Lamming in *Water with Berries* and *Natives of My Person*; Brodber in *The Rainmaker's Mistake*; Dabydeen in *Turner*; James in *The Book of Night Women*; Harris in *Palace of the Peacock*, and Scott in *Night Calypso*). In *Turner*, for example, Dabydeen powerfully argues his contention that empire was a pornographic project, with the erotization of power becoming a key weapon in the colonizer's arsenal. If we agree that the very materiality of the human body invites the impingement of dominance relations violently inscribed with flesh on flesh, this can have significant implications for incest. The issues are: How does the global phenomenon of incest manifest in nations which have been spawned in the bowels of imperial processes, and grapple with legacies of racism and oppression? How does the dynamic unfold when victims and perpetrators bear the woundedness of self-denigration, and manoeuvre crossroads between vilified Indigenous and ancestral cultures and contemporary cultural innovations?

In Lawrence Scott's *Night Calypso*, the traumatized child narrator responds to extreme sexual violation by spending his days in silence and his nights in tortured trances, during which he ventriloquizes troubled familial and personal histories and reenacts experiences so horrific that he cannot bring them into waking articulation. Demonstrating classic symptoms of trauma – hyperarousal, silencing and dissociative amnesia, Theo grapples with the absent presence of intrusive fragments of memory, which block normal daily communication. At night time, his halting, encoded and enacted revelations are of multi-generational patterns of incest, perpetrated by the Marineaux plantation masters who impose racial ascendancy on their enslaved and labouring offspring and half-caste siblings, at the grim crossroads where white supremacy and white-on-black disciplinary actions intersect with desire for the racialized other. The toxic and inherently abusive Dellacourt/ Marineaux lineage is initiated in 1802 when the Master/Mister encounters the narrator's great-grandmother, the twelve-year-old enslaved Christiania, on her knees, scrubbing floors. Naming her "puppy", he forcibly mounts her. The appellation speaks both to the depersonalization and degradation of the child and the bestiality of the rape. Thereafter, successive generations of Marineaux men systematically rape their half-sisters. Violation, shame, rage and even murder/suicide roll out when Christiana's daughter, Alice, kills her youngest child, Mercy, to rescue her from this horrific fate. Thereafter, gripped by guilt and shame, she turns the murderous impulse against herself. Silencing and evasion of the root of her tragedy is the societal response. Even infanticide/suicide is insufficient to activate the community to finger the abusive system and demand acknowledgement of culpability.

In this novel set in the 1930s, incest and miscegenation are perpetrated in the service of dominance relations based on race differentials, which are perceived as foundational to the social order. If black women are essentialized as the natural targets of sexual dominance, the task of maintaining the purity of the seed requires white women to be essentialized as boundary markers of ethnic superiority. The incest dynamic is not interrupted when a bastard son is born. The potential for incestuous cross-ethnic interface surfaces when young Theo is poised to take up the male privilege of sexual initiation in relation to his white half-sister, Chantal. The potential of this youthful albeit incestuous love interest to replace cycles of abuse with a measure of mutual affection and reciprocity is reflected in naming, which acknowledges Theo's autonomous identity. Chantal calls him by his name, while his father /abuser names him Coco after the bird cocorito. Nocturnal whippings and sexual batterings are the agents of subordination deployed by the father to effeminate and punish his son for daring to entertain a desire which threatens the social hierarchy. The psychic wounding finds its parallel in the physical mark of the father, a rope-like scar which mars his back.

Incest in this text speaks to the interface of unjust national and domestic power relations. In "Profiles and Myth and the New World", Wilson Harris argues that "all cultures are subject to the ravages of unjust conventions which may take the form of stereotypical purities" (Harris 1999, 196). He references contradictory socio-symbolic positionalities of incest as state-tolerated royal privilege "countenanced" to preserve the purity of dominions and blood lines, but also as a heinous predatory act within ordinary families, which the strong and the privileged perpetrate against the weak and vulnerable. Harris argues that legislative protection for victims of family incest may be overridden by "unconscious legacies of perverse linearity that seek to frame the identity of the family into an absolute convention". This impulse can harden into "projected incest, so to speak, projected violence by the state upon others to preserve stereotypical purities. The stranger is targeted, the foreigner is targeted, the refugee is targeted, as impure" (Harris 1999, 196).[5] And the enslaved and their progeny are targeted. In "Figuring the Father", Jennifer Rahim astutely reads assault perpetrated against Theo through Harris' theorization of incest, concluding: "Miscegenation thereby secures the plantocracy's elite racial purity on which its right as the 'ruling line' is founded, even as the wanton fathering of 'outside' children is a means of flaunting proprietorial entitlement and justifies the claim to a superior masculinity. In Theo's case, rape cements his inferiority to a male planter class that violently enforces its rule/law against any native socio-political and/or sexual challenge to it" (Rahim 2011, 11).

The bottom line is the social entrenchment of incest as lustful excess and disciplinary action perpetrated by plantation masters and their agents within slavery and post-emancipation is intended to teach successive generations of its progeny to know their subordinate position as the twice possessed. In this socio-symbolic terrain, substantial challenges exist in terms of even recognizing incest as a criminal act and moreso of prosecuting incest, entrenched as the right of privileged men within the hegemonic order. Saidiya Hartman, writing on "Seduction and the Ruses of Power", speaks to the theatrics of terror in the racist imaginary, including rape of women, castrations and assault of men, and lynching spectacles, all feeding into an erotic of power. She identifies rape and sexual violation of the enslaved in nineteenth-century America as "crimes licensed and disavowed by the law by highlighting the state's crimes of commission and the categorization of negligible injury" (Hartman 1997, 81). The social construction of the enslaved as property, whose raison d'être is to serve the master class, nullifies any question of availability for sexual labour. Moreover, the construction of enslaved women as lascivious, hypersexual and a threat to public morals nullifies any question of unwillingness to perform. Indeed, if any blame is to be imputed, it is attributed to the victim.

In Shani Mootoo's *Cereus Blooms at Night*, the interface between incest and preservation/despoliation of ethnic superiority within subordinate masculinity plays itself out with an even more perverse twist (Morgan and Youssef 2006). Chandin Ramchandin, adopted into a family of Presbyterian missionaries to better facilitate cultural assimilation, is subjected to intense socialization. Predictably, he comes to loathe all things East Indian and to desire all things Caucasian, including his white, adoptive sister, Lavinia Thoroughly. Reverend Thoroughly thinly disguises his abhorrence of this prospect and his disparagement of his racially despised "son" by taking recourse to the fiction that such desire for his sister is incestuous and therefore against God's will (Mootoo 1999, 37). He points the lovesick young man to the brown-skinned convert, Sarah, as a more appropriate love object. Chandin's undesirability and shame are doubly magnified when Lavinia, saved from the "disgrace" of consorting with a brown man, chooses Sarah as her lover. The two run away, leaving Chandin bereft, both of his love object whose rejection intensifies frustration and shame at racialized embodiment, as well as the woman whom he had married to mask his shame. Rape is an act of violence against his daughters in which he exerts patriarchal privilege to possess his daughters with impunity, unhindered by social blame. By defiling their bodies and souls, which are an extension of his wife's, he punishes Sarah for her desertion. He slakes his sexual hungers, arguably predicated on the tacit assumption of the right of men to sexual outlets within their homes, whether or not their wives are available. The dynamic is facilitated by the siege mentality and insularity of the Indian rural community, which would not readily give over its own to the national judicial system, especially over a family matter involving as undervalued a being as a girl child. Alongside all of these causal factors is incest as revenge to punish his daughters as extensions of his own property, his own flesh. Swearing "What the ass . . .? . . . A man tiefing my baby? . . .

I ent go let nobody tief my woman again" (Mootoo 1999, 222), he stages an orgy of destruction of property, beating and violent rape. In the process, the enraged Chandin glimpses and seeks to obliterate the image of his raced embodiment, the root of his psychic dis-ease: "He turned around and saw himself in the full-length mirror on the armoire door. With the heel of his foot he attacked it with a lightening blow. The mirror shattered and fell in a hundred brilliant shards" (Mootoo 1999, 222). Rather than serving as an unjust covenant intended to safeguard against pollution by an undesirable, racialized other, Chandin's is an act of vengeance rape against his own polluted flesh for its unworthiness and undesirability. Despite apparent differences, both fictional scenarios share in the same dynamic.

In relation to contemporary incest scenarios, arguably representations of sexual victimization can lead to greater understanding of abusers and their targets. Narratives, mediated through authorial perspectives, language, cultural systems, including ideologies and symbols, convention of genres, intertextuality and reading practices, are useful for locating characters at the interface of domestic, communal and national histories, and for teasing out power and gender relations within familial and social scenarios. Poverty, frustration, shifting unions, anomie and social dislocation, the absence of wives or the presence of stepfathers without strong affective ties to children in the home have all been identified as risk factors for sexual abuse. The reality is that conditions within prosperous two-parent households can also lead to incest. A 2009 study on "Perceptions of, Attitudes to, and Opinions on Child Sexual Abuse in the Eastern Caribbean" indicates that despite widely held assumptions about the prevalence of incest in particular ethnic and religious groups, and within isolated rural communities, f indings are that incest occurs in "both rich and poor families, in all communities, cuts across social class, and is not affected by levels of education, religious affiliation, professional status or social standing" (Jones et al. 2009, 12).

We also turn to a fuller discussion of the incest dynamic in Nalo Hopkinson's futuristic narrative, *Midnight Robber*, which delivers us back into the future. Hopkinson deploys the science fiction genre, with its strategies of defamiliarization, cognitive estrangement, strategic mimesis and perspectival shift, to evoke strange interactions, values, worldviews and practices that have in many societies become normative. The text plays with narrative conventions, disrupting binaries associated with postcolonial fictions, the science fiction genres and broader implicit fictional contracts in relation to utopias and dystopias. Its ideologically infused "strangeness" emphasizes empowering and disempowering societal and familial frameworks. Toussaint, with its safe, orderly existence, in which there is no shortage, no need, no poverty and no back-breaking labour, falls short of being utopian. Its shadow parallel the penal colony of New Half Way Tree in which there is widespread disorder, ugliness and struggle to seek out the most basic of livings – falls short of being dystopian. Echoes of imperialism and enslavement, and the quest for freedom run throughout the narrative.

By inscribing the consequence of sexual abuse on the body of a young girl uneasily poised between a recognizably Caribbean, technologically enhanced and enabled world, and a rugged, pre-technological natural environment, Hopkinson addresses some old issues and new. Within this futuristic framework, what is the likely impact of the insatiable pursuit of new technologies on productive, sexual and reproductive labour relations within human societies? What are the cultural norms which make the domestic space unsafe for the vulnerable female child? How does a young girl deal with intimate interpenetration of her budding body and illicit possession of her womb space? How does the process of enlargement and externalization of her internal boundaries impact the child's sense of self and being in the world? How do folkways of healing address the psychic hurt generated by incest? And most significantly, what is the correlation between Hopkinson's configuration of a brave new world and the potential for a social order free of predatory sexual abuse and oppression?

Midnight Robber deals with a multiplicity of crimes. At the bedrock of the social order is the dynamic interplay between masters and subordinates, in both benign and malignant forms, as reminiscent of imperialism's crimes against humanity. The abusive father is mayor of the Cockpit County of Toussaint planet, which has been colonized by the Marryshow Corporation and kept safe and peaceful by an artificial intelligence, the Grande Nonotech Sentient Interface known as Granny Nansi web, or more affectionally, Granny Nanny. The artificial intelligence governs through implantation of nanonites into the human bloodstream. These give operational agency to Granny Nanny through robotic presences named Eshus. The Marryshow Corporation may be benevolent in its governance, but this is achieved at the cost of absolute surveillance. This relatively mild, intrusive colonizing presence gives way to a more extreme shadow reality on the penal colony of New Half Way Tree. Here, it is the recognizably Afro-Caribbean outcast who oppresses and denigrates the racialized other – a servant class of douens. Imperialism's violation of virgin territory for economic gain and technology's rabid exploitation of natural resources is countered by the ecologically balanced interdependence and minute footprint of the Indigenous population of douens.

On the colonized planet Toussaint, gender identities are fluid, and open unions are practiced, with resultant conflicts kept in check by the Granny Nanny surveillance system. Slippage notwithstanding, the cultural norms are fashioned by an androcentric system, embodied overwhelmingly in Antonio Habib, who, as mayor, stands at the interface of civic authority and familial authority, and abuses both in his deadly passion games. The patriarchal system allows men free rein for sexual adventurism, but makes it a matter of deep dishonour if they are made cuckolds by their wives. When his wife's infidelities become public, the philandering Antonio, motivated by jealously and public embarrassment, rigs an elaborate charade of chivalric defence for his wife's honour. When the fight goes awry, he faces prosecution for murder, which he evades by escaping, with his daughter in tow, in a shift pod through a dimension veil into the savage, pre-technological penal planet, New Half Way Tree, peopled by douens, criminals, renegades and misfits. A decade later, the sexually abused and severely beaten child commits patricide and is hunted mercilessly by her stepmother, Janisette, in revenge for killing her husband.

The text yields rich insights into the complex familial dynamic which accommodates incest. The seeds of the incestuous impulse were planted from birth. The vain, self-centred mother, Ione (I/one), who conceives the child as a pawn to attract the attention of her husband, withholds maternal love and devotion. From Tan-Tan's birth, the father, entranced by her beauty, vulnerability and dependency, vacillates between sporadic bursts of excessive attention and withdrawal, when he is obsessed or angry with her mother. Together, they produce a child who is starved for mother and father love. Her yearning and emptiness destabilize her at the core, and rob her of the ontological mooring which forms the basis of healthy individuation. Consequently, she exists in disequilibrium and hyperarousal, constantly alert to produce the catalyst which will attract and hold her father's intermittent and intense bursts of attention. The child's attachment trauma is only partially mitigated by the steady attention of Eshu, the non-humanoid caregiver. This makes her vulnerable to abduction, and subsequently, to incest.

At sexual initiation, the vulnerable nine-year-old copes with pain and shame of rape/abuse by enlisting two passive withdrawal strategies – doubling and dissociation. This reaction aligns with the research findings of Spencer Eth and Robert S. Phynos, in "Developmental Perspectives on Psychic Trauma in Childhood" (Eth and Phynos 1985). They argue that younger children, because of their helplessness and dependence, are more inclined to dissociative responses, such as detachment, fantasy, numbness and compliance, whereas older children are more inclined to hyperarousal responses, such as hypervigilance, anxiety, hyper-reactivity, flight and panic. The scenario also illustrates a major issue in grappling with child sexual abuse – the deleterious impact on the immature value-processing system of the youngster, intensified in the case of father-daughter incest by the child's dependence on the abuser to teach right from wrong. She also suffers betrayal trauma, defined as the hurt generated by the violation of trust within a close, dependent relationship by those who have a responsibility to extend protection and nurturance. This, in turn, can produce suppression of the horrific memory or betrayal blindness which occurs when a child fails to understand adult sexual advances as abusive; or, conversely, the child may recognize the abuse but may either avoid reflecting on its meaning or may be incapable of doing so. Tan-Tan distances herself from the horrific event, while blaming herself so as to retain some semblance of a positive image of the father, whom she desperately needs in order to survive. She reasons: "Daddy was two daddies. She felt her own self split in two trying to understand and accommodate them both" (Hopkinson 2000, 140). The physical ripping of her prepubescent body induces a psychic split. She splits into good Tan-Tan, who wants to please her father, and bad Tan-Tan, who must have done something bad to elicit his horrific attention. She is silenced both by the horror of what he is doing and by shame: "Shame filled her, clogged her mouth when she opened to call out to Janisette for help" (Hopkinson 2000, 140). If Good Tan-Tan is silenced, Bad Tan-Tan becomes an intrusive and condemnatory inner voice, thereafter an absent presence which speaks to the disjuncture between the inner and outer self. Internally, she is taunted by "a silent bad voice like an insane eshu" who cackles and screams condemnations, cursings, defamations and even truths, which good Tan-Tan does not want to entertain.

Hopkinson's representation of the impact trauma induced by sexual abuse differs somewhat from that inscribed by Mootoo and Scott. Yet silencing emerges as a common denominator in all texts. The dumbstruck children of Scott's *Night Calypso* and Mootoo's *Cereus* can be best understood through the filters of classical trauma theory. The incestuous rape, and even more so when followed by patricide, overwhelms the cognitive capacity of the children. Their immature brains and thinking systems, "as carriers of cognitive schemata", are unable to "encode and properly process" the events (Balaev 2008, 151). Unadmitted to the conscious mind, these catalysts become unrepresentable fragments of undigested memory; unspeakable acts that evade articulation. Unknowability and irrepresentability lie at the root of cycles of intrusive memory, distorted temporalities and uncanny repetition. Their absent presence in the case of the young protagonist of *Night Calypso* leads to a form of dissociative amnesia and silencing. Theo, who can only speak the horror of intergenerational cycles of incest during nightmares and night trances, and through disturbed reenactments. In the case of Mala Ramchandin, her loss of language speaks to the loss of a meaning system, sociality and being in the world. Her abuse and shattered world view are so extreme that, for her, language loses symbolic referentiality. Her communications are reduced to grunts, sighs, whistles, insect and animal sounds; and later, when recovery begins, isolated meaning-infused words and snatches of songs.

In *Midnight Robber,* complex cultural norms and practices takes precedence over psychobiological factors. The child protagonist shares with the other protagonists under discussion unresolved histories of oppression and denigration. Her budding notions of sexuality are permeated by private and public cultural enactments of sensuality, excess and infidelities. She is silenced during her father's incestuous penetrations by shame, moreso than by cognitive processes leading to submerged memories, distorted temporalities and silencing. Her healing processes are similarly enmeshed with cultural norms, rituals and formations. This fictional representation fleshes out the call for extended definitions of trauma that shift focus away from an event-based model to broader, more culturally applicable paradigms. These include safe-world violations, insidious traumas, oppression-based traumas, postcolonial syndrome, postcolonial stress disorder and post-traumatic slavery syndrome. Of particular relevance to this enquiry is Craps' contention that notions of an essentialized, universal, psychobiological response can lead to practical Western interventions, which are disrespectful at best, if not downright harmful to deeply entrenched Indigenous practices of remembrance, mourning, healing and reconstruction.[6]

Tan-Tan's eventual avenue for her liberation surfaces from inception of the abuse. Even as she distracts herself during the sexual assault by fastening her attention on the Midnight Robber Doll, she begins to conceive a transcendent possibility by ditching a discourse of self-blame in favour of appropriating onto herself an empowering discursive and socio-symbolic identity embedded within a female Midnight Robber folkloric figure: "She wasn't Tan-Tan, the bad Tan-Tan. She was Tan-Tan the Robber Queen, the terror of all Junjuh . . . and strong men does tremble in their boots when she pass by. Nothing bad does ever happen to Tan-Tan the Robber Queen. Nothing can hurt she" (Hopkinson 2000, 140). Whereas her withdrawal links her to the Midnight Robber fantasies, from inception Tan-Tan's resilience surfaces in her focus on the knife: "she watched the new dolly on the pillow beside her. Its dress was up around its waist and she could see its thigh holster with the knife in it . . . it would be nice if the little wooden knife were inside it were really sharp steel" (Hopkinson 2000, 141). As she matures, she begins to fall into the pattern of sexual manipulation using beauty and sensuality to receive sexual attention, as a panacea for low self-esteem and unworthiness. In the process, she veers dangerously close to her parent's passion games: "You could rule man easy, with just one thing" (Hopkinson 2000, 151). Intergenerational cycles of vulnerability and sexual manipulation are set to begin anew.

Hopkinson represents in the characterization of Antonio Habib a profile of an abuser whose public success and performance of hegemonic masculinity masks weakness and vulnerability, which erupt in excessive need for manipulation, prestige and sexual control. Unsatisfied yearnings for home, safety, shelter, belonging, love and nurturance permeate the narrative. The interplay of spatiality, sexuality and domestic and public power plays are introduced from the opening frame, which finds the mayor making his way home through side roads and entrances to stage an ambush: "Mayor Antonio, the most powerful man in the whole country, opened up his own parlour door that afternoon to behold his wife lounging off on the settee with her petticoat hitched up around her waist, and both feet wrapped round Quashee waist" (Hopkinson 2000, 15). Obsessed with his frivolous wife, he cannot exclusively commit to her since to do so would be to admit his vulnerability and neediness, which are at odds with his powerful public profile. Manipulation through sex and passion games, as opposed to love and mutual respect, are the unstable adhesives of his marriage. Arguably, Antonio, with his philandering ways, demonstrates deep insecurities and fear of the sexual power of women and their capacity to captivate men via their sensuality. His passion games smack of fear of intimacy and attachment so great as to disallow him peace in his marital relations. Vacillating between desire for oneness and merging, and desire for separation and autonomy, he assuages his need for her in explosions of physical passion, which ultimately leaves him empty and more in need of her than before. His antidote is to punish her for his need of her by withdrawal into work and a series of superficial liaisons. Work and sex soothe and persuade him of his virility and potency for a moment, but do not facilitate true fulfilment and intimacy. His insecurities, and strong compulsion towards control, drive him to use and abuse a number of women. Antonio uses Tan Tan to soothe his bruised ego from birth. Initially, the connection satisfies without the pyrotechnic stimulation of passion. The incestuous penetration awaits their exile to the penal planet and her prepubescence.

Antonio Habib offers his daughter an incestuous liaison that feeds into her yearning for father love. He initiates an affection-based engagement. He sets the stage to gratify his lust and longing by paying court to her beauty, her resemblance to her lost mother, and finally gifting her his wedding ring in a bizarre pseudo-marriage ritual on her ninth birthday, the night of her defilement. Accompanying this gift is the articulation of his delusional rationalization, in a bizarre parody of a marriage vow. Erasing the fact that he selfishly dragged his young daughter through the dimensional vale when escaping the consequences of his crime, he rescripts his sacrifice of his child into a valorization of his sacrifice for and commitment to her: "Is yours now. I give up everything to come here so we could be together, Tan-tan; my wife, my home, everything. And look how big you get. The ring is yours" (Hopkinson 2000, 139). Tan-Tan is defiled at nine, impregnated at twelve, and again at fifteen in the sexual encounter in which she commits patricide.

The motivations of Antonio Habib and all of the other fictional constructions of perpetrators of incest align with the motivational categories of incest proposed by Maddock and Larson as follows:

- Affection-based: the incest provides closeness in a family otherwise lacking in nurture and affection. There is an emphasis on the specialness of the relationship, within which otherwise unavailable caring is given and received.
- Erotic-based: the family atmosphere is one of chaotic pansexuality, and it is not uncommon for many members to be involved. Its norm is the erotization of relationships. The term "polyincest" is often used to describe such multiple-perpetrator situations.
- Aggression-based: the incestuous acts involve the perpetrator's sexualized anger. The perpetrator vents their frustration and conflicts on a vulnerable individual, and physical mistreatment is often involved.
- Rage-based: the perpetrator is hostile and may be overtly sadistic. There may be great danger to the victim.

The incest dynamic explored in *Night Calypso* meets and exceeds the category of "chaotic pansexuality"; hence, we would propose an additional type, the erotization of power-based incest, in which the sexual conquest directed towards the vulnerable, weak, dependent and denigrated affirms illusory notions of superiority and dominance based on class, ethnicity and gender. The fictional representations point to salient parallels between abusers across periods, ethnicities, and hegemonic and counter-hegemonic masculinities. Hopkinson's representation of the abusive father who manages to transform a loving and caring daughter into a murderess bears comparison with Mootoo's evocation in *Cereus*. Despite their divergent social locations as examples of hegemonic and counter-hegemonic masculinity, both men possess fine prospects and promising high-profile lives which fail to alleviate their low self-esteem and lack of ontological security. Both of them love obsessively and lose their primary love objects. Both anaesthetize their frustration and impotence with alcohol. Both seek affirmation and control by slaking their sexual appetites on their daughters, constraining the children to bear the weight of their father's pain, vulnerability and neediness. Both prove incapable of sustaining long-term reciprocal relationships with adult women. Both react with excessive control and violence when young rival lovers come courting and seek to reassert their right of possession by hammering their children turned sex partners with penile weapons, hardened by rage into battering rams. Both trigger murderous responses during the rape of their daughters, who have been, until then, serving as faithful, long-term sexual partners.

Feminist readings would account for this dynamic as patriarchal privilege and paternal rights of possession. According to Judith Hermon, in *Father Daughter Incest*, gender asymmetries pay a key role when fathers commit incest and effectively prostitute their daughters by making them pay in sexual services for the care and attention which should have been the basic duty of paternity (Hermon 2000). Both fictional perpetrators feed off unarticulated societal assumptions, which generate understanding, if not acceptance, of the rights of men to sexual satisfaction, even if it is through predatory relationships with other dependent females within the home, and especially so if wives are absent and unavailable. Yet another element surfaces. The ageing men seek to assert their right of ownership of the children/women whom they have made for themselves, through violent displays of what they project as the primary benefit which the maturing teenagers are seeking in their young partners – sexual potency. The acts of sexual violence address the perpetrators' feelings of anger, fear and impotence, and produce an immediate rush of agency and potency, which, when mixed with sexual release and satiation, becomes a heady drug indeed. Most significantly, both emotionally needy fathers cannot admit the depth of their suffering as a result of the desertion and infidelities of their love objects/wives. They cannot bear recurrence of humiliation, rejection and abandonment. In the case of Antonio Habib, moody, narcissistic, habituated to the trappings of power and recognition, his daughter becomes a bridge to the power, privileges and the pleasures of a past from which he has been exiled.

Chandin Ramchadin practises aggression and rage-based incest from inception, which makes it easier for his daughter to detect his hostility, and despite her enduring concern for his emotional well-being, to articulate early her hatred and death wish in relation to this father turned aggressor. Habib's affection-based incest confuses the nine-year-old love-starved child and induces a psychic split as she seeks to grapple with offerings of love in this most horrific of forms. The act of patricide becomes possible only when the older child, with greater self-sufficiency and agency, responds to the surfacing of a young suitor; Habib's jealous rantings unmask the latent hostilities and the erotization of power. The long-term interaction tips over into rape, aggression and rage-based incest.

SOCIAL AND CULTURAL CONTEXTS

Incest invariably becomes a familial secret shame; it also becomes a national open secret shame. Jones et al. open their study of *An Integrated Systems Model for Preventing Child Sexual Abuse: Perspectives from the Caribbean* by highlighting the plight of Amber (name changed). Amber's disclosure of her brother's rape and molestation, which she suffered from age nine, generates denial from her brother; apathy from her mother – herself a victim of abuse; rage from her father, who beats and accuses his daughter of lying, falsely accusing his son, sexual impropriety and defiling the honour of the home. Her attempts at securing legal redress result in her loss of the case. She nevertheless charged all three with abuse, arguing that the infringement extended to her mother and father for prioritizing the illusion of their exemplary family above her safety and well-being. By extension, her stance implicated the nation's values and norms, in this case acting through its judicial system, for failing to safeguard its young citizens. The one redeeming factor was that Amber came to the point of recognizing that she had been wronged on multiple fronts; she was entitled to tell her story and to seek redress (Jones et al. 2014, 1–2). This is an assertion on the legal front. On the literary level, Jennifer Rahim, in "Figuring the Father", argues that Caribbean writers are collectively "redrawing the lines of death-wielding gender ideologies that contrive to keep us incarcerated in the 'duppy-bowl' of their destructive systemic reign" (Rahim 2011, 16). She contends: "By placing the sexual stories of the young at the centre of the journey towards adulthood, children's bodies are not merely the symbolic agents of that process. They are situated within the literary nation as sites of tension where the societies' most guarded gendered subjectivities can be challenged or recalibrated, and their histories of shame exorcised and hopefully healed" (Rahim 2011, 8).

Hopkinson's narrative reaches for a just and equitable order in which children would be nurtured, cherished and protected from the ravages of neglect and abuse. She does so by engaging the socio-psychological positionings of humans as gendered beings, and particularly women's location as sexual, productive and reproductive labour in increasingly technological environments. The narrative presents two worlds, whose shape-shifting evocations are contradictory and paradoxical. The further Tan-Tan migrates away from a not-quite-idyllic civilization – kept in order by constant surveillance, which has nevertheless not altered the dark desires of the human – is the more she migrates away from entrenched, skewed value systems. The passage through the dimension veil represents a spatial shift into a shadowy existence and a backward shift into a prior evolutionary stage marked by bodily transitions which emphasize human convergences with animals and foreshadows the incest debacle:

> A next veil swept through them, slow like molasses. Tan-Tan felt as though her tailbone could elongate into a tail, long and bald like a manicou rat's. Her cries of distress came out like hyena giggles. The tail tip twitched. She could feel how unfamiliar muscles would move the unfamiliar limb. *The thing standing beside her looked more like a man-sized mongoose than her father. He smelt like food, but food she wasn't supposed to eat. Family.* Tan-Tan sobbed and tried to wrap her tail tightly around herself (Hopkinson 2000, 74; emphasis added).

Both Tan-Tan and her father become unglued when transversing the dimension veil. The process strips civilizing accretions and constrains heightened recognition of human embodiment. Like the sweaty, muscular, back-talking pedicab runners, who privilege their autonomy and raw physicality above the comforts proffered by Granny Nancy web, Tan-Tan must painfully learn that that "back break" may be for humans after all; communal relations can be cooperative; and predatory sexual relations are not a default response to poverty, disempowerment and social isolation. Entry into the New Half Way Tree reconstitutes the human as needy and dependent on the wisdom to be derived from collaboration as opposed to conquest. Moreover, survival is impossible without acknowledgement on interdependence between human, animal and natural worlds. This is the base line for the functionality of the douen world. It is a leap that Tan-Tan, with her humility, agility and openness to the new, proves capable of making.

This is not the dynamic which operates for the humans in New Half Way Tree. In "Race and Technology", Elizabeth Boyle argues that "the act of decorporealisation of the 'black body' in a futuristic setting identifies, critiques and resists dominant representations of race and gender constructed within generic science fiction spaces" (Boyle 2009, 177). While this may be valid in relation to intertextual interface of genres and texts, this is not always the case in Hopkinson's intra-textual world. The savagery of the penal colony is played out in terms of gross physicality on bodies with overdetermined markers of race and gender. Entry into the penal colony and the stripping away of Granny Nanny's constraints unmasks Antonio's heart and inner being. He is transformed from a socially adept and swaggering communal leader into the deficient, self-indulgent, untrainable man that he has always been. The portrayal of the ugly, savage, abusive mother and her emasculated, browbeaten son plays out gender caricatures which have certainly survived and even heightened in human interaction. Indeed, for the most part, humans do not fare positively on the downside of the dimension vale. The place of primacy in New Half Way Tree belongs to Hopkinson's douens.

FOLKWAYS OF HEALING

What then is the just, equitable and safe social order which Hopkinson evokes? A major issue with incest and sexual violence in domestic environments is the loss of home – a space of safety and peace, nurturance, flourishing and rest. The destabilization, which leads the unhomed and deterritorialized father to seek shelter though his illicit sexual intrusion, sets Tan Tan adrift on a journey that alters her construction of home. Driven into exile on the penal planet and marronage, first within the sheltering Daddy Tree of the douen community and thereafter in the bush, she discovers and embraces natural and animal domains; learns – along with drudgery – the joys of inhabiting a labouring body; and contends with the task of enforced spatial expansion and illicit possession of her body as reproductive labour and home to the unborn.

As surely as the novel exposes the deleterious psychosocial dynamic which can play itself out between the sexes in human families, the narrative disrupts deliberately and systematically any connection between home, biological parenting and nurturing, at least in the humans. Indeed, in Hopkinson's forceful disruption of hierarchal relations between human and animal dominions, and between human and artificial intelligences, human beings come to occupy the lowest rung of the ladder. Giselle Anatol's perspective is instructive: ". . . recognizing "maternal power" and affectionate bonds that are separate from biological reproduction are also crucial to validating the transhistorical experiences of people of the African diaspora, and necessary for rebuilding a communal identity that refuses to be bound by individualism and potential isolation inherent in biological models (Anatol 2000, 120).

Hopkinson's futuristic world valorizes an Afro-Creole folk sensibility that would traditionally have been seen as backward and superstitious. Folk elements intersect with discourses of mothering and modalities of parenting and childrearing, and avenues for therapeutic intervention. Douens, according to folkloric traditions, are characters with feet turned backwards and large, floppy hats. They are liminal beings, housing the souls of children who die before they are baptized and hence, they are constrained to remain earthbound. They are known to lure children away from their parents and villages, and lose them deep in the forest. Hopkinson's douens inhabit a large, complex civilization, and possess a lively interest in human metallurgy and other technological inventions. They provide a lifeline for the innocent adolescent running from incest and the consequences of her murderous response. Hopkinson's revisionary construction of douens is a subset of the multigenerational literary project of shifting Afro-Creole civilization and sensibility from margins to centre, with a particular focus on its potential to produce healthy and wholesome families as the kingpin of the social order.

The douendom into which Tan-Tan enters is a refashioning of a stable domestic domicile governed by mores which bear remarkable resemblance to traditional moral family values. Love, shelter and protection are afforded by the Hinte, who, as a foil to the vain, distant human mother, constantly draws her children, including Tan-Tan, into her ample, feathery bosom. The adoptive douen father, Chichibud, is the soul of kindness, goodness, patience, protection and discipline. He stands in opposition to the drunken, sexually abusive Antonio. Together, they refute skewed ideals of male breadwinners and female homemakers to function as exemplary citizens of a viable alternative community, who reside in a mighty, sheltering Daddy Tree. Families with strong affective ties gather for meals of worms, tree frogs and other delicacies; there is peaceful, harmonious and complimentary interface between loving husbands and wives; the leaders have clear moral authority and disinterested strategies for leading the community; teenaged children vociferously articulate their defiance and are allowed a measure of experimentation, but are also gently curbed and taught compliance. Within this economy, there is a valorization of the life of the unborn as a gift from the Daddy Tree. Notwithstanding the violent and repugnant manner of impregnation, in the eyes of the teenage douen, Abifeta, there is no room for moral relativism and debate attending abortion of the product of incest.

To derive the benefits of douendom, Tan-Tan must undergo a shift in sensibility and an affirmation of difference, which may well be the most consistent ideological thrust of Hopkinson's narrative. Countering familial and societal incestuous in-breeding, a turning in on a self that is rooted in delusions of superiority or erupting as effects of ontological inadequacy, the narrative works in favour of recognizing an alternative world view characterized by what Harris terms "a profound and unusual treaty of sensibility between the human presence on this planet and the animal kingdom" (Harris 1999, 194). Simply put, the douens teach Tan-Tan the meaning of home. By inscribing their viable and resilient culture in opposition to that of restless, aggressive and violent humans, Hopkinson presents multiple meanings of home: as body, family, community and nation; as physical and psychic sanctuary; as complex of values and aspirations; as life-giving interface of gendered and raced subjects; as a complex socio-political organism resting comfortably within intersecting ecologies; as a network of intergenerational power relations and interdependencies governed by bonds of love and codes of honour, which privilege communal well-being above destructive individual impulses.

If douendom speaks to the potential for ecological, national and spiritual integration, Hopkinson also extends her notions of communality and therapeutic intervention to cover modes of mothering and home-making generated by non-humanoid forms. Writing against received science fiction genre assumptions of the fear of artificial intelligence, Hopkinson crafts Granny Nanny as an autonomous artificial intelligence with affective impulses rooted in Caribbean folk ways of caring. Named after the legendary folk freedom fighter, Nanny, leader of the maroons, and Anancy, the Caribbean folk trickster and obfuscating storyteller, the artificial intelligence Granny Nanny is the most faithful and efficient mother within the narrative. Working through her shapeshifting executing agent, Eshu, himself named after the god of the crossroads of the Yoruba pantheon, she is the quintessential hover mother. Robbed of the negative associations that would obtain in Western ideologies, this mother cares for and protects all, knows all and permits much, intervening only where there is risk to life and limb. Occupying the void generated by Ione's neglect and desertion, and the terror generated by the stepmother's jealously and murderous hatred, Granny Nanny becomes the quintessential other mother, pursuing her lost child, Tan-Tan, across the dimension veil and intervening into the birthing process of Tan-Tan's son, thereby creating redemptive purpose for the monster issue of incest. Imaged *androgynously* as the nurturer, protector and capacious womb, the discipliner and bringer of peace, she is also the father/generator of a new race, who scatters seed into Tan-Tan's womb to implant nanonites into Tubman's blood, to create the first cyborg. Giselle Anatol reads Granny Nanny's wide-ranging mobility and agency as signifying maternity as a hindrance to woman's full potential: "The s/mothering nanny possesses the power of influence through nurturing but also political power; she can be centred and grounded; and yet mobile and active; she can stifle and yet she can also free" (Anatol 2000, 114).

By loosening any psychic and symbolic connection between human biological parenting and child rearing, Hopkinson replaces the erring mother with numerous mother/father figures, who fulfill the substitutionary functions. This alleviates grief over the loss of mother/motherland with persistent underlying associations between biological parents with the imperial mother/motherland. Both oppress and reject their children. It is Granny Nanny who fulfills Tan-Tan's wish that her mother will come to find the exiled father and daughter, and by implication relieve her from the distress of being the substitute wife. Signifying on the science fiction tradition, which traditionally focuses on civilizing the alien, using the technologies and rationale of Western invention and world view, Hopkinson's universe generates spatiality, ideology, world view and parenting that valorizes safe and empowering Caribbean cosmologies and Indigenous world views.

The third healing stream that is carefully laid out is the power of narrative structured around African-Caribbean folkways. Those who have suffered rape/incest traumas invariably suffer an element of self-blame for having caused the assault; complicity when the body betrays some form of enjoyment; silencing when discovery of the deeds done in secret threaten the stability of the family home and the loss of its primary breadwinner. Dominick La Capra terms the process of engaging trauma and arriving at reengagement in life which allows one to begin anew an "articulatory practice" (La Capra 2001). The rape/trauma victim's capacity to own and tell her story is pivotal because it a re-appropriation of control and repositioning in terms of location within the signifying system as subject, as opposed to an object to be used to satisfy another's lust. Narrative asserts the power of the victim, who has been silenced by abuse and eroded by shame, to tell her story. Given the belatedness of trauma and its intrusive cycles of uncanny repetitions and disrupted temporalities, the narrative generates a sense of order by ordering chaos through the act of narrative self-fashioning.

Affirming the agency of folk personas and symbols in crafting therapeutic interventions, Hopkinson evokes the Midnight Robber figure of elaborate ritualistic dress and language, famous for its verbal communal engagement, framed in grandiloquent terminology and boastful self-fashioning.[7] Tan-Tan inhabits the folk character of the Midnight Robber to create a viable life narrative, and a personal and social self that is effective enough to halt her sense of psychic dislocation. In the process, she speaks new possibilities into being and rescripts herself as a victor. Posing a critique to the efficacy of a talking cure for trauma induced by sexual abuse, Tan-Tan's dynamic curative process begins in praxis and only thereafter rolls out in speech. This process begins with her excursions from the bush into human settlements, where she sets out to impose justice and order. Feeding the poor, chastising the oppressor, adopting and mothering the demanding, orphaned rolling calf and punishing the thief, she becomes a costumed figure working towards systematic imposition of a rule of law on anarchic settlements. As talk travels, the flesh and blood Tan-Tan is amplified by her discursive replica. Her exploits are exaggerated and retold as a series of cautionary tall tales and legends which flow beyond her natural reach to work in the service of preventative and retributive justice. Tan-Tan, recalibrated by her exposure to the norms, values and systems of douendom, becomes variously symbolic of deep-rooted violation and justice, punishment and retribution. Her work constitutes a triple rebuke to human modes of (non)engagement. She rebukes the failure of nation states to protect their young and vulnerable citizens from sexual abuse. She intervenes in real-life injustices, including those traditionally classified as private domestic affairs. She dips into denigrated folkloric repertoires to undermine socially endorsed silencing and erasure, and to project a larger-than-life discursive presence.

Tan-Tan's case plea for justice staged before the court of public opinion deploys carnivalesque performative traditions. The case to be debated is what is the just punishment for patricide committed by children in response to incest? The day of reckoning comes when she is hunted like an animal by her stepmother for capture and submission to Junjuh justice – an eye for an eye, a life for a life. When condemned by her stepmother's allegations of lasciviousness and seduction, which replicate age-old practices of victim blame, Tan-Tan deploys a countervailing theatrical narrative self-fashioning to integrate her split psyches and worlds. Countering victim blame, Tan-Tan's grandiloquent speech reformulates the case and persuades the assembled audience that she was just a child in need of adult intervention. In the process she strips away the masking and hypocrisies, which would have the said adult passing on weaponry to the child, in keeping with the tacit assumption that she was culpable for the incest and responsible for her own protection and retribution: "I name Tan-Tan, a 'T' and 'AN', I is the AN-acaona, Taino redeemer; the AN-nie Christmas, keel boat steamer, the Yaa As-AN-tewa; Ashanti warrior queen; the N-AN-ny, Maroon Granny; meaning Nana, mother, caretaker to a nation. You won't confound these people with your massive fabulation (Hopkinson 2000, 320).

The naming signifies multiple female figures of resistance and empowerment, whose acts have become legendary sources of courage. Tan-Tan's narrative appropriation draws strength from generations of warrior women who valiantly fought oppressions and won victories for themselves and their peoples. She established herself within a lineage which extends from Annie Christmas, folk heroine of antebellum New Orleans, reputed for her strength and skill at taming bullies, to Taino chief Anacaona, who negotiated with the conquistadors and chose to be executed with her people, rather than accept sexual servitude and concubinage to a Spanish intruder.

The intervention shadows the numerous dualities and doublings which emerge throughout – civilized worlds and shadow worlds; real Ione and shadow Ione, which is what Tan-Tan becomes to her father; the loving father and the incestuous father, the good Tan-Tan and bad Tan-Tan. The midnight robber persona, whose verbal violence and grandiloquence of the speechifying tradition enlarges the psychically diminished Tan-Tan, heals the split between good Tan-Tan and bad Tan-Tan. The Midnight Robber performance unifies her habitation of her abused and impregnated body; roots her identities in a series of ancestral legendary and mythic doubles and forerunners; and ultimately allows her to achieve a coherent self. The impact is the recuperation of a usable past and a viable being in the world. And there is a sense in which the freedom that she crafts extends beyond herself and points a liberatory pathway for the legacies of slavery, which are ever present in the futuristic, post-capitalist world, driven by obsession of powers, self-aggrandizement and the exercise of imperial longings, this time on the part of Caribbean citizens who would reach tentacles of technology-based violence and dominion across indices of difference. Hopkinson's complex deployment of the fantasy genre speaks to a nostalgic longing for a brave, new, futuristic world order and a resurgence of Indigenous cultural forms with the capacity to heal, revitalize and instruct in empowering ways to be human.

chapter 5

Baby Mama Talks

Motherhood in Childhood, Caribbean Style

LATIN AMERICA AND THE CARIBBEAN IS the only region in the world where adolescent fertility rates are stagnant or increasing, instead of decreasing. A 2012 World Bank study on teenage pregnancy ranks the region as having the third-highest fertility rate in the world, with seventy-two births per thousand between the ages of fifteen and nine. There are significant variations from nation to nation within the region, with Trinidad and Tobago, the subject of this chapter, ranking lowest, with fifty live births per thousand for the same demographic (World Bank 2012, 8). The majority of these young mothers come from rural or impoverished areas, and a substantial cross-section have suffered some form of sexual violence. The report indicates that early pregnancies – within or outside of marriage or common-law unions – increase the vulnerability of the girls, with potential consequences of underdevelopment, school dropout, impaired employment prospects, enhanced dependence on men, and health challenges, including exposure to maternal and infant mortality risks, and sexually transmitted diseases.[1]

There is also a stronger likelihood of perpetuating the cycle of poverty and violence. This chapter explores self-perceptions and lived experiences of a now mature woman who entered a residential, common-law union at age thirteen, and gave birth to her first child before she was sixteen. The early "consensual" encounter answers to the definition of statutory rape. Privileging the maternal voice, this enquiry uses discourse analysis to explore perceptions, in retrospect, of the experience of early motherhood and its outcome, with a particular focus on the interface between self-perception, gender prescriptions, cultural assumptions and the vulnerabilities identified above. The chapter posits that individual case studies of this nature, used in tandem with other quantitative and qualitative forms of scholarly enquiry, can enhance bottom-up understanding and provide useful data as a basis for intervention.

SOCIO-CULTURAL CONTEXT

A 2013 World Bank report identifies the onset of sexual initiation in the Caribbean as the earliest in the world, except for Africa, where early sexual exposure tends to take place within marriage. Early initiation into sexual activity predisposes young people to early pregnancy HIV/AIDS and sexually transmitted disease (World Bank 2013, xiv). In a 2010 study on "Adolescent Fertility in Selected Countries of Latin America and the Caribbean", Cristina Gomes indicates that "teenage pregnancy and fertility persist and even is increasing in some countries, contributing to interrupt adolescent educational and labor development and expectancies, and exposes teen girls to risk conditions associated with abortion, delivery complications and maternal death – particularly poor, undernourished and Indigenous adolescents, among them who live in rural areas, poor and less developed states, regions and countries" (Gomes 139). The socio-cultural dynamic which leads to motherhood in childhood in the Caribbean is complex and multi-faceted. The dynamic of colonialism and plantation economy, with its construction of enslaved adults and children alike as productive, reproductive and sexual labour, lies at the bedrock of modern Caribbean societies. Centuries later, its patterns of familial and interpersonal interaction, cultural assumptions and codes of violence are still bearing its strange fruit within the social order (Morgan and Youssef 2006; Morgan 2014). Prevailing gender constructions in the region perceive femininity as synonymous with sex appeal and masculinity with sex seeking (Jones 2013, 46). Systemic transgenerational poverty, with its coping strategy of matrifocality, intersects paradoxically with male privilege, accorded even to men who abdicate their responsibility to provide and protect within the home.

Historical dynamics, which led to privileging the mother child bond, accommodating absent or distant fathers, celebrating the coping strategies of the female-headed household, make single parenting acceptable, if not valorized in the Caribbean context. Overall, childbearing is not necessarily restricted to marriage. Women may, by choice or necessity, forgo becoming wives, but the notion is that they ought to become mothers because mothering will make them into real women, and secure care and provision for them in old age. Although this dynamic is operative within all strata, it is particularly virulent within Afro-Caribbean lower-strata households. Multiple male partners, traditionally engaged in a process of serial monogamy, have been perceived as potential providers by single mothers and female heads of households. Childbearing is seen as cementing the process by giving potential, if not actual, access to multiple streams of income from multiple child fathers. All of this adds up to inadequate protection and provision for children of both genders and particularly for girls (Senior 1997). This trend is catching on in the middle and upper strata. Independent professional women are increasingly opting for single parenting.

Among certain populations early sexual initiation may even be perceived as a rite of passage which ushers one from girlhood to adulthood. There are households in which children may be coerced or even conscripted into providing sexual services for visitors or residents to whom they may or may not be linked by blood – boyfriends, stepfathers or "uncles". Girls are also covertly socialized into trading sex for economic and material services, for example, taxi drivers or "uncles" who provide school supplies. In a cross-section of Indo-Caribbean households, male violence and terrorism over households with minimal familial and police interference has traditionally been accepted. This cultural acceptance of the male right to exert violence over his household speaks to embedded patterns of male privilege. In a few particularly bizarre instances, this notion extends to sexual privileges of the male in relation to the female children of the household. Anecdotal evidence and common lore also point to select communities in which incest or statutory rape have become normative and are seen as rites of passage into female adulthood.

In the Caribbean, both the pregnancy scenarios and how they are perceived are diverse and nuanced. Drayton argues: "Sexual activity *per se* is, however, not the real issue: it is sexual activity that *leads to pregnancy* that is the problem" (Drayton 396). Drayton asserts teenage fertility was never actively encouraged: ". . . the Church preached against it; parents discouraged the idea and punished the fact; schools expelled pregnant girls from the classroom; (and) national governments have set up family life education units to deal with the problem" (Drayton 396). Drayton draws attention to another common Caribbean perception: "Many pregnancies may be unplanned but few babies are unwanted" (Drayton 33). This applies even in highly prescriptive environments, such as churches and deeply religious households.

In relation to Trinidad and Tobago in particular, then Minister of Education, Dr Tim Gopeesingh, raised a national alarm in February 2014 over this complex of issues. Gopeesingh indicated approximately five hundred teenage pregnancies are reported annually. The majority of victims are impregnated by men between the ages of twenty-five and forty, hence they are victims of statutory rape (Lord 2014). Only rarely do these men face prosecution. The minister also indicated that there are numerous cases of multiple teenage pregnancies, with some girls bearing as many as four children before the age of twenty. Dr Gopeesingh, a gynaecologist, indicates, based on his extensive experience dealing with teenaged mothers: "It is an issue of socialization and what these teenagers are looking for is . . . some degree of love."

Although the vast majority of these pregnancies occur out of wedlock, the issue was complicated by the existence of contradictory laws in relation to the legal age of consent. Up until 2017, the age of consent for sexual intercourse was set at sixteen years, and child marriage was legal in Trinidad and Tobago, with no fewer than four marriage laws. The Muslim Marriage Act 7 of 1961 had – until the 2017 amendments – legalized marriage for girls from the age of twelve and males from sixteen; the Hindu Marriage act legalized marriage for girls from fourteen and males from eighteen. While recognizing the cultural specificities at work in defining childhood and youth, this project adopts the delimitations of the United Nations Population Fund (UNFPA), which defines adolescence as between the ages of ten and nineteen, and youth as between the ages of fifteen and twenty-four (UNFPA 2019, 3)

This chapter will explore a case study of motherhood in childhood. It speaks to the subjective dimension of the call issued by Gomes for the "integration of objective and subjective indicators, which consider also the perception of adolescents about their decisions and needs" (Gomes 140) The research addresses the following issues:

- Does the narrative point to factors which predispose girls to becoming mothers in their childhood?
- To what extent is the interviewee impacted by varying levels of awareness, access and agency?
- What does the case indicate about the impact of cultural norms, societal perceptions and self-perception?
- What coping strategies were deployed and what values does the interviewee impart as a result her experience of teenage motherhood?

THE CASE

Cecelia Beharry (name changed) is an articulate and attractive forty-eight-year-old domestic helper with multiple jobs, at times as many as three a day. Her major assets are her quick intelligence, pleasantness and willingness to serve.

The data was conducted in an interview of approximately forty-five minutes. It took place at Cecelia's workplace, where she is comfortable. While the power relations implicit in an employee/employer relationship must be taken into account, there were no issues of establishing trust and rapport. Moreover, the interviewee owned the process, expressing pride at having her story told, while insisting on the use of pseudonyms to protect privacy. The analysis adopts the approach of an interview as negotiated text, generated by interaction between two participants to produce contextually based meanings. It treats the interview as an avenue for narrative self-fashioning, the piecing together of a life narrative centred around a series of traumatizing triggers, which in themselves generate disrupted chronologies. Arguably for Cecelia, the traumatizing catalyst of domestic violence, extreme enough to become murderous, was present from birth, coming to a head in a life-transforming event at age five. This is within the period when the child's cognitive processing systems were undeveloped. The interviewee began weeping some three minutes into the interview and wept more or less intensely for its entire duration.

The investigation uses discourse analysis as its methodology and takes regard of proxemics – use of space; chronemics – pacing of speech and use of time as a variable for communication; kinesis – body language; and paralinguistic elements variations in volume, pitch and voice quality. It also takes note of what is included and excluded. The interview was treated as an act of self-disclosure, in which revelation and understanding are enhanced through the requirement for reflection and bringing suppressed information to articulation.

FINDINGS AND DISCUSSION

Theme 1: Death of mother due to domestic violence

Cecelia: "My childhood . . . my childhood was hard . . . it was hard. Mother died at the age . . . when I was the age of five. Father was an alcoholic. So, me and my two sisters and my brother we were more or less left to fend for ourselves."

Q. "How did your Mom die?"

Cecelia: "From abuse . . . from my father."

Q. "Do you remember anything about it?"

Cecelia: "About the abuse?" (musing) "Well, at that age the only thing I really remember was running on a Thursday night . . . every Thursday night because that was the day he get pay . . . so he get pay and he would start to drink and it was the same drama every week."

The pattern described is a common one of the father working until pay day and then using a substantial portion of his income for drink, after which he unleashed violent abuse on a weekly basis (Morgan and Youssef 2006). Although Cecelia remembers the maternal grandmother providing shelter for the family running from the drunken father, there is no recollection or mention of any intervention to break the cycle of drinking, beating and begging on the part of the father; and flight and return to the abusive partner on the part of the mother. The father's drunken abuse and constant beating of the mother caused a brain haemorrhage, from which the mother eventually died at age twenty-six.

Cecelia, who is usually articulate and voluble, was not forthcoming in her response to the question: "How did your mom die?" She expressed no anger and attributed no blame to her father. Her language and expression, when dealing with her father's part in her mother's death, was indirect. Aided by passive voice construction and nominalization, she foregrounds the fact that her mother died. Only when pushed did she mention her father's part in the matter and even this she related in a gentle, childlike voice. Never once did she directly state "my father killed my mother".

Theme 2: Paternal abandonment and vulnerability to sexual abuse

Q. "What was your father like (pause) when he wasn't drunk?"

Cecelia: "Nice. He was nice. I remember even after she died, he would drink and ting, but then I would remember hearing him crying in the night. And then he would get up early in the morning and he would cook, wash (losing composure) go to work. (Tears beginning to flow). And then it would be all the same thing on a Thursday (sniffling) . . . Well, there was nobody to beat because by that time my mother was dead. He would stay out all weekend drinking and he would come back sometimes Sunday morning." (Weeping, long pause)

The abandonment of young children takes multiple forms. The first layer of absence and loss experienced by the four children was the loss of their mother when Cecelia was aged five. The wounding, grief, fear and confusion, which must have been generated by this tragic mother loss, were exacerbated when the father continued his weekly cycle of drinking and deserting the home, leaving the children unprotected and without food, adequate shelter or guidance. The young children were often left to fend for themselves, foraging food from fruit trees and living in a structure without doors, windows, electricity, or pipe-borne water. The warm climate and the rural environs, with open lands and fruit-bearing trees, facilitated their survival. Paternal abandonment left the young girls vulnerable to attack. An intruder entered the unsecured house and threatened to rape the eldest sister:

> Cecelia: "Um hum. Ahm . . . there was a point in time when it was every weekend he would be out and then there was a Saturday night when the three of us, me and my two sisters – one older, one younger – ahm, we in the house. It didn't really have windows and doors . . . there was no electricity. Somebody came in the house behind my sister, Karen. Well, we managed . . . after we started to bawl and ting in the middle of the night, the person left. And after that, my grandmother took us from there . . . we went to live with my grandmother."

Reflective of the then vulnerable child's need to create an affirmative picture of an abusive parent, on whom she depends, Cecelia saw it as very important to paint a positive picture of her father. With a mournful smile and an affirmative nod, she justified her conscious choice to affirm her father as nice when he was not drinking – rising early, caring, washing and cooking for the children after the mother died – until the weekly Thursday to Sunday drink, abuse and desertion cycle kicked in. Cecelia clearly indicated that the father's physical abuse did not extend to the children. She inferred indirectly some sorrow on his part after her mother's death. She did not mention his ongoing aggression extended to her mother unless she was pressed and even then, her revelation was oblique. In response to a question of whether she remembered her mother's face, she said "no", with her head bowed. Again, only when pressed about the absence of photographs, she responded tersely, "My father burnt all after she died." The father eventually found another partner and a measure of recovery through the intervention of Alcoholics Anonymous.

Theme 3: Inadequate Care from the Extended Family

Historically, the extended family network in the Caribbean has provided a safety net and takes responsibility for its children. In this instant, only female family members are mentioned – an ageing, impoverished grandmother and a succession of aunts. There are apparently no men in the safety network. Again, Cecelia is quick to make excuses for familial inability to extend adequate care to the needy children – "It was too much for them, too many mouths to feed." So it was from one home to the other, week after week, until the big sister took the family back to the yard with the unsecured, unfinished house. The abandoned children were shifted from home to home among female relatives, with all the vulnerabilities which this entailed, but they were never actually made to feel at home. Eventually, the eldest sister took them back to the home, with its dilapidated structure. There was no mention of intervention by state authorities.

Theme 4: Early Sexual Initiation and Childbearing

Q.	"Your dad used to come to see you?"
Cecelia:	"Ahm, off and on, off and on, and then he end up getting sick. By that time, I was thirteen and because there was nobody to take care of me, I end up with husband (voice softer and weeping more intense). So, at the age of thirteen, I went to live with somebody and I had my first child at sixteen."
Q:	"Was he good to you?"
Cecelia:	"At the starting, yes." (Long pause and intense weeping)
Q:	"If you want to stop at any time, it's okay, you know."
Cecelia:	"No."
Q:	"So, at thirteen years old . . . how old was he?"
Cecelia:	"Twenty."

Severe physical deprivation and the absence of a sustaining, nurturing environment were instrumental in driving Cecelia, at age thirteen, into a cohabitational "consensual" relationship with a twenty-year-old man. She became his "common-law wife" and went to live in his family home, enduring problematic relations with the other female members of his extended household. Motherhood came early at sixteen. Cecelia recalled: "I guess not knowing much about that kind of life at the age of sixteen, you telling yourself you is a big woman, you proud to be pregnant . . . not even know what to expect when you reach in the hospital . . . All of that was . . . I guess it was like a little girl getting a dolly, you know. Yuh happy, proud to be a mother because that's all you know . . . Yuh is a mother now."

This statement, expressed very slowly and in a contemplative manner, reflects a clear division between the experiencing younger self and the reflections of the adult speaker. Multiple distancing devices are deployed. Repeated use of "I guess" indicates uncertainty. The use of the second person, instead of the first person, to describe the flawed and unrealistic assumptions of the youthful mother is telling. The insights of a mature, experienced self are voiced in the first person, as in "I guess it was like a child getting a dolly." Cecilia foregrounds ignorance: not knowing about birth control, not knowing what giving birth entails, not knowing about the demands of motherhood. Despite the use of multiple distancing devices, which reflect, retrospectively, hard-won wisdom for the happenstance of early motherhood, Cecelia records a shift in self-identity in the young mother, which leads to a sense of pride, self-affirmation and positive self-knowing.

Theme 5: Coping Strategies

Cecelia told of decades of back-breaking domestic labour because the common-law husband, who eventually married her, refused to work to provide for the young family. The second child came when she was seventeen. She was constrained to work multiple jobs to make ends meet. Hard work and dogged determination enabled her to build a small room and, eventually, a small house in the yard of her husband's family compound. Even so, she was careful to record her husband's positive care and attention to the children, which allowed her to fulfil the function of primary breadwinner and initiator of all measures for familial enhancement and improvement. Her husband's penchant for sexual relations with minors continued unbated. Eventually, she left the marital home when she became exasperated with his ongoing infidelities, extending even to sexual relations with underage minors who were the same age as her daughter.

Theme 6: Ongoing Vulnerability to Abuse and Violence

Reflecting the propensity of women who have endured lifelong abuse and violation, Cecelia, after leaving her husband, connected with another abusive partner. They set up house on land that she worked hard to purchase. She was not forthcoming about the events that led to him burning down her small house and knifing her in the shoulder.

Analysis

Despite the valid and oft-repeated assertion that risks, vulnerability and potentialities open to adolescence and youth vary from place to place and culture to culture, Cecelia Beharry's narrative reflects a substantial cross-section of the factors that lead to and result from teenage pregnancy. Cecelia was predisposed for early motherhood by the broad sociocultural framework; the family into which she was born; and the nature of life that she endured from birth. Firstly, she was born into a social order generated through a violent and violating history, in which labour abuse in all of its forms – productive, reproductive and sexual labour – have been endemic. Although it would be impossible to connect the dots with a straight line, continuities exist between Cecelia's life circumstances and the values, practice and customs generated on sugar estates. Patterns of alcoholism, violence and wife beating are a case in point (Brereton 2010; Hodge 1974; Morgan and Youssef 2006; Morgan 2014). Moreover, the requirement for child labour in all forms within the dynamic of plantation society has contributed to the blurring of the boundaries between childhood and adulthood. In the Caribbean, perceptions of childhood and the age at which one may consent to, legitimately engage in, and profitably enter sexual activity and marital relations are not self-evident and are not subject to broad-based societal consensus.

Cecelia Beharry presents a textbook case, manifesting practically all of the risk factors for early initiation of sexual activity identified by Rohan G. Maharaj, Paula Nunes and Shamin Renwick, based on their survey of ninety-five relevant peer-reviewed papers published between 1980 and 2005, entitled "Health Risk Behaviours Among Adolescents in the English-speaking Caribbean: A Review." In relation to specific risk factors for early initiation of sexual activity, they indicate "a history of physical or sexual abuse was found to be a predictor of having sexual intercourse as an adolescent" (Maharaj, Nunes, and Renwick 2009, 10). Additional risk factors were "less family stability, single-parent family households, low socioeconomic status, and poor knowledge of STIs" (Maharaj, Nunes, and Renwick 2009, 43).

Awareness

The child came to self-awareness in an impoverished environment with an alcoholic, abusive father and a compliant, apathetic mother, who apparently lacks the wherewithal – financial and otherwise – to choose an alternative life pathway for herself and her children. From her earliest childhood, Cecelia came to self-knowledge within the framework of the murderous abuse and violence endured by her own youthful mother, which ended her life when she was in her twenties, by which time she had already borne four children. Reflecting unwholesome generational continuities, children born to teenage mothers are similarly likely to have teenage pregnancies as well. Cecelia, whose life path was rife with continuities of domestic and sexual abuse, was exposed from childhood to a multiplicity of traumatizing catalysts – domestic violence, maternal loss at the hand of the father; paternal abandonment, bringing vulnerability to sexual assault; poverty; hunger; insecure shelter; inadequate access to guidance, education, healthcare, and the list continues.

Although at one level she is aware of the ill done to her mother and her family by the drunken, abusive father, she chooses to gloss over this. Whereas this may be readily attributed to the child's needs to think well of the adult on whom she had to depend, Cecelia upholds selective memory as an antidote to bitterness and sadness as a lifelong coping strategy. In relation to her father, she suppresses memories of violence, pain and abuse, and opts instead to foreground memories of her father's pain, caregiving and nurturance. In relation to her former husband, she extends forgiveness for his infidelities and pities him for the current emptiness of his life. Although abuse-generating stress was normalized from infancy, becoming an inescapable, taken-for-granted facet of life, Cecelia has chosen to be cheerful, upbeat and strong, and overall, a capable manager of painful memories. Since the interview, she has mentioned repeatedly how helpful it was to tell her story, and to receive empathetic listening, and to recall and chart her journey, which affirmed the depth of her suffering and the effectiveness of her strategies for rising above them.

Agency

Cecelia's residential, common-law relationship with a twenty-year-old man at age thirteen aligns with the societal value system in which it is common for girls and women to have successive, more or less binding relationships before they legally marry. Cecelia interpreted this action paradoxically. On the one hand, she constructs it as reflective of her agency in terms of "getting husband". Given the scenario of severe deprivation, her attraction of the sexual attention and care of a twenty-year-old lover at age thirteen may have brought her a measure of relief because she had a "husband" and a "home". This notion holds, despite her intensified weeping at this point of the interview, for the frightened and needy child who embarked on this course of action. She is very clear, in retrospect, that this came about because of lack of parental care and protection, and secure shelter. And the law defines such relationships as child sexual abuse, based on the notion that children are not mature enough to make informed decisions about consensual sex. The values and perceptions of the broader social groups were evident in the fact that there was no apparent censure for a young male cohabiting with a thirteen-year-old in his mother's home. Several key events reflect a hard-won growing agency on the part of the young woman. At seventeen, when she fell into the category of repeated teenage childbearing because of sheer ignorance, Cecelia gained agency in relation to sexuality and fertility when she learned about contraception. This knowledge came not as a result of structured institutional intervention in relation to the risks of teenage pregnancy, but through the friendly casual advice of nurses, who warned of the consequences of ongoing childbearing and advised her about the availability of free contraception.

Becoming a mother brought increasing levels of vulnerability and need, and exacerbated an ongoing problem. The husband's unwillingness to become a provider for the young family became far more problematic in the face of the requirement to provide for two infants. It was this that brought Cecelia to awareness of the impact of a lack of education. Sporadic schooling ended with the start of the common-law union at age thirteen. Though highly educated in the school of hard knocks, she found herself devoid of any educational certification whatsoever; and hence, employable only at the lowest levels of unskilled employment, at the lowest levels of renumeration, and the highest levels of vulnerability to mistreatment and abuse by employers. It was from this level that she began the slow, arduous process of working as the primary breadwinner to provide basic necessities for her family, then, eventually, over the long haul, the addition of rudimentary living space on the family compound.

Maternity increased need and motivation. Cecelia charted a difficult pathway towards financial agency, won through mammoth sacrifice, backbreaking labour, consistent saving, cautious spending, frugality and creativity. Arguably this confidence in her capacity to provide for herself and her children was instrumental in Cecelia Beharry finding the agency to leave her husband after some twenty years of cohabitation, having endured years of exploitation and mental abuse when he refused to work steadily to provide for his growing family. Eventually, when he once again began to engage in sexual relations with underage minors – the same age as his daughter, she decided to leave him. The age of her children was a contributing factor because she waited until they were sixteen and seventeen years old. She respects the choice they made at the time to remain with their father. Arguably, also though she was not forthcoming on the matter, it is apparent that Cecelia did not demonstrate the same level of compliance in the subsequent relationship with the other abusive partner. She stated succinctly: "He put me in the hospital with a stab wound in my back. I ended up building a little house on the land but he burnt it down flat. So I end up by my sisters."

Access

Cecelia's narrative demonstrates the growing inadequacy of the extended family networks to care for its own. This exacerbated a crippling lack of access to institutional intervention at pivotal stages of the family misadventure. The state systems, and their intersections with deleterious cultural assumptions, failed Cecelia Beharry from infancy. There was no mention of police intervention when her mother was being regularly beaten. The cycle of alcohol consumption come payday followed by extremes of domestic violence is well documented. The strongest possibility was that the beatings fell under the conceptual purview of "husband-wife business", which tacitly accords to the husband, as head of the home, the right to govern his household and discipline his wife and children by acts of violence, should he deem it necessary. The narrative affirms the persistence of cultural patterns – the fatalistic notion that women should endure domestic abuse, encapsulated in the saying "Is yuh husband is yuh luck" (Morgan and Youssef 2006). Since there was no identified perpetrator of an illegal act of violence, it stands to reason that there was no investigation of cause of death when Cecelia's abused young mother succumbed to brain haemorrhage due to severe, repeated beatings. Most telling of all, there was no formal intervention when the underaged child appeared at the public health clinic to deliver the baby conceived through statutory rape. There were no state authorities to check on mandatory school attendance. Arguably, the educational process could have facilitated training, enhanced self-esteem, promoted values clarification, and fastened the eyes of the vulnerable girl on the potential of education for self-empowerment and upward mobility. There was no social service intervention when the abandoned children were scratching out a tenuous existence on their own.

The lack of access does not end there. Given her total ignorance of sexuality and childbearing, Cecelia Beharry bore her children and was catapulted into motherhood in childhood through happenstance. Her ignorance of the workings of her body meant that she was deprived of the choice of whether to conceive a child. In other words, pregnancy occurred because of a lack of choice due to a lack of knowledge. Cecelia indicates that she had no knowledge of contraception until she had had her second child, even though her first child was the result of statutory rape. The access that does come to her comes through informal encounters with nurses. The ability to swiftly act on this intelligence is a credit to Cecelia.

This dynamic interplay of causal factors begs the question: Could the multiple distresses endured by Cecelia Beharry have been addressed by interventions focused primarily on behavioural modification? Executive director of the United Nations Population Fund, Mr Babatunde Osotimehin, argues that "From a human rights perspective, a girl who becomes pregnant – regardless of the circumstances or reasons – is one whose rights are undermined" (Williamson 2013, iii). This case supports the UNFPA contention that approaches to addressing teenage motherhood, which traditionally focus on behavioural modification of girls, assume that the girls have agency and responsibility, and hence are liable for blame in terms of preventing pregnancy. Osotimehin indicates that these approaches "fail to account for the circumstances and societal pressures that conspire against adolescent girls and make motherhood a likely outcome of their transition from girlhood to childhood" (Williamson 2013, iii).

In the absence of an effective institutional support system, maintenance of tight family ties is a pivotal coping strategy. Cecelia remains, until today, deeply appreciative of her sisters. Significantly, apart from a brief mention of her brother at the beginning of the narrative and again at the end, he disappears for most of the account. The narrative of family pulling together to cope with deep adversity is a female version – girls and women coming together to form family and to generate a safety network. The male family members are simply not there.

Self Perception

Cecelia measures her eventual success in relation to the glaring inadequacies of her childhood. Her greatest treasure is her relationships. By dint of hard work, she has educated her children, who are thriving. She has built a stable home with her second husband, who takes care of her. The house itself is large and impressive, extensive enough that there are rooms which she does not even enter. The enduring legacies of a traumatic past are pain and a certain hypersensitivity that she is not valued or cared for. There is also a sense in which her capacity to rise above adversity is dictated by her careful management of her troubled past, which determined the kind of person who she became, and is becoming. In the service of this objective, she opts to have highly selective memories. As a coping strategy, she minimizes the disadvantageous circumstances and focuses on the positives. Highly empathic, she constantly makes excuses for all, including her murderous father, implying his acknowledgement of culpability in his weeping at nights after causing his wife's death through domestic violence. She only admits evidence to the contrary (he burned all the photos of her mother after she dies) when it is elicited. Cecelia's life narrative ends on a triumphant note:

> The good thing in my life is that my two children are able. I put them through school. My son, he is now a supervisor at the *Trinidad Guardian*. My daughter, she is married and she has a son, good husband. She is not employed out there, but she does her little thing at home to make ends meet. It's good when I see them. They're happy and I know that they did not go through what I had to go through, to suffer as I suffered. I have an extremely good relationship with my two sisters and my brother, and I have a marriage that I am determined to make work. And this time, I have a good husband.

Having suffered the loss of her mother and desertion by her father, Cecelia measures the success of her life in terms of her ability to care for her own family and to see them successfully established in their careers and life paths. The herculean task and deep sacrifices that enabled her to deliver them to this stage of their lives is interpreted as a positive investment. Note how often she sums up her present life circumstances as "good" – she uses the term to denote how beneficial the children's ability to make their way is; applies it to her husband to describe him as faithful, kind and generous; to describe her relationship with her sisters and brother, to indicate it is mutually supportive, open and sustaining. The closing statements of the interview reflect a clear ethical compass, unwavering notions of good and bad, and a strong determination to work diligently for the "good" things in life. Although she does mention accomplishments in terms of the acquisition of material things, including her house and land, this does not figure high on her list of successes. It is not what brings "goodness" into her life.

The findings of this analysis lend flesh-and-blood support to several recommendations made by agencies dealing with teenage pregnancy. Girls are victimized by the cultural mores and community perceptions, as well as family histories of abuse and deprivation, poverty, lack of moral and secular education, which make them vulnerable to teenage pregnancy. Effective intervention must address societal and cultural factors, and not simply focus on individual behavioural modification. In the absence of responsible parenting, the state has a responsibility to create safety nets and to give young girls access to the knowledge needed to avoid vulnerabilities and the risk of adolescent childbearing.

In terms of self-perception, the immature value-processing systems of adolescents can lead them to embrace stances, attitudes and notions that are deleterious to their long-term well-being. More specifically, perceptions of agency, readiness to embark on sexual activity, and the significance of motherhood are all subject to immature value-processing systems and skewed ways of making meaning of adolescence. This is exacerbated in children who have not been subjected to stable and consistent parenting, broader family involvement and engagement with community, secular and moral educational systems, reading programmes, support groups and so on. The risk is that the choices made in youth leads to consequences that may well be difficult or impossible to reverse. These perceptions and thinking processes can be expected to change as the individual matures; hence, intervention in terms of imparting educational and developmental opportunities, family life education and values clarification, which are crucial in childhood, stands to be beneficial at all ages. Most significantly in this case study, the existence and maintenance of supportive family networks has proven to be the most valuable resource of all.

chapter 6

"Killing Don't Need No Reason"

Trauma and Criminality in *A Brief History of Seven Killings*

> The only thing that ghetto people can fill a void with is a void.
>
> —*Marlon James, A Brief History of Seven Killings (2014, 14)*

INTERVENTIONS INTO CRIMINALITY IN THE CARIBBEAN and beyond tend to focus on recuperating the individual as well as alleviating societal conditionalities which lead to criminal behaviours (Ayres 1998; Verner 2006). The complex cause-and-effect network of Caribbean gang violence has been particularly resistant to intervention. A major issue is how to alleviate the scourge of gang violence which, particularly when imbricated with political processes, devastates individuals, families, communities and nations, and spreads its tentacles transnationally and trans-generationally. This chapter reads Marlon James' sprawling epic, *A Brief History of Seven Killings,* through the filters of trauma theory to demonstrate correlations between criminality and unresolved traumas on multiple levels. It explores the manner in which unrelieved historical, national and cultural traumas drill down into the lives of individuals, families and communities. We argue that trauma and crime are complex, resistant, multinational and multicultural issues that cannot be grasped through a linear, individual focus. James' narrative exemplifies the manner in which individuals are unwittingly caught up in lingering, intrusive, contemporary legacies of historical and national atrocities. Effective intervention must therefore excavate and address these rhizomes, while tackling more immediate individual and communal societal conditions. This enquiry illustrates the power of narrative, in this case, a sprawling polyvocal narrative, to promote interdisciplinary dialogue on the causes, consequences, control, culture and representation of crime in anglophone Caribbean societies.

The 686-page novel is divided into four segments and covers five days. The core incident is based on an actual event – the shooting of reggae star Bob Marley in 1976, prior to the staging of a peace concert, intended to unite warring political factions – the People's National Party (PNP) and the Jamaica Labour Party (JLP), as well as the gang lords who supported them through violent interventions. True to the book title, each segment of this far-from-brief history is centred on death. The first two segments – "Original Rockers December 2, 1976" and "Ambush in the Night December 3, 1976" – are set in Jamaica and focus on the assassination attempt on the Singer. Death of the key players involved in the attack pervades all other segments. The third segment of the novel, "Shadow Dancin' February 15, 1979", is also set in Kingston; while the fourth and fifth segments, "White Lines/Kids in America August 14, 1985" and "Sound Boy Killing March 22, 1991", are set in New York. The novel is peopled by a huge cast of characters and voices, which circle and provide fragmentary, subjective, mediated exposure to the antecedents, occurrence and outcome of the central crisis in which the Singer – treasured son of the soil, mediator, supporter of the oppressed, bringer of healing and peace – is attacked and wounded. This attack against the Singer can be read as exemplary of the depth of societal woundedness and the challenge of establishing therapeutic intervention. In the process James performs an act of assemblage which frames the incident and contextualizes the personal histories of all actors and contributors. The complexity of the trauma narrative is heightened by the multiplicity of perspectives, the skewed mentalities, the drug-induced hazes, the chaos and confusion, the disrupted spatialities and temporalities surrounding the core event, and the haphazard lifestyles of the characters.

Much of the horrific immediacy of the novel is crafted through its astute incorporation of a series of bizarre real-life occurrences, and the blurring of boundaries between fantasy and reality, thus filling in gaps left by distant life histories and media reportage in a disruptive and disturbing manner. The result is a fictional recreation of unspeakable acts – generated by wildness, which emanates out of unspoken and unspeakable histories and creates gruesome scenarios that are stranger than fiction.[1] It traces the rise and fall of Storm Posse don, Josey Wales, modelled after real-life Kingston Shower Posse don, Lester Coke. Fictional and real characters experience gang-style execution of their children in identical fashions. This is also the case for the incident which triggers the downfall of both the fictional and the real don – the threat of extradition to the United States for his mass slaughter of occupants of a crack house in revenge for a robbery by an addict on the streets of New York. A British reviewer of the novel recalled:

> In the mid-eighties, Lester Coke, the boss of Jamaica's Tivoli Gardens neighbourhood, was the victim of a street robbery in Miami. He responded by tracking his assailant to a nearby crack house where he single-handedly killed everyone inside. The FBI only realised what had happened several years later. Their attempt to extradite Coke set in train a string of events that led to Coke being burned alive in a prison cell in Jamaica, his son Jah-T murdered while riding a scooter in central Kingston, and his youngest son, Christopher Coke, known as Dudus, becoming the boss of Tivoli Gardens (Blincoe 2014).

Like his real-life counterpart, Lester Coke, Josey Wales is subsequently mysteriously burned to death in a Jamaican prison cell while awaiting extradition. The major accomplishment of the novel is the manner in which it plausibly evokes the complex and irrational physical and mental worlds of the host of players, which constitute a criminal community and those who fuel its machinations. This goes beyond the criminogenic nature of ghetto existence, where the communal welfare depends upon criminal networks, which the community, in turn, has a vested interest in shielding. The network figured in *A Brief History* includes law enforcement officers, transnational operators, politicians and, moving magically among all, the Singer, who seeks always to build bridges and join hands.

The correlation between trauma and crime has been decisively made. These are the givens. Modern Caribbean societies were spawned in the crimes against humanity – a terrorist imperial system founded on the bedrock of the *encomienda* system, which led to the genocide of Indigenous tribes, followed by the largest mass labour migration in human history – slavery and indentureship, both of which were buttressed by incredible enactments of mass terrorism. The attendant rupture of ancient cultural systems of gender and familial relations proved devastating. Cultural traumas are the inheritance of collectivities that envision themselves as wounded by historical violations (Morgan 2014). Mediated by knowledge and cultural workers, like the iconic Bob Marley, cultural traumas manifest in group assemblages and antipathies to sufferers, who have had no direct experience of the traumatizing catalyst, and impact the potential of collectivities to fully inhabit and realize the potentialities of their present-day existence.[2] These historical forces have thrust their rhizomatic roots over time and transnational space to produce social worlds of incredible savagery, violence and violation. The epistemic violence of racism, colourism and classism, which have become the kingpin of the postcolonial social order, relegates segments of the society to entrenched poverty and underdevelopment. Cultural trauma, in turn, feeds into insidious trauma – minute traumatizing catalysts inherent to the social framework layer –incrementally to bring the individuals and communities to the breaking point. Insidious trauma is implicated in mental health challenges, which may include the onset of neuroses.[3]

The fact that trauma theory emerged out of the imperative to understand the Nazi Holocaust begs the question of what literary trauma can bring to the table, in terms of addressing mind-boggling violence and resistant social issues. On the simplest level, trauma theory speaks to psychic and societal woundedness that intrudes into the conscious mind, seeking articulation and ordering into narrative. The pivotal facet of this narrative is not fidelity to the facts surrounding the submerged, fragmented and dissonant traumatic experience, but fidelity to the experiential truth of what Cathy Caruth terms, "the moving and sorrowful voice that cries out, a voice that is paradoxically released *though the wound*" (emphasis added). She continues, "[I]f Freud turns to literature to describe traumatic experience, it is because literature like psychoanalysis, is interested in the complex relationship between knowing and not knowing" (Caruth 1966, 2–3). Dominick LaCapra, building on this connection, argues that literature is particularly useful for grappling with trauma because of its capacity to gesture towards excess. LaCapra indicates that writing trauma, as distinct from writing about trauma, "involves processes of acting out, working over, and to some extent working through in analysing and 'giving voice' to the past – processes of coming to terms with traumatic 'experiences', limit events, and their symptomatic effects that achieve articulation in different combinations and hybridised forms" (LaCapra 2001, 86).

Reacting to the impulse of evasive histories, contrived archives and other official repositories of collective memory to sanitize and homogenize national narratives, Ramu Nagappan points to the paradoxical potential of fiction to give voice to fragments: "The fragment is a contingent narrative, a record that until now has remained unacknowledged or undiscovered" (Nagappan 2005, 28). This, in turn, can impact public discourse, cultural reception and, perchance, even spark constructive conversations about complicity and blame. While none of these positions adequately addresses the problematic of languaging social suffering, all speak to the power of the literary imagination to strain towards the unknown and the unknowable, which is the stuff of trauma.

Marlon James' fiction points to narrative fragments and wounds that speak culpability and complicity as he maps an inhospitable location, where rhizomes of oppressive and unjust transnational histories sprout intergenerationally, venomously and fatally in nations, communities and individuals. He gives voice to a multiplicity of intersecting narratives and worlds, which demonstrate how poverty and harsh social conditions, compounded by political exploitation of the impoverished and disempowered for partisan advantage, and by brutal day-to-day abuse by state authorities, give rise to savaged and savage individuals, who are ghettoized victims of cultural trauma and dread perpetrators of direct trauma. This dynamic is fuelled by US involvement in the internal politics of developing states, as well as the gang's involvement in transnational criminal networks.

Copenhagen City don Papa-Lo muses gently that "ghetto people not used to full night sleep" (James 2014, 90). The very peacefulness of the night becomes a basis for hyperarousal, an imperative of alertness because the quietness must be masking mayhem. In this scenario, to inhabit time and space is to inhabit an inhumane domain that disallows rest and peace. People of the ghetto chronically experience all of the stressors which the American Psychiatric Association's manual for assessment and diagnosis of mental disorders defines as generating direct psychological trauma: "Exposure to actual or threatened death, serious injury or sexual violence in one or more of following ways: through 'direct experience'; through 'witnessing in person' the traumatizing event occurring to others; through coming to terms with the impact of the traumatizing catalyst on a close family member or friend; and through experiencing "repeated or extreme exposure to aversive details of such events" (American Psychiatric Association 2013). Layered on historical violations, this tightly interrelated web of trauma catalysts can, in turn, produce monstrous modes of being. Deborah Thomas argues that the spectacular, exceptional violence of slavery's terrorist system, with its focus on visuality and performativity, has generated repertoires in collective memory, which nourish unjust social relations and virulent gang violence in contemporary times (Thomas 2011, 106).

James is careful to take on board a vast array of catalysts that produce the grim social phenomenon. The gangs are comprised, for the most part, of young persons traumatized and abused by poverty, inadequate parenting, and state injustices. Several young black males attempt to choose a nonviolent pathway, only to find this intention short-circuited by a corrupt and brutal police force (Watson et al. 2018; 2019). They, in turn, join pseudo families of paternalistic dons and, by extension, become pawns of politicians, who set out to use gangs for political advantage, only to find that they have triggered incendiary violence that they can no longer control. They are also used by international operators planted on the islands to secure the objectives of foreign governments.

This chapter takes its title from the musings of a street child of the ghetto named Bam-Bam:

> And killing don't need no reason. This is ghetto. Reason is for rich people. We have madness . . . Madness is walking up to a good street downtown and seeing a woman dress up in the latest fashion and wanting to go straight up to her and grab her bag, knowing that it is not the bag or the money that we want so much, but the scream, when she see you jump right into her pretty up face and you could slap the happy right out of her mouth and punch the joy right out of her eye and kill her right there and rape her before or after you kill her because that is what rude boys like we do to decent women like her (James 2014, 9).

The madness of the ghetto, which does not yield to rational and linear explanations, becomes accessible if one focuses on traumatic outworking of psychic pain as an explanation for the irrational, murderous violence of the veritable army of rude boys. It signals how the narrative works, both to figure out underlying causes and to undercut the same.

Even in Bam-Bam's understanding, the robbery, rape and mayhem constitute madness. On the other hand, it is eruptive violence spawned in the ruptures in his early family life and his tenuous relational connection to his whoring, hyper-sexualized mother and her murderous man friends, and to his frustrated, wife-beating, emasculated father. Within the trigger-happy adult male, there remains the terrorized child, who witnessed the slaughter of both his parents in a single night as they beat, maim and facilitate the murder of each other, in blind rage, like puppets jerked around by deep-rooted, death-dealing impulses and horrific life circumstances: "My mother run back in and start to laugh and kick my father and Funnyboy go up to her and shoot her in the face. She fall right on top of me, so when he say find the little boy they look everywhere but under my mother" (James 2014, 13). In a complex image of rebirthing, the child is saved from the murderer whom his mother brings home to take revenge on his father, when her lifeless body falls on him and hides him. The bloodied orphan later crawls from under the mother's dead body to flee into his fate, carrying his only legacy of value – his father's oversized Clarks shoes. Savaged in infancy by grim societal conditions and parental death, the street child suffers symptoms of separation and individuation trauma, including dissociation and distancing, leading to the incapacity to connect and empathize with, or feel the pain of, others. This fictional representation fleshes out medical research that points to a dose-related correlation between childhood trauma and adult criminal activity: the higher the number of traumatizing catalysts, the greater the propensity for the victims to drift into adverse criminal activity (Reavis et al. 2013, 44–48).

As parentless spawn of the ghetto, the orphan is picked up by the gang network, which gives him the only sense of belonging that he knows. Given excellent tutelage, he is wielding a gun by age ten, under the substitute authority and pater-familial protection of the gangland don. Bound on cycles of uncanny repetition, Bam-Bam – whose name echoes the sound of gunfire – is beyond trigger-happy. His entire being is set on swift and automatic resort to violence. The metonymic association between the gun and the street child-turned-bad man is so tightly fused that he has no other identity or name. The wounded, fragile self, propped up by bravado and ego retrieval, is further buttressed by the power of the gun, which assumes its own God-like agency through its power to take life. Fitting neatly into the void left by the incapacity to form secure human attachments, the gun, through a grotesque intimacy, is personified as a live-in partner, which in turn changes the terms of interaction within every other actual and potentially intimate and chance encounter: "*Is a hell of a thing* when a gun come home to live with you . . . Everybody talk to you different when them see a new bulge in you pants . . . When a gun come to live in the house it's the gun, not even the person who keep it, that have the last word" (James 2014, 72, emphasis added). Together, Bam-Bam and the gun enter into an unholy union that produces a provocative bulge in his pants, a fitting appendage to his edgy and violent hypermasculinity. It refashions all other relational connections, eliciting new levels of obedience and deference within the most mundane of interactions because it infuses the most innocuous conversation which does not go his way with the potential for swift and irreversible reprisal, meted out through the barrel of a gun. Personhood, communicative ability, communal affirmation and male authority shift from the diminished man to the overdetermined gun. The gun has a particular potency, as opposed to the weapons which it has supplanted. There is no longer a need for the hand-to-hand engagement, as is the case of the stick, machete, razor and switchblade. It allows for a measure of distance, just in case proximity invites recognition of shared vulnerability and humanity.

This unholy union, built on the foundation of a lack of moral sense and empathy, combines with fragile hypermasculinity, hyperarousal and underlying hopelessness. To anaesthetize the pain and emptiness of the past, and the inescapable hopelessness of the present, Bam-Bam succumbs to drug addiction, which provides the only momentary anodyne for his pain and the only ecstasy that he can experience. Add a snort of cocaine and Bam-Bam is placed on automatic pilot as rapist and killer, overcome by the indiscriminate desire to "fuck fuck fuck" and "kill kill kill" (James 2014, 244). The death-dealing impulse to inflict pain, which acts as momentary anodyne, is translated in his psyche as power. Given this dynamic, the mere existence of decency, joy, beauty, order, prosperity – as reflected in the unknown happy woman on the street – is emblematic of loss that begs to be violently snuffed out. James' narrative thus puts a different spin on the affective responses, the fear, withdrawal and distancing predictably manifested in middle- and upper-strata women in response to a rude boy's proximity in a public place. He suggests that the latter also experiences affective responses, such that the mere sight of the secure, happy woman can generate impulses towards violation and murder.

James produces an evocative representation of the mutually reinforcing connection between childhood trauma and youth victimization, and the perpetration of violence. While distancing and dissociation protect trauma victims from immediate psychological distress, the desensitization, and the overwhelming void at the core of their beings, alongside the drugs which they use to anaesthetize their pain, make them deadly perpetrators of violence, and the cycle continues. The outcome is an evocative fictional sketch of disturbingly real scenarios, in which gang violence is not seen as an aberration or a deviant choice. Indeed, for the street spawn of the ghetto, the death-dealing dynamic becomes so normalized, their prevailing perception is that there is no choice. For this population, their lives are a constant round of grief, death, anxiety, depression and fear, which, in turn, exacerbate and deepen trauma symptoms of hypervigilance and hyperarousal, avoidance, dissociation and void. The gang is family. Its stringent standards of loyalty are violently entrenched. The performative, banal, daily acts of violence answer to an inherent theatricality – a deadly play enacted before a collective gaze – which infuses empty lives with skewed meaning. These collective meaning systems, though distorted, read for the participants in the play as clear and uncompromising.

Even the gang's impulse to turn on and eat its own answers to a skewed logic. Bam-Bam is bewildered when the gang leader turns on him, but not before his crazed mind repeatedly contemplates killing the emerging gang leader for rushing in for a kill and stealing his thunder. The community is so diseased and counts life so cheaply, that slaying its own sons and daughters gives no pause. Bam-Bam dies as he has lived. The pathway that leads to his youthful, bewildering death at the hands of fellow gang members parallels his rebirthing experience – flight from murderous gang members, wallowing through masses of filth and garbage, ravenous hunger, all the while bemoaning his lack of understanding at a loss of meaning and place within the brutal pater-familial network, on whose behalf he has killed and maimed since age ten. Ejected from the hostile and indifferent shelter of the gang and hunted like an animal, he is reduced to a bundle of base appetites that externalize his absolute abjection and unbelonging.

James' criminals, sketched fulsomely in *A Brief History*, exist in a nightmarish twilight zone, enacting stylized and even pre/scripted half-lives which, to borrow Judith Butler's formulation, are not perceived as "grievable" (Butler 2009). The gangland ghetto charted by James is not simply a site of social death, unrealized potential and truncated life chances; it also constitutes a swift pathway to physical death. Any opportunity for alleviation is denied when painful personal experiences and memories of abuse, abandonment and loss are multiplied myriad times over for multiple gang members. Individual anguish is mirrored in collective anguish. These repressed, unarticulated psychic pains flow into collective pools of cultural memory of loss – mother loss; father hunger; raw, basic, physical need; spiritual vacuums; abandonment; and pain. Psychological trauma, emanating from life-threatening events and psychosocial locations, overlaid on collective cultural violations, feeds into skewed communal worldviews. For the majority, there is no vision of an alternative lifestyle. There is no other life.

James's narrative also lends credence to notions posited by Dessa Kristen Bergen-Cico and others. These researchers argue that explorations of participation in street life, including gang activity, criminal behaviour, and illicit drug sale and use, tend to use theories of psychological deviance and anti-social behaviour as rebellion against dominant values of the majority. The researchers point to the fact that where these behaviours flourish, they are perceived as "normative social behaviours serving as one of the most visible forms of authority" (Bergen-Cico et al. 2014, 15–26). They argue for the application of behavioural addiction theory if one is to disengage from street life and to avoid recidivism:

> While chaotic environments with high crime can adversely affect many community members, the type of "street action" explored in this study can also create an alluring "rush" that draws young unemployed men, and to a lesser extent young women, into the action of the streets, yielding outcomes that mirror behavioural addictions. Street crime and gang activity, if

> neurobiologically reinforced, might initiate a behavioural cycle for many of the participants, with negative consequences for the wider community. Framing the draw of gang involvement as "street addiction" recognizes both the environmental influence of street life and its potential to create psychological dependence in the analysis of such criminal behaviour (Bergen-Cico et al. 2014, 2).

In addition, insights drawn from trauma filters would draw attention to affect – submerged repressed anguish that elicits emotional pain and affective responses, which do not answer to reason; and therefore, intervention based on thought and reason cannot readily address and reverse the toxic behaviours.

Never distant from the equation are colonial and neocolonial geopolitical forces that drill down into the ghetto to produce the gang. Deborah Thomas argues persuasively that a focus on the complicity of US underworld political operatives in generating contemporary gang violence obscures connections between today's grim scenarios and imperialism's abuses. James' focus disallows any summation which does not take regard of collusions among the neo-imperial state, Caribbean governments and politicians, an avaricious upper and middle class, and throwaway ghetto dwellers. Rhone Fraser, in his analysis of the novel, concludes: "Overall the novel is a cautionary tale about internalizing hegemonic narratives that teach us to conform to an economy that profits from gun sales and drug addiction in order to create what Bob Marley has described in 'Redemption Song' as 'mental slavery'" (Fraser 2017, 79).

While we may be prepared to take on board criminals who have been traumatized in their childhood and have consequently turned to a life of crime, we are not as accepting of the notion of perpetrators who have been traumatized by their own acts of violence. Saira Mohamed, in "Of Monsters and Men: Perpetrator Trauma and Mass Atrocity", identifies perpetrator trauma as an "outlier in the scholarly judicial and popular understandings" (Mohamed 2015, 1163). The definition of perpetrator as one who chooses to inflict suffering in an attempt to twist the meaning system of the victim, such that the perpetrator's capacity to exert pain becomes an affirmation of power, does not readily admit a diagnosis of trauma. Acknowledgement of the trauma of the victim establishes the right to bear witness, to be heard, to strip off victim status and to access a shared meaning system, which signals reincorporation into the family of man. To accord such rights to perpetrators is perceived as unjust to victims and untenable within the broader societal order, which would prefer to envision the perpetrator as monstrous and deserving of exclusion from grace, forgiveness and acceptance.

Papa-Lo, the loquacious don of Copenhagen City, is traumatized when he viciously attacks an innocent schoolboy, whom he mistakes for a 'rudie'. At one level, his action breaches the unwritten moral code by which he and rival leader Shotta Sheriff maintain the order of their jungle – the morality which disallows the raping of church women and the murder of schoolgirls for their lunch money. It also comes after he stumbles upon an enviable scene of intergenerational love and respect – a grandson helping his aged and infirm grandfather – and realizes that there are no old men in the ghetto. The scene inspires a hope for intergenerational connection and longevity, which is incompatible with his life work. The immediate horror of what he has done to the boy holds him enthralled in a close face-to-face encounter with his agency as an engineer of death. Empathetic identification seeps into his consciousness as he witnesses the slow and desperate demise of this innocent schoolboy, unmediated by physical and psychic distance. His dying enters Papa-Lo's sensibility through numerous doors of perception: "[I]s one thing when you kill a man and he just dead. Is another thing when he too close when you shoot him and he grab you and you see the way he looking at you" (James 2014, 86). He feels death through the tactile sense when the boy grips him as in an attempt to "hold on to life". The nightmarish incident of his own taking lives haunts him, surfacing into his consciousness unbidden. This intrusive re-experiencing lies at the root of his subsequent incapacity to function effectively in a context in which authority is maintained by the ability to murder unflinchingly and in cold blood.

Within the framework in which early and or violent death is an imminent probability, as opposed to a distant possibility, the community is also peopled by ghosts – spirit-presences of the departed, bereft of bodies through which to enact vengeance against their killers. This vision is reflective of the African cosmologies, which envision the universe as peopled by the living, the dead and the unborn. Embodied and disembodied spirits interface with each other, and determine the concourse of life on earth (Mbiti 1990). This assertion about individual existence after death fails to give comfort, because in James' universe there is decisively no rest for the wicked. The ghost of the murdered Sir Arthur Jennings is reflective of the societal trauma at numerous levels. Serving as a chorus on the unfolding action, and empowered to speak only to the reader, he manifests most decisively when a character is about to die, which makes for his repeated intrusion into this far-from-brief history of killings. His ghastly wounded apparition externalizes the function of trauma. He himself becomes its haunting, absent presence, which never is fully digested and appropriated. In a bizarre reversal, he is the member of the privileged, hegemonic class, those who arguably, in this life, are spared the heinous ignominies of poverty and humiliation. In death, he haunts the boundaries of impoverished and violent communities. It is Jennings who becomes the marginalized, ignored, silenced, powerless. His quest for vengeance is bound to fail, since he is bereft of even a despised, raced body, which would facilitate enactment. In James' symbolic economy, death is indeed a great leveller. The cautionary tale signals the possibility of an eternal realm in which the wealthy, the empowered, the corrupt and the secure, engineers of this living hell, will reap the wages of their anarchies.

James' *A Brief History* raises a multiplicity of troubling issues. Writing a savage society, inhabited by impoverished, cynical, verbally and physically violent people, James raises issues about the nature and value of the human. His gangland characters inhabit alien meaning systems that only one living within their own unique hell can validate. James' work begs the questions: Are these throwaway people or do they possess inherent value, and to what extent are their strivings and murderous actions and intent related to a quest for significance? If, as we argue, this epic of violence and violation can be read as a trauma narrative, in which the major perpetrators are themselves represented as victims of cultural trauma, which runs through the bloodstream of their inheritance, and of the insidious trauma inherent to their social order, then the writing, which can be read as an attempt to "save order from chaos" (James 2014, 343), demands an affective response, as we bear witness.

This is not unproblematic. We read as situated subjects, bringing to the engagement individual sensibilities produced by positionalities of time, space, ideologies, national and personal histories, and more. Trauma narratives demand empathetic attention and identification. Some deal with this by eluding or erasing representations of perpetrators so as to soften or alleviate the psychic pain of reading and writing. Jean Rhys' *Wide Sargasso Sea* (1966) subtly and evasively explores this problematic. Antoinette plays the innocent when the husband questions her about a location named Massacre. This is juxtaposed to a consistent symbolic identification between Antoinette and the enslaved, culminating in her leap from the battlements of the cold English mansion to an illusory hope of her black, childhood playmate's welcome. Not so for Marlon James. He delves into the evil savagery with apparent relish, while seeking to elicit measured empathetic identification with his traumatized perpetrators. Our task as critical readers is to enter into the narrative world and yet avoid appropriation of indirect trauma in a manner which eclipses the sufferers, substituting in their place a fixation with the discomfort of bearing witness. Conversely, the task is also to avoid unchecked empathy and idiopathic identification, characterized by immersion into the alien and alienating value system, and a psychic absorption into and possession by the violent and violating characters and scenarios. The requirement then is to read, understand and retain ethical self-awareness so as to frame an effective critical response to James' worlds. Our own persistence in reading this excruciatingly violent and violating narrative was alleviated only by the conviction that there had to be a gem to be mined out of the muck. The gem we sought was the ideological framework or worldview which accounts for the making of self and community within the savage scenario; the social enactments and material practices that support these diverse and brutal modes of being and becoming.

Judith Butler's notions of precarity and grievable lives prove helpful in this regard. She argues that although precariousness is a fundamental facet of all human lives, our capacity to read some lives as possessing value and therefore as grievable is determined by the framework through which we apprehend, or fail to apprehend, persons as losable and injurable. Butler indicates that the power dynamics which craft knowledge economies, shape epistemological and ontological approaches to targeted groups. The ontological queries indicate ways we interrogate what is a human life; or we determine, given adverse and inhumane life conditions; or we construct a way to be human (Butler 2009, 13–15). This becomes more relevant when dealing with populations who enter into the world within enclaves already tainted by social death. Bam-Bam testifies, "By the time boy like me drop out of my mother, she give up. Preacher say there is a god shaped void in everybody life but the only thing ghetto people can fill a void is with a void" (James 2014, 9). To use Butler's formulation, since the ontology of the body is social, only social and political forces give the body its meaning: "The body is exposed to socially and politically articulated forces as well as to claims of sociality – including language, work and desire – that make possible the body's persisting and flourishing" (Butler 2009, 6). For Bam-Bam and his fellow travellers, their framing within the hegemonic order and even their essentialized counter-discursive stance to their persistent marginalization both point to death and not life. This is the impulse which drives the "fuck and kill" (James 2014, 244) mantra. Hence they enter into what Gordon Rohlehr terms a culture of "terminality" (Rohlehr 2013, 4).[1]

Butler's analysis of conditions under which contemporary wars are waged is relevant for this war as well:

> shared condition of precariousness leads not to reciprocal recognition, but to a specific exploitation of targeted populations, of lives that are not quite lives, cast as "destructible" and "ungrievable". Such populations are "lose-able", can be forfeited, precisely because they are framed as being already lost or forfeited; they are cast as threats to human life as we know it rather than as living populations in need of protection from illegitimate state violence, famine, or pandemics. Consequently, when such lives are lost they are not grievable since, in the twisted logic that rationalizes their death, the loss of such populations is deemed necessary to protect the lives of "the living" (Butler 2009, 31).

Butler argues against such othering and scapegoating, and for a recognition of a common position of vulnerability and precariousness shared by the entire human family.

This chapter argues that we cannot afford to relegate criminals to the dung heap. This assumption is predicated on hypocritical notions of pristine innocence of the engineers of the transnational, regional, state and hegemonic social orders. That aside, the hardened criminals' inability to rest, their agitation and hyperarousal, their cold-bloodedness, lack of empathy and emotional connection, their incapacity to experience guilt and remorse, their dissociation and cyclic repetition of murderous violence, their culturally accepted repertoire of brutal practices and social enactments arguably manifest the complex overlay of traumas which stand in need of targeted therapeutic interventions. By deploying the fictional strategy of polyvocality and stream of consciousness, James gives voices to myriad sensibilities and demonstrates the extent to which persons may inhabit the same spaces, but live in vastly divergent mental worlds and meaning systems. The strategy lends voice to those who are generally silenced within hegemonic discourse, who live in accordance with meaning systems that only inhabitants of that hellish nightmare can validate. Arguably, entry into voice may well be a welcome alternative for those who currently act out through violence, in the absence of an alert and respectful audience, and a capacity to tell. The narrative strategy conveys a sense of the ordinariness and humanity of the perpetrator of mass violence. To borrow Saira Mohamed's formulation, James' fierce and enraged monsters are fragile men, and his capacity to persuasively and simultaneously sketch their monstrosity and their humanity is testimony to his craft. His vast canvas demolishes carefully constructed barriers between 'them' and 'us', and constrains acknowledgement of collective responsibility, which, in turn, carries a responsibility for collective intervention. James' provocative representation disallows the facile solution of relegating monsters to the outer darkness beyond the pale of social order, excluded from the commonwealth and well-being. Cycles of abuse and violence are also spatialized in the subsequent chapter, which zeroes in on a close reading of Nalo Hopkinson's complex deployment of the fantasy genre in an incest narrative with a focus on the lived experience of poverty, early pregnancies and the vulnerabilities attendant to these realities.

chapter 7

A Chorus of Resistance

Hurricane Narratives of Loss and Resilience

> Even when the hurricane rode in and the wind rose cracking its whip upon the land, twisting, breaking and uprooting, still, when the screaming died away, the soft shoots sprouted again their chorus of resistance.
>
> —*Barbara Lalla, Arch of Fire (1998, 3)*

BUILDING ON THE PREVIOUS CHAPTER'S EXAMINATION of domestic violence as a persistent and pervasive threat within the home, another major facet of vulnerability that confronts the small island states of the Caribbean is the risk of natural disaster, specifically, the annual looming threat of hurricanes. David Longshore defines a hurricane as "a weather system in which winds move in a circular direction around a warm centre of low barometric pressure" called an eye (Longshore 2008, 397). Indeed, the phenomenon has travelled in myriad ways and is invariably called a typhoon in the northwestern Pacific regions, and a cyclone in Australia, the South Pacific and the Indian Ocean. Despite their etymological mutation, hurricanes contribute to a most vivid, unforgettable and harrowing experience for landscapes and human communities, as they signal profound physical and social vulnerabilities. As effectively as they slaughter and maim people, they topple buildings, damage infrastructure and can devastate agricultural and tourist-based economies in a day. In the Caribbean, their ferocious nature is often associated with global trade networks and Western expansionism in the fifteenth and sixteenth centuries, which historically contributed to the rise of modernity and its violent enterprises in the Indies.

In contemporary times, hurricane intensification, catastrophic storm surge events and rising sea levels are associated with global warming. Here again, developed nations' industrial practices generate calamities, while small, economically fragile island societies absorb impact. In this sense, the memory and collective experience of hurricanes become a locus from which to track the ways that the region's creative writers and cultural architects have discursively engaged natural disasters; the effects of risk-reduction efforts; and the manner in which communities anticipate, prepare for and recover from these violent experiences. This chapter reads a cross-section of hurricane narratives to probe both the trail of devastation and mindsets; coping mechanisms; and the resilience of peoples, for whom to possess their island homelands is to be poised for the annual threat of potential devastation.

In Caribbean narratives, devastating storms are granted anthropomorphic associations and mythic dimensions.[1] This mythical element is embodied in the term hurricane, which derives from the name Huracán (also Hurakan, Jurakan), the Mayan god of the storm. Huracán means "one-legged" and represents "all three attempts to create humanity, in which he completed most of the actual work of creating human beings under the direction of Kukulkán, known by the Aztec name, Quetzalcoatl, and Tepeu."[2] Hurricanes are thus endemic to the Caribbean geophysical landscape and frequently figure in Caribbean literary and cultural expressions as markers of the interface between man and nature, cultural assumptions and practices in relation to ecological and social conditions.

The hurricane as a trope of resistance against unjust hegemonic domination is a recurrent theme in the literature. From the inception of the imperial colonizing impulse, the eruptive violence of the hurricane has been associated with the restless volatility of the tropical landscape, the ungovernability of the enslaved populations and their resistance to Europe's global enrichment project, thinly veiled as a civilizing impulse. A case in point is Erna Brodber's allegory, *The Rainmaker's Mistake* (2007), where the colonizer, Mr Charlie, religiously spreads the originary myth that the enslaved entered the world as brown yams, the issue of his solitary masturbatory acts buried in the patient earth.[3] The imperial masculinist myth of origin is dispelled when Mr Charlie's protégé, the overseer, Woodville, the erased stud who seeded the erased women to create the child labour force, rises up after emancipation and laughs a devilish laugh, which becomes a typhoon.

The meteorological context of the action is important, and yet, for all the critical energy devoted to the novel, it seems that little attention has been given to the point that the major catalyst for its unfolding action is a typhoon. The winds operate as a social leveller and insurgent force that eliminate the great house and blow Mr. Charlie and his deceptive governance away; thereafter, he dies and rots in a cave. A bizarre time-lapse occurs and the plantation is broken into three continents, which is Brodber's innovative re-assembling of the African diaspora: "The water from the river overflowed the man-made banks and spilled over into the area where we stood, and so heavily did it spill, and so constantly did it flow that it made small rivers separating us – Woodville on one side, I-Sis and Sallywater on the other, and the rest of us in-between. Three separate continents. Three sides of each washed by water, the fourth connected to our past" (Brodber 2007, 16). In "Metaphors of Underdevelopment: A Proem for Hernan Cortez" (1985), Edward Kamau Brathwaite tropologizes natural disaster as a discursive mode through which to address the historical catastrophe of the transatlantic slave trade and to illustrate a "much wider cycle of destiny" (Brathwaite 1985, 454). He contends that "the history of catastrophe . . . requires *a literature of catastrophe*", which is figured via the eye of the storm. For Brathwaite, the cyclone motif problematizes the ways in which typhoons embody the nature of turmoil, chaos and the "explosions that create symbolic fragments of continents that we now call islands and inhabit" (emphasis added). In other words, he is framing the archipelago in psycho-geographic terms and examining how the processes of diasporic formation resist monolithic, imperialist discourses on culture and history. In *Rainmaker*, Brodber certainly enacts the call to shape the world of the text in such a way that it actualizes a material and physio-cultural explosion, which she constructs to unveil the occluded histories and hitherto unseen violences concealed behind the high walls of Charlie's estate.

Adrift in time and space, Queenie and company are on the brink of a preempted future. Queenie, as self-appointed leader, seeks to gather information on the group's history. What unfolds is Brodber's epistemological undoing of the group's neutering and lobotomy surgical procedures that altered their minds and bodies, and ensured compliance with their function as labour units. Living "in the free" means discovery of creativity, inventiveness, responsibility, and significantly sexual potency. Eventually, a nearly dead Woodville returns to the community as an ejaculating corpse, a heuristic device intended to lead the community into life. He is: "old, dried up, existing in two dimensions, ready to be replaced" (Brodber 2007, 29). Latterly revealed as the rainmaker, he dualistically represents acquiescence to Europe's civilizing order and the survival of African cultural forms. He squirts semen on his children, Jupiter and London, which initiates a process of self-discovery through the embrace of mortality: "And with that carcass rotting in the cave, goes the eternity and peace he offered. We have no choice. . . It is naturalness twinned to mortality, accompanied by hope, and duly tempered by responsibility. I embrace them with both hands . . . and continue the search . . . In the free" (Brodber 2007, 150).

The multiplicity of voices participates as speculative presence in each of the stories, which reflects a collective desire to formulate a coherent account of experiences previously erased in one way or another. While Queenie must navigate through the intense seas, mooring between spectacular currents, aquatic ecosystems, atmospheric circulations, and move between the domains of I-Sis and Sallywater, Essex and Luke take to scientific and mechanical inventions to grapple with the terms of their newfound consciousness. This assertion of freedom rejects any fixed definition; rather, the group's post-emancipation enterprises invoke a sense of liberation that is as perpetual as it is promising. Embracing the mythic, dualistic, destructive and creative power of the typhoon, Brodber selects the agency of a devastating storm, working in partnership with an enlightened overseer, to destabilize and distance the oppressive imperial order and to create the preconditions for emergence "in the free". The myriad assemblages are thus exemplary of the inventions that are curated to counteract the ideological wars that have been waged against a people who have been systemically depersonalized. These nebulous links and mythical inventions illuminate a latent but potent dimension of a people group, who relied on alternative modalities to contest the impact of erasure and amnesia, and to procure a different kind of ontological self-engineering.

Perhaps one of the most iconic representations of the association between hurricanes and resistance in the wake of imposed sub-personhood is to be found in artistic and scribal expressions stimulated by the infamous 1781 *Zong* massacre, in which one hundred and forty-three enslaved Africans were dumped alive in the ocean by Captain Luke Collingwood to enable the ship's owners to collect insurance for property lost at sea. The nineteenth-century painter, J.M.W. Turner, immortalized this moment in the lurid seascape, *Slavers Throwing Overboard the Dead and Dying – Typhoon Coming On*. The painting, whose naming encapsulates the spurious rationale for this mass murder, was highly praised by noted art critics, such as John Ruskin,[4] as a quintessential example of the nineteenth-century's aesthetic of the sublime. Turner's painting invokes stereotypes of the tropics as a space of fiery damnation, pestilential rage and intemperate emotion, excited by the terror of slavery. The massacre and the insurance case that followed became touchstones for the abolitionist movement, as exemplary of the inhumane savagery of the trade in enslaved Africans.

The case has become pivotal to a Caribbean literature of resistance as successive generations of writers engage an experimental type of discourse to unsilence the drowned Africans, who, according to Guyanese writer David Dabydeen, have been adrift in Turner's seas for centuries. This powerful image and event become an archive, and the writer a tomb raider in pursuit of submerged knowledge possessed only by these spectres of the Middle Passage.[5] For Dabydeen, Ruskin's perverse and admiring review of Turner's art undermines the outrageous subject – "the shackling and drowning of Africans" (Dabydeen 1994, ix) carried out in the name of financial self-interest. As Dabydeen contends, such an appraisal is doubly problematic because it effectively renders Ruskin complicit in the actions he ignores: the atrocious historical truth of Turner's image. In a radical, counter-discursive manner, Dabydeen invokes the image of the sea with its "encumbered . . . corpses" (Ruskin 1903, 575) before proceeding to reawaken "the submerged head of the African in the foreground of Turner's painting" (Dabydeen 1994, ix) and a "stillborn child tossed overboard from a future ship" (Dabydeen 1994, x). Apart from Dabydeen's polemical critique of Ruskin's review, the images articulate the story of the slave-mother and the infant she throws overboard to spare it a life of servitude and unthinkable trauma. The infant who washes towards its mother rekindles a memory that remains bound up with the Atlantic crossing and hence becomes typically "obscene" (Dabydeen 1994, xi and 17). The memories of death and the violence of the Middle Passage flow freely, one into the other, and Dabydeen's run-on lines dramatize a drowning that is as literal as it is metaphoric and voluntarily sought by a suicidal mother.

The sea becomes a shifting ground of meaning and memory, as Dabydeen enters an aquatic mortuary and unburies facets of black memory as a basis for more empowering cartographies of self and community. By contextualizing his discourse around the critical terrain of the typhoon, he crafts new expressions that curate an intuitive, reclaiming response that heralds the afterlife of those lives lost at sea. While the typhoon that undergirds the *Zong* Massacre may be evinced as an agent of divine retribution and judgement against the unjust slave traders, it reflects a process of arranging those submerged histories of the extensive community of ocean dwellers. Up to today, their spectral presences demand materialization and their silenced voices demand articulation through narrative. Generations of Caribbean writers have responded to their hauntings.

Striking a more pragmatic note, Grenadian/Trinidadian raconteur and social commentator Paul Keens-Douglas relates "Story of a Storm – Ivan", a didactic cautionary tale spiced with incisive humour. Noting that "Ivan was an education" before, during and after the hurricane, Keens-Douglas creates a polyvocal narrative incorporating gossip, rumour, folktales, media reporting, tall tales, disaster advisories and even the voices in the wind – in short, tapping the diverse sources of knowledge to reassemble fragments generated by the chaotic disaster into interconnected vignettes. Keens-Douglas makes it clear that whatever else disaster produces, it generates lots of talk. His narrative equally reveals the challenges of cross-cultural communication. One can witness, for example, the woman who responds to a query about her well-being: "'I still in shack boy, I in shack!' So dey say, 'Okay, she still have house' (23:57), while another claimed, 'Well, boy, at least I ain't dead'" (22:42). A distant voice also declared, "It could've been woss [worse]" (22:45). It seems that Keens-Douglas is putting forward a passionate argument for mounting a collaborative resistance to the trajectory of Hurricane Ivan via the counter-wind of collective storytelling. He provides copious examples of how stories drawn from multiple perspectives can be harnessed towards internal configuration of individuals, communities and nations, and the myriad factors which determine mass vulnerability to risk and potentialities for resilience. This polyvocality also allows those who have not experienced disaster to indirectly enter into the experience of others, while enabling a vivid recollection for whom the event is too close a means of vicarious speaking.

Moreover, Keens-Douglas' narrative posits that a generic lack of preparedness for natural disaster prevails because of an inherent unfounded optimism, a philosophical notion of being invincible, an illogical "faith" that since God is variously a Trini, a Bajan, a Grenadian and so on, the hurricane would be averted. When this is combined with the sure conviction that preparing for a natural disaster that is not likely to touch down is a profound waste, for which populations invested in operating by "vaps" readily and irrationally blame "the government". The outcome is a lack of readiness for natural disaster that is embedded in deep-rooted, irrational cultural assumptions. Any attempt to generate change in the collective level of disaster-preparedness needs to go beyond timely dissemination of accurate and helpful information to address the root of these underlying cultural assumptions and practices. The narrative also illuminates a collective mindset that is more invested in anthropomorphizing than understanding destructive weather systems. Ivan is portrayed variously as "a little boy with short breath" who turns into "a big man with big wind to blow way Grenada". Experientially, the people hear in the storm "voices in the wind" and the rampaging of hostile and dangerous supernatural forces, like "demons and devils howling for blood" (8:27). Through the mass mediated distance of television screens, the storm manifests as a "big white beast, with flashes of red and yellow, the eye spinning in the middle of the head spreading across the screen", heading to eat up the islands.

Arguably, in terms of the battling to stay alive during the disaster, notions of the storms as possessed of spirit, voice and malicious intent spur the vulnerable to fight vigorously; even more so, if the embattled are people of faith who can call upon God for help to defeat this evil onslaught. In the post-disaster phase, Keens-Douglas portrays urban dwellers negatively as they wait passively for help to arrive, or alternatively, spawning gangs of pillaging looters, while the country folk take charge of disaster recovery and demonstrate greater resilience. However, while the narrative illuminates the deficiencies of preparedness and the paucity of post-disaster organizational machineries, it certainly paints the island states and peoples as profligate in their generosity in terms of aid. The narrative celebrates the Caribbean community's kindness and readiness to give. Despite the enormity of the "mashupness", the story of the storm culminates in laughter and transcendence.

Olive Senior's "Hurricane Story, 1903" (1944, 1951 and 1988) equally demonstrate the devastating consequences of hurricanes on social equilibrium, and more specifically, on gender relations in Jamaica, over an eight-decade span. This period, which spans post-emancipation to post-independence, saw significant events and broad social trends in the national history. It was a season that marked the emergence of the formerly enslaved communities as proud and self-sufficient peasant farmers, who sustained their families on the rich earth tilled by the strength of their hands. Children of the rural peasantry painstakingly climbed into literacy and lower middle-strata status based on access to white-collar employment. By the 1950s, there had been substantial urban drift to produce overcrowded cities and jostling for daily necessities. Moreover, metropolitan migration that favoured female migrants had emerged as a major coping strategy for families in dealing with crises and disasters.

Senior's stories coincide with a series of actual hurricanes. The unnamed 1903 event made landfall at Port Morant with winds of 201 mph and brought destruction, or near destruction, to Port Maria and Port Antonia, and mass damage to Kingston. The 1944 hurricane touched down on 4 August, when the agricultural sector was recovering from drought and some 40 per cent of the crop was destroyed. Hurricane Charlie in 1951 was eclipsed by Gilbert in 1988, the largest cyclonic system ever observed in the Western Hemisphere, which caused forty-five deaths and generated a storm surge of nineteen feet. Gilbert caused an estimated $4 billion in damage. Senior's hurricane stories trace both the impact of natural disaster on the nation and the manner in which the evolving social order undermines the resilience of the people to deal with the ravages of these storms. The deceptively simple narrative poems also chart the interface of resilience in the wake of disaster with rural, urban and metropolitan locations, as well as class and gender. Whereas "Hurricane Story, 1903" testifies about the closeness to the land, simple coping strategies rooted in faith, family and knowledge of environment, the final 1988 account speaks of unmitigated loss, isolation and despair. In the majority of the poems, the narrative voice is a simple, childlike one, embedded in family and community or grieving at its loss.

"Hurricane Story, 1903" is metaphorically associated with Noah's ark – the sustained biblical narrative of transcendence despite the certainty and destructive power of the flood. The opening of the poem foregrounds the cyclic nature of the disaster:

> Time and time again, Grandmother plucked
> bits of fowl coop from the pinguin fence
> Grandfather drained his fields, shored up
> their lives against improvidence.
> When the earth baked hard again, into
> the forest he walked to cut thatch
> to patch his house (Senior 2005, 19).

The resilience is based on simple, self-sustaining lifestyles and aspirations, and possession of an extensive range of skills using natural materials derived from the surrounding environment. The child narrator envisions the grandmother and the grandfather who operate as a team with clear complementarity and division of labour. In the season of crisis, food survivalist strategies take precedence, so the trunk of good clothes is emptied, to be replaced by basic food stuff, inclusive of chocolate bars, milk, cinnamon and nutmeg to "give courage" (Senior 2005, 19) when the storm has passed. The capacity to survive the onslaughts in "Hurricane Story, 1903" is also rooted in a closeness to the nurturing earth, faith in a loving and caring God, and in supernatural capacity to read the environment. Deploying the wondrous skills deployed by the Indigenous Indians, who read the signs and took to high ground before landfall of the 2004 Asian tsunami, which killed more than 225,000 people, Grandfather, "the seventh son of a seventh son", could read the signs in the natural environment – the flight pattern of the birds, the glow of the sky, the stillness of the winds – to know when it was time to batten down (Senior 2005, 19). Senior's narrative speaks of rooted, Indigenous ways of knowing, patterns of generational continuity passed through the male lineage (as opposed to more traditional Caribbean association of Indigenous knowledge with female matrilineage), and executed in intimate partnership with a lifelong partner.

Significantly, given the persistent matrifocality of Caribbean social orders, Senior evokes patrilineal lineages and legacies:

> . . . on Grandfather's bed
> we rode above it, everything holding
> together. For my grandfather had learnt
> from his father and his father before him
> all the ways of orchestrating disaster (Senior 2005, 20).

The poem revises the biblical narrative of the ark, which was built when human wickedness had become a stench in his nostril and God determined to begin human civilization anew with one righteous family. The animal kingdom (so the biblical narrative relates) is reconstituted through pairs of animals, who came at God's command to create a floating gene conservation bank. This element is recreated in the poem as the child peers curiously, awaiting the offspring of the sensay fowl and the strutting red horn rooster, who spent the night of the storm together in the hole of the cotton tree. Senior, it seems, is indicating that disaster responses are to be orchestrated. Indigenous, grounded cultural pathways of knowing and being, accrete over time in this poem, shape and alter how people groups think, understand, act and respond in times of crisis.

The poem, "Hurricane Story, 1944", represents the season in the sociocultural landscape of Jamaica, which saw a shift away from dependence on the land. Aspiration for upward mobility based on education and jobs that did not dirty one's hands takes precedence over agriculture's intimate connection to the sustaining earth. What happens to disaster preparedness and resilience when education for social mobility, the holy grail of generations of West Indians seeking escape from lives of poverty and back breaking labour, throws up early success stories? The narrator peers into the gender dynamic that emerges when the father replaces ancestral schooling in the orchestration of disaster, with a formal colonial education, which beglamours him in the eyes of his country brothers, frees him from manual labour, and equips him for illustrious employment as an assistant (white-collar class) in Solomon's Dry Goods and Haberdashery.

This father proves impotent in the face of disaster and its aftermath. Senior plots the downward spiral of the family, whose coping strategies are initiated by the mother, who is despised by the paternal family as plain, dark and a match that would bring the eminent, upwardly mobile father down. Indeed, the mother maintains unwelcome connections to the land:

> But through her
> they got the house
> for though he was a gentleman in good employment
> (first class) it plain to see
> (she of few words said)
> one body money can't stretch
> She turned back to the soil (Senior 2005, 25).

When the storm hits and flattens the haberdashery and the roof, it is the mother who orchestrates recovery from the disaster, ordering the children to nail salvaged bits of roofing back in place; to thank God for the paltriest of nourishment "black cerasee tea and water crackers" (Senior 2005, 25); to assist in the garden, and to grow straight like scallion. She expresses faith and resilience through the melancholy crooning of old hymns, working the land consistently, and fulfilling her marital duties, as manifested by an endless stream of pregnancies, evoked in the narrator's statement:"Nothing like a pregnant woman to encourage melon and pumpkin" (Senior 2005, 25).

Senior points to the skewed values inherent in a colonial education unto social mobility which replaces the Indigenous knowledge that generates self-sufficiency and wisdom for practical living. The outcome is a vast disparity in the capability of the man and his wife, and male inequity and dependency, which the husband addresses with regular outbursts of violence:

> Monday Tuesday Wednesday our mother worked in the fields
> Thursday Friday she went to market
> Saturday she left him money on the dresser
> He took it and went to Unity Bar and Grocery got drunk
> came home and beat her
> Sunday she went to church and sang (Senior 2005, 27).

"Hurricane Story, 1944" paints an unwholesome picture of gendered interface with disaster outcomes. The father, a dandy defeated by his aspiration for upward mobility and disdain for the land, becomes a pathetic, drunken wife beater, ashamed and wallowing in the disgrace of the loss of white-collar employment, the need for his wife to turn "back" to manual labour and reliance on the land, and his own dependence on his wife's income, generated by farming and selling produce. Normalization of a cycle of work and violence and worship speaks also to the tacit acceptance of this scenario within the communal order.

To offset the closing portrait of the beaten, near silent (as opposed to silenced), sexually subservient, continually pregnant wife, Senior subtly interweaves muted pictures of female empowerment. The mother's ability to clap her hands and order diverse things in the face of the maelstrom of disorder wrought by the hurricane – material necessities; grateful hearts; faith and positive outlook; character development – produce resilience in the face of disaster. All of these are lacking in the educated and dandified father. The shift is complete when he loses his mobility because his bicycle tires have been sold to buy school books; and his family headship as breadwinner when his elegant straw boater, now battered, reappears "jauntily" atop his wife's head "as she strode off to market one day".

"Hurricane Story, 1951" continues along the trajectory of diminished resilience. The wife is now firmly established as the decision-maker in the ambitious couple, with a fine son. Senior combines, in this hurricane story, three of her overriding concerns. The impact of the hurricanes is incorporated here with the impact of metropolitan migration, and the effects on the child who is left behind. Here again, as is the case with "The Country of the One-Eyed God", a child is left bereft of parents who are seeking to make their way through the hazards and disappointments of metropolitan migration and eventually abandon their son. Margaret believes that training for better employment in England will allow her to support her family. This is evoked when she says: "Plenty people going in for nursing now" and "build a good life for my son" (Senior 2005, 35), but migration is not the solution she thought it would be. Margaret finds out that England is not the land of easy opportunities that she had imagined it was going to be, and she becomes depressed that she is unable to send home money for her young son.

In this case, the boy, who succumbs to madness more so than badness, develops an uncanny connection across the ocean with his mother. The mother, numbed by foiled ambition, dashed hope, coldness of weather and hearts in the country of her migration, grapples with alienation, anonymity, humiliation and back-breaking labour, without commensurate advancement. She also takes leave of her senses and steps into the ocean when she hears the voice of her son calling her over the seas. The water motif swirls around the poem, mixing and blurring the lines between communities and places. Time elapses so that the abandoned child is an adult at the end of the poem and the scene shifts from a mono vision of an isolated young woman caught in the throes of self-imposed exile and alienation, to a two-fold vision of a young man's persistent effort to communicate with his mother via the ocean, and the whispers that she hears across the Atlantic. First, he blew breath across the water:

Ah-
Then
Ah o
Ah-o
Ma (Senior 2005, 41–42).

In these phonemes, Senior seems to be exploring the metaphysics of breathing – in and out – like the tides, coming in and going out, which are important predictors in the event of a hurricane. The poem is thus a layered sonic narrative, composed of storm-related noise, intended to provide listeners and observers with the dispersal and fragmentation that natural disasters bring. It concludes on a fatal note as both mother and son walk across the water to meet each other.

In "Hurricane Story, 1988", the persona's mother, with no mention of a partner, family or community with which to confront disaster, is a higgler engaged exclusively in transnational merchandising, as opposed to production. She is placed in the wake of the post-hurricane Gilbert turmoil and there is the memory of a personal and emotional prosperity that cannot be recovered. A transnational trader peddling on sidewalks goods purchased from Miami, Haiti, Cuba and Panama, she lives in the urban informal sector, banking between her breasts. Faith is reduced to complaint, "Lawd life so soak up/and no bail out. Too raatid!" (Senior 2005, 56). The shift to the Creole voice, battered and neglected, wails at the exasperation of life's injustices. The poem's closing exclamation may be a cathartic release for the mother and her daughter-narrator, who assert their voices after the storm. While the mother gets the final word, the reader wonders whether domestic and commercial recovery is even possible after the ravages of Gilbert. Senior's chain of hurricane narratives ends sadly with a broken woman in intense isolation, comforting herself at nights with marijuana spliffs in the face of a grim existence. This is a devastating picture of loss.

Thus far, this chapter has tracked the fictional representations of hurricanes in Caribbean literature and the symbolic association between these natural disasters and resistance. While hurricanes encompass experiences of destruction and loss, they also reveal liminal spaces of rehabilitation, where the fury of the wind propels acts of positive human and communal interactions. A close observation of the symbolic relationship between storms and human community is detailed in Derek Walcott's *Omeros*. The hurricane is a prevailing metaphor that encircles the poem and persists until book seven. Walcott draws on the figurative energy of the hurricane as he imagines a symbolic resistance to the desecration of primal landscapes and the usurping of native spaces. These new forms of violences are encoded in the running analogies to the tourist industry and the larger history of Western economic and territorial expansionism. Philoctete's smiling for the tourists, who seek to steal his soul with their cameras, is an apt example. As a natural form of protest against the prostituting of the St Lucian landscape (long deemed the Helen of the Caribbean)[6] for material gain, the violent storm that ensues not only evokes a sense of divine retribution to the icy hand of new empires that attempt to process the life out of everything, but exposes the design of the more-than-human world that is operational in the text.

The sky in book one becomes the colour of violence and a space that seethes with the presences of history. While the atmospheric changes are evoked painstakingly in stages, the aftermath of unrelenting rain is pictured even more graphically:

The Cyclone, howling because one of the lances
of a flinging palm has narrowly grazed his one eye
wades knee-deep in troughs. As he blindly advances,
Lightning, his stilt-walking messenger, jiggers the sky
...
His wife, Ma Rain,
hurls buckets from the balcony of her upstairs house.
...
After their disasters
it was he who cleaned up after their goddamned party...
In the grey vertical forest of the hurricane season...
all the village could do was listen to the gods in session,
... the abrupt Shango drums
made Neptune rock in the caves ...
Erzulie rattling her ra-ra; Ogun, the blacksmith, feeling
No pain; Damballa winding like a zandoli/lizard...
[T]he gods aren't men, they get on well together
holding a hurricane-party in their cloud-house
and what brings the gods close in the thunderous weather,
where Ogun can fire one with his partner Zeus.
Achille in his shack heard chac-chac ...
in the telephone wires
[...]
In the devastated valleys
... antlers of trees tossed
past the banks
the rivers ... had joined in a power so massive
that it made islands of villages ... Too much had been forgotten
Achille bailed out his canoe under an almond
that shuddered with rain.
There would be brilliant days still, till the next storm,
and their freshness wonderful (Walcott 1990, 51–53).

The comingling of myths (Greek, West African and Indigenous) echoes Walcott's personal searches and quest to locate himself between cultural and poetic traditions. Change is therefore associated with the power of Caribbean mythic and meteorological activity. The merging of myths – Zeus, Shango, Ma Rain, Neptune, Cyclops, Zando-li-lizard – suggests that the New World is a hospitable host to these influences.

Moreover, the dance between the gods enables a syncretic merging of forces, where the skyscape is inspirited with supernatural forces who act on human history and repel the spiritual drought of the island. Walcott is aligning the climate as energies that throw obstacles in the path of those who enable the banal operations of capitalism and punish the community for the dearth of ancestral traditions. A close observation of the atmospheric changes and the islanders' awareness of the storm risks are evident in the fishermen who secure their canoes on the deck, Achille's hermetic isolation in "his shack" (Walcott 1990, 53), Plunkett's "bolt[ing] up the house" (Walcott 1990, 55) and the villagers who "roofed their shacks with tins" (Walcott 1990, 57). The hurricane moves in several stages: atmospheric and oceanic activity; change in temperature and wind speed (embodied in the howl of the Cyclone); torrential rain and flooding (as in Ma Rain's hurling of the buckets from the balcony of her upstairs house); destruction and collapse (signposted in the images of "devastated valleys" and "trees tossed"); and finally, the calm, when the low pressure weakens prior to the recuperation stage (epitomized in Achille's emergence from his shack and trek to the coastline to bail out his canoe from under the almond tree).

As the hurricane devastates the land and structures, the impact of the violent winds also finds concrete expression in the shape of each character's psychic and physical maladies. Helen has a wound in her heart as she is caught in an intoxicating love triangle with Hector and Achille. Achille endures the heel-prick of love lost, while Hector suffers from intense jealousy. The implied narrator shares a wound with Philoctete, as embodied in their search for roots, while Plunkett has an old head wound and loses his wife, Maud, who suffers homesickness (another kind of psychical wounding) and death from cancer. The image of the "coral sores" (Walcott 1990, 151) and the eruptive Sulphur Springs volcano of La Soufrière signify the psychic damages of history, which still haunt the island. Yet while historical and new traumas circulate throughout the poem – embodied most evocatively in the trope of the storm – Walcott provides spaces where refuge is sought and rebirth is immanent.

The oxymoronic nature of "natural disaster" is thus symbolic as its conflation with ordinary phenomenon and the social impacts on human populations can produce recuperative outcomes. They can break a drought, and operate as an assembling agent to coalesce into a knowable wholeness the splintered and fragmented stories of a people. The storm in *Omeros* operates as a zone that yields new understandings of self and enables each character to ride out their own crisis and chart a communal response to the forces that seek to threaten their psychic and physical health. When life returns, Plunkett visits Ma Kilman – the village sibyl – to contact his dead wife, who makes peace with him. Philoctete reveals a newfound assertiveness and refuses to tell his story to the tourists, while Achille undergoes a spiritual rebirth and returns to Helen with new understanding that is epitomized in the fresh catch that concludes the book. The Sulphur Springs return to calmness and the tree branches begin to burgeon. Nature, like the human world, reclaims its rights to go on. The hurricane for Walcott, not unlike Brodber, Dabydeen, Senior and Keens-Douglas, is at once an agent that exposes the hidden geographies and histories of Caribbean peoples, while operating as a testing ground from which the strong emerge triumphantly, and the weak wasted.

The narratives demonstrate that resilience is greater in the context of community and intimacy with the land. Intuitive ways of reading the environment, passed from generation to generation, constitute effective early warning systems that are not necessarily effectively replaced by high tech, televised, mass-mediated warnings, which stand to be ignored for a multiplicity of reasons, often rooted in irrational cultural assumptions. The fictional representations point to a fascinating though commonly observed phenomenon: that occurrences as regular as hurricanes, which constitute an annual threat, can seem to come upon vulnerable nations and populations as a surprise. Fictional representations of disasters thus provide a rich repository of insight into attitudes and cultural assumptions, values and priorities, past and contemporary modalities of disaster management. The mythic associations attached to hurricanes and their contemporary deployment as rhetorical strategies with Caribbean literary traditions also prove a treasure trove, revelatory of how people groups make meaning of their lives and calamities, which can be mined for pragmatic present-day applications. These insights can prove to be priceless as the vulnerable nation states of the Caribbean seek more effective modalities for managing trajectories of risk and vulnerabilities, and orchestrating responses to life-threatening and economically debilitating disasters.

The works of Walcott, Brodber, Dabydeen, Senior and Keens-Douglas certainly shine a light on how carefully one needs to proceed with the aftermath of natural disasters.

chapter 8

Harrisian Narratives of Environmental Degradations and Indigenous Healing[1]

> It have a flower somewhere, a medicine, and ways
> my *grandmother* would boil it. I used to watch ants
> climbing her white flower-pot. But, God in which place
> Where was this root? What senna, what tepid tisanes,
> could clean the branched river of his corrupted blood,
> whose sap was a wounded cedar's.
>
> —*Derek Walcott, Omeros, 19 (authors' emphasis)*

IN THIS CHAPTER, WE TURN ATTENTION to the works of Wilson Harris, who has long emphasized in his fiction and theoretical writing the myriad ways in which the Caribbean and South American human and natural worlds are interwoven. The deep impact of the Guyanese topography upon Harris' psyche has its roots in his early vocation as a government land surveyor during the 1940s and 1950s. His connection between the fluidity of the South American landscape and his creative imagination served to unfix reading habits that divided the world into colonial binaries. Inspired by the ancestral faces that he perceived in the ravines, rapids of rivers, tides, waterfalls and rocks, Harris developed a literary methodology that encoded this reality. This critical process is emphasized in fluid time scales in the narrative, the coexistence of the dead and the living, juxtaposed images and a dreamlike universe.

Historically, European capitalists designated the Caribbean and South American territories as destinations for capital flows and resource extraction. The vast volume of water, hectares of thick tree canopies and giant freshwater lakes were prime attractions for Spanish, Dutch and English imperialists.

This historical backdrop encapsulates the deterministic cycles of conquest and disempowerment that decimated the Caribbean's Indigenous people groups and landscapes. From the colonial gaze, the New World was fundamentally perceived as monolithic, one-dimensional and incapable of independent creativity and self-productivity. This led to the European scientific objectification of the Caribbean universe, which translated into conquest and mastery.

Many communities and ecosystems were sacrificed on the altar of relentless production. Although Harris' main focus has been on the South American hinterlands, his planetary and geological turn opens up ways to think about the global, historical and modern dynamics of neocapitalism – marked, for example, by forms of debt and bonded labour, territorial dispossession and ecological plunder. He searches for a radical change to these tragic fates through the cultural horizons of myth. In his essay, "Profiles of Myth and the New World", Harris defines myth as the sedimented aspects of culture, which pertain to every ethnic group in the Caribbean and South America (Harris 1999, 201). He avers that these foundational vestiges, which have been lodged in the Caribbean and South American maternal womb of space, can certainly be re-tooled in literature as identified in settings or locations that contain spiritual gateways, sacred figures, archetypal characters, totems, spirit companions and a sense of time that is fluid – all for re-building a viable reality (Harris 1999, 201–11). This is not unlike the time-bending enterprises of Brodber, Brand, Scott and others.

The way in which Harris intermixes a diversity of cultural histories in his fiction is significant and has been documented by many critics, including Sandra Drake. Drake notes that Harris' specific deployment of dualities, conjoining motifs and ambivalences can be read as his rejection of any perspective that resembled tyrannical paradigms (Drake 1986, 177). Michael Gilkes also observes that Harris' poetics of "heterogeneity" and "radical dialectic", with its intersecting expressions of Greek deities, West African limbo and Haitian vodun, Meso-American bush babies, resurrection motifs in Christianity and Indo-Caribbean mythologies (as in the multi-limbed Kali goddess), enable a rethinking of earth-bound dynamics (Gilkes 1989, 10). Guyana's vast socio-cultural and ethnically diverse position can consequently be seen to have inspired his global approach. The aim of this chapter is, in part, to build upon the multi-cultural and theoretical value system of Harris' aesthetic markers.

In this vein, Harris is not alone in his literary experimentation with multicultural theoretical models. In *Caribbean Man in Time and Space*, the Barbadian writer Kamau Brathwaite conceptualizes the wholeness of the Antilles as "the curve" (a womb image), sweeping from Florida to the Amazon and Brazil (Brathwaite 1974, 1–14). This sweeping curve, which is evocative of a maternal embrace, signals new directions in anglophone Caribbean literature, as Brathwaite attempts to harness an idea of Caribbean space as a site of multiple, intersecting spatialities that connect with North American historical realities of globalization through forced migration and the rise of the global economy. Similarly, in "Caliban's Guarden", Brathwaite asserts: "I also began to recognize that these broken islands were the sunken tops of a mountain range that had been there a million years before. That in addition to the death of the Amerindians I was also witnessing the echo of an earlier catastrophe. That the islands had been part of a mainland" (Brathwaite 1992, 4). His archipelagic emphasis and multicultural disposition – not unlike Harris' cross-cultural poetics – seek to understand the complex imperatives of space.

In other words, the Atlantic's crosscurrents, for Brathwaite, reveal the Americas (North, Central and South) to be connected by an enduring ecology long before it was grouped together by colonialism. Importantly, this worldly approach moves away from nation-centric understandings of space, which arguably cannot account for the ecological ties that bind each territory. Some of the solutions to the present constellation of global crises could come from the long-dismissed voices of Indigenous peoples, who, historically have been at the forefront of its economic, social and political fallouts. It is therefore critical to note that Brathwaite is tracking how the co-existence of ancestral elements within the already hybridized moorings of each nation works towards the production of cultural newness[2] and resilience.

This attunement to the relations of space and time via cosmological perspectives is evoked, for example, in his story "The Black Angel", when he perceives that the Jamaican and Barbadian woodland territories contain the calcified memory of the dead: "It was as if my spirit was waking up in the middle of/a very dark night/as if I was alone in a wood of presences and powers/vague enraged personalities I could not see or name" (Brathwaite 1994, 28). In this regard, Brathwaite's theoretical and creative works fulfil the socio-cultural and geological imperative of reclaiming stolen territories through the creative imagination. Cynthia James fittingly states, "The Black Angel is a story of affirmation in which the landscape [is] a private and personal talisman" (James 1994, 759). Brathwaite shares the ideology that Caribbean space is a vast womb of sorts, as it houses the vestiges of every ethnic migrant culture. The landscape, in this sense, functions as an indomitable entity that will continue to intensively regenerate itself through acts of remembrance and ritual contact.

In close proximity to Brathwaite's archipelagic formulation, J. Michael Dash puts forward the idea of the "other America", which creates a bridge between the different geographies of the Americas. Dash invites the reader/critic to envision the diverse historical, economic, political and cultural realities of the Caribbean and South American continent as important sites, which offer alternative articulations of the Americas within an aggressively globalizing world. Although Dash concretizes the connection between the Caribbean and North America via the image of the mid-Atlantic sea ridge (Dash 1998, 3) – a maternal umbilicus that nourishes the region's historical and cultural continuities – he cautions that this dimension of inter-cultural criticism does not seek to neutralize the strong, visible signs of internal difference and diversity, but rather, facilitates important, visceral connections based on similar historical origins. He provides the paradigms of liminality and tropicality to capture the common history of movement, myriad self-expressions, travel and the workability of a hyphenated identity to enable planetary insurgency against hegemonic forms of power that seek to pauperize, restrict, oppress and undermine developing nations and their peoples (Dash 1998, 149–51).

Jan Carew notes that any critical turn to the multicultural interests of the Americas would do well "to look back at . . . [the] seminal cultural developments . . . in Guyana over half a century ago, for these were replicated in many islands and mainland territories around the Caribbean Sea" (Carew 2006, 23). Taking a lead from Carew, we look at a selection of the Indigenous fables written by Harris in 1970. Guyana is often linked to the origin of the term meaning "land of many waters" (Ludewig 2019, 79). In a symbolic sense, the definition emphasizes the liquidity of Guyanese social and cultural identity, which is usually divided into various ethnic groups – Indo-Caribbean, Afro-Caribbean, the First Peoples, and a sprinkling of Chinese, Portuguese and Caucasians.

Harris' short stories in *The Age of the Rainmaker* focus on the First Inhabitants/Amerindian peoples who occupied the region before the advent of any other ethnic group. The original inhabitants are further sub-divided into the Taino, Carib and Warrau communities of the South American basin. Indeed, an extensive anthropological overview of the Guyanese First Peoples would require another discussion altogether. However, this overview serves to contextualize the springs of Harris' thoughts, which interrogate the manner that Indigenous cultural and religious traditions are wielded to repair a vision of the Caribbean/South American environment as multivalent. His utility of the mythic imagination, with its focus on the deeply felt ideology that the land is a physical and psychic sanctuary, provides an alternative approach to envision new ways to be human. It is also worth noting at this point, that while this chapter extends existing theoretical standpoints on Harris, oeuvre, it also proposes and sharpens the argument that intergenerational or ancestral memory is so powerful in the psyche of each protagonist in the selected narratives, that it begins to command its own attention, and each individual is made to listen to its power. Interestingly, in "Tradition and the West Indian Novel", Harris distinguishes his New World epistemologies from Eurocentric structures by deconstructing ideas of linearity (Harris 1967b, 28–47). Instead of monolithic paradigms that elided the complex spiritual tapestry of Caribbean experience, he presents the novel of fulfilment, which is characterized by its aesthetic features of geological motifs, mythic time scales, embodied characters, spatial metaphors and gateways through which the wreckage of colonial history is manifested.

This elaboration on the tapestry of Caribbean ecology via literature reflects the imperatives of liberating the human imagination from predetermined reading habits. Harris' critical practice eschews monopolistic analyses of texts for alternative readings that are attuned to subtle resonances, fossils, buried clues and opacities. Anita Patterson aptly notes that Harris seeks to re-enable a vision of the "continuity [of life that] appears to have vanished in the New World" through the intuitive imagination (Patterson 2008, 138). In *The Sleepers of Roraima & The Age of the Rainmakers* (Harris 1974; 2014), he recuperates Caribbean Indigenous ontologies as a way of resisting empire's depersonalizing instincts and cultural severance from Caribbean ancestral epistemologies. Elizabeth deLoughrey and George Handley contend that Harris' eco-socialist convictions of nurturing the wounded landscape give rise to incisive cultural forms with the power to instruct and heal the psyche of the generations in the wake of neo-imperial dispossession (deLoughrey and Handley 2011, 26). They postulate that he accomplishes this through extensive flashbacks (allowing the narrated time to cover strategies for survival against eco-imperialism) and the construction of the landscape as an ineradicable presence (deLoughrey and Handley 2011, 26). In *The Sleepers of Roraima & The Age of the Rainmakers*, and in particular, "The Laughter of the Wapishanas" and "The Age of Kaie", Harris appoints the environment as both a vessel of memory to repurpose the lifeways of Indigenous communities and impart modalities of healing in a post-industrial era.

INTERCONNECTED VISIONS AND FORESTS OF THE IMAGINATION

The narrative "The Laughter of the Wapishanas" portrays a series of excursions into Guyana's heartland by a young girl called Wapishana, who is desperate to return humour to her people, whose habitats have been repeatedly destroyed by colonial and neocolonial violence. It is written from the third-person point of view and the plot enacts the female protagonist's journey into the hinterlands to "search [for] the colour and nature of the laughter . . . which she was determined to restore to the lips of her people" (Harris 2014, 143). Wapishana's very name is symbolic; it means the branches of trees that encompass myriad forms of life: bird, fish, animal and god. Through Wapishana's symbolic embodiment of the tree's branches, Harris presents a vision of resilience rooted in the natural and maternal world – where the act of reclaiming laughter is akin to the regeneration of life itself. The fable thus invites readers to consider the ways in which cultural survival is ultimately tied to ecological consciousness.

This ecological awareness is further developed through an ethnographic framing, which expands the critical horizon of the text. Harris' introductory note provides some evidence that the group was indeed solemn and laughter-loving (Harris 2014, 141). He likewise records the period of the 1960s, which marks the tumultuous years of transition from British colonial rule to an independent government under Forbes Burnham, whose Soviet leadership style exacerbated racial and ethnic rivalries. The backdrop of violence and brutality of tyrannical regimes destroyed the hope of the ethnic communities, who remained perennially exploited and controlled. Frank Birbalsingh cites George Lamming's sentiments that "the long survival of Mr. Burnham as Prime Minister and President of Guyana depended on the manipulation of race as a device" (Birbalsingh 1997, 11). In light of this chain of historical events, the story reflects on both colonial and postcolonial expropriation and disillusionment.

Subsequent to the author's insightful introductory remarks, a complex plot emerges: the narrator journeys into a primordial landscape to make known her complaint about the loss of ancestral territories, the abrogation of her community's ways of hunting, fishing and grazing rights, and the de facto cancellation of their interaction with nature. It is an allusion to the First People's struggles against (neo)colonial extractive activities in Guyana, namely the degradation of oil reserves, logging, polluted landscapes left by bauxite mining, the contamination of watercourses and deforestation. Harris posits, "The predicament of the Indian continues to deepen with new uncertainties as to the authority which governs him. Such authority has been at stake for centuries with the decimation of the tribes. And a political scale is still lacking: the land under his feet is disputed by economic interests and national interest" (Harris 2014, 141). Harris' attention to the despoliation wrought in the name of national interest hints at the enterprises of postcolonial governments that acted upon its Indigenous population in similar ways to previous colonial rule. With the future of the geophysical world under threat, Harris subsequently sets up the coping mechanisms of the Wapishana woman – a survivor of colonialism – who does not accept the evil of conquest and sets out on a journey to reclaim her territory. The fable opens with "The Sermon of the Leaf", which refers to the place where the Wapishana people live – the savannahs and forests – and the magico-religious quality of plants that the Wapishana women use in their healing practices. Nádia Farage describes the initial chant of the Wapishana shaman who escorts the young protagonist to a staircase of consciousness. According to Farage, the staircase is a "chain [or] bridge" that connects and facilitates movement, while the journey itself is a sign that obstacles are being gradually overcome (Farage 1997, 260). Dream, chant and shamanic passages initiate the journey of the young woman, who "dreamt" to cradle "the dry mourning of the elder tree of life" (Farage 1997, 63). As the plot unfolds, Wapishana searches out the gift of laughter, which carries imperishable healing properties, and which she believes, will revoke the "years of drought" that plague the island (Harris 2014, 143).

The narrative divulges that not only did colonial and postcolonial foreign experiments disrupt Indigenous ecosystems, but equally devastated a symbiotic relationship between human and habitat. This inextricable connection between Amerindian ontology and the environment is underscored by Harris in the essay, "The Question of Form and Realism in the West Indian Artist", where he observes that the "cosmic [interface] brings . . . authority [. . .] in terms of understanding and protect[ing] the kind of world we build, the kind of living substance we realize and cherish" (Harris 1967, 19–22). For Harris, the fates of creation, the people and the woodland itself rest in a vision of cosmic inter-relatedness. An appreciation of the living cosmos is echoed by Wapishana, who assumes a maternal role herself by repurposing the function of native archetypes and myth in times of crisis. As she embarks upon her journey, she inspects the fate of the dying trees and the brokenness of "hunted bird and fish, animal and god" (Harris 2014, 143). She laments the poaching of species, which deranges the natural population growth of the wildlife. As the narrative unfolds, she climbs the secret staircase, while making her way deeper into the ruined heartland. While bravely ascending the staircase with the help of the shamanic figure, she learns that it is only through navigating a spirit-infused terrain she will be able to locate the right dosage of tonic to bring healing to her people. Thus, it is through her labouring movements and commitment to defend the livelihood of her community that the process of social and ritual support is set in motion.

In his conceptually insightful essay, "Tradition and the West Indian

Novel", Harris expounds on the appearance of spirit-guides or shamans in the world of the living, whose particular functions are to warn, instruct and bless (Harris 1967, 30). Brazilian anthropologist Eduardo Viveros de Castro[3] observes that Amerindian[4] perspectivism integrates ideas of the human world with spirituality (de Castro 2012, 117). He asserts that this "conception [of a] universe . . . inhabited by different sorts of . . . human and non-human [entities]" (de Castro 2012, 83) predicates a standpoint of "ecosophic [or intuitive] knowledge" (de Castro 2012, 95). He is describing a reality where the region's first inhabitants were in constant partnership with forces who occupy the cosmos (de Castro 2012, 94–95). It signposts a revolutionary horizon, which advances the point that despite modernity's growing instincts towards accelerating violence and sterile life forms, a path to knowledge is enacted by way of a cosmically attuned and eco-critical imagination. It is a perspective that has existed for eons longer than colonialism. Demonstrably, the elder's instructions in the narrative propel the young protagonist into a path of extremities, which involve her crossing multiple difficult thresholds. This sense of terrestrial simultaneity creatively connects with a nuanced understanding of Caribbean/South American historiography, since the region's history cannot be expressed through images or ideas of linearity. The physical and psychic shape of the environment, in itself, is a map of the impact of the past as a broken set of miles. The present reality is therefore caught in a circuit of relations that generates a multiplicity of possibilities. This pluralism is associated with the assemblage of realms and energies in Harris' story.

In terms of fictional methodologies, Harris opposes the machinery of imperialism, which produced taxonomies of the self that sought to negate mutualities, parallel time and ancestral faiths. The logic of historical materialism, with its heavy focus on the concrete universe, produced the effect that the corporeal and social world must be commensurate with ideas of linearity. Damien Grant, in *Realism*, explains that the human world, according to Western realist narrative conventions, thrives on a hierarchy that compartmentalized communities and people groups, based on caste, rank and consciousness (Grant [1970] 2019, 9). It is a reading practice that divided the sacred from the material and omitted the creative power of spiritual intermedialities. In a counter-discursive manner, Harris assembles the haunting presences of history in the current milieu of the Wapishana woman, who, very much like the land, carries the weight of history and the potential of renewal. This style of narrative hybridity (as delineated in the pursuit of material and immaterial realms, the melting pot of human and non-human knowledges, and a merging of past and present times) foregrounds creative insights and provisional modes of freedom. When Wapishana arrives at the top of the staircase, she hears a cacophony of spirit voices that coalesce into one reality.

Several interesting ideas emerge at this point. The spatial metaphor of the staircase facilitates a new treaty of relations between spiritual energies and earthly beings. It also transposes the protagonist into a time tunnel of history and a world of the dead. Embedded in the concept of the steps that connect earth to sky, and the image of a self-determined woman climbing the staircase, is the sense of numinous intercourse. The ladder imagery provides the apparatus for establishing a dialectical relationship between heights and depths, not simply in content but in form. The vision that she receives is extreme – a vista of drought and rain, suffering and contentment. However, at the heart of the battle between entities, Harris is presenting a new genesis or vision of reconceiving the landscape as an entity with agential significance. For Wapishana, the vibrancy of her ancestral past and an original time is heard across the seemingly dying landscape, which invigorates her consciousness. In this vista, she observes a "cloud of rain . . . [and] on one . . . horizon [there is a feathered man with a] yellow beak, crest [and] claws" (Harris 2014, 144–45). The fictional use of bird-headed figures unfolds as an imprint of immortality. The kinship with animals and constellations suggests the ways in which Harris' cross-cultural imagination is activated to reverse the burdens of imperial, monolithic history. Interestingly, his pursuit of folk images, as outlined by Hena Maes-Jelinek, encapsulates the myth of the feathered serpent god, Quetzalcoatl,[5] to signify the evolutionary wedding of earth and sky, as well as outward and inner space (Maes-Jelinek 2002, xix). The Mesoamerican myth of Quetzalcoatl – a prime creator-deity who provides rainfall for the fertilization of the earth – carries the idea of regeneration incurred through a merging of the elements (de Montellano 1990, 46–48). This reliance on mythical forms supports Harris' philosophical interpretation of the revitalizing dimensions of Caribbean space, which sets in motion avenues for Wapishana's self-fashioning. Accordingly, in this spiritual force-field, her consciousness expands and she is able to metamorphose into a communal self. This is evoked when "[s]he recalled how she seemed part and parcel of the . . . fabric of space – as if she herself . . . moved [through] inner and outer horizons [. . .]. Each step she made . . . corresponded to inner and outer crenelations of [the] psyche" (Harris 2014, 145). This movement through interlaced spaces is also consonant with shamanic passages, which bring to the scene multiple personae – mystic plants and deceased shamans – that enable the discovery of new possibilities. Shamanic encounters thus energize the quest for liberty from the inside of rituals and ceremonies.

It comes as no surprise that in the ceremonial space of Guyana's interior, Wapishana enters into a mythic consciousness, which undermines the silencing and erasure of oppressive practices. It is worth considering Harris' attention to psychic intercourse on the facets of the protagonist's journey. She must abolish the material or corporeal self that has been over-exposed to imperial forces and embrace the heightened consciousness of the mythic beings, who imprint upon her mind the knowledge that she desires to restore her community's health. In this nirvanic or transcendental state, she observes young trees or seedlings rooted deeply in the timberlands, breathing life into the earth and channelling an imperishable balance and cohesion into the community. The balm that grows from the knowledge of the earth (a knowledge passed down through generations of nurturers) has the power to heal the chaos caused by external forces. It is the earth's wisdom, deeply connected to the maternal and generative, that holds the potential for recovery and restoration. Harris continues to bridge the divide between the earthly plane and the cosmos, the material and the spiritual. This intimate rapport with ancestral connections to the land offers the protagonist transformational tactics for the benefit of the tribe. As Wapishana garners knowledge of the source of laugher, she encounters the "Elder Tree of the Fish" (Harris 2014, 146) and sees through the mists of time, the "bridegroom of conquest" (p. 147), whose bargaining schemes of gold and silver precipitated the space takeover of the hinterlands. The images of the "scissors of light" (p. 146) that cut through her legs, the conquistador's arms that "clasped her to his breast" (p. 147) and the "tyrannical" flood which "pull[s] her down into the depths of the pool" suggest the logics of vulnerability, seduction and entrapment. Such encounter is sexual and resonates with the assault that is cloaked in Europe's global civilizing projects. Indeed, Harris' fable takes up the ambiguous connection between physical and sexual violation and hunt, which entangles human and feathered species. There is a tension of flirting and mockery between female and male principles "whose pliant quarrel drew her to taste afresh an inexplicable humour of self-mockery" (p. 65). Such language and images locate capitalist ideology in its position of predator and conqueror. However, the girl is saved by the retributive rainfall that the shaman induces, and she swiftly advances into a reunion with the "Elder Tree of Animal" (p. 148).

The periphery of the rain and the watchful shamanic figure provides a site of complex interconnection with a variety of agencies. Harris is building new discourses about ecological renewal rituals, aimed at facilitating awareness and validation of alternative healing pathways, which were condemned by imperial and neo-imperial powers. At this phase of her quest, Wapishana is confronted by a thick veil, behind which the laughter of her people is audible. She is advised by her spirit guide to attune herself with the music of the living landscape so that entry can be gained. As she obliges, the veil is torn and she enters into a horizon of spirits. Harris is evincing the potentialities of partnering with alternative systems of knowing as a precondition for the emergence into a new state of consciousness. While crossing into the arch of space, Wapishana encounters the Elder Tree of God, who offers her a token that contains the "maiden juice of . . . laughter" (Harris 2014, 151). The remedy is rumoured to awaken the human senses from the inhibitions of colonialism. As her primal instincts are aroused and the cheer penetrates the cells of her being, "the rain [begins] to fall from the elder tree of life" (p. 151) and the land is fertilized.

This experience reveals cogent aspects of interlapping connections among human expression and the natural world. Harris is conveying the pre-colonial mixture of landscape, hinterland, collective history and personal geography. As Farage proposes: "Personhood, among the Wapishana, does not subsume to be a simple dichotomy between body and soul, since . . . body and soul are proposed as a gradient; a balanced dosage of these components is what makes up the human condition" (Farage 1997, 105). Wapishana,

Harris' protagonist, discovers the elixir of life in the dual elements of nature and in the very substances in which nature is produced. By affectively reorienting herself within the landscape, Wapishana, as a human archetype, plumbs the material topsoil of the land to locate the remedy that will dispel the spiritual and material drought that plagues her community. The ritual of laughter is presented as a vital force, which is necessary to repair the fragmentation induced by historical amnesia and geological dislocation. The impact is the repurposing of a usable past and a viable being in the world. The events in the narrative illuminate the extra-human qualities of the environment and the ceremonial knowledge of deceased shamans, who become instrumental in restoring the soul of the tribe. At the narrative denouement, Wapishana's actions prove effective: the drought ceases and the exuberance of the community is restored. It is a demonstration of the sustaining power of trans-historical unity and inventiveness. Through this fable, Harris, in Sylvia Wynter's words, pits "against those various faces of domination [. . .] the creative determination of women, workers, dominated races, and other groups to . . . affirm themselves" (Wynter 1995, 64). Certainly, utopias are not found in Harris' narrative, but its ingredients are perceptible in the alliances with the material and non-material world; the act of claiming communal responsibility; the establishment of networks of solidarity and alternative ways of knowing, which are essential to any form of psychological and physical healing for the once-colonized.

ANCESTRAL PARTNERSHIP

In keeping with Harris' thematic concerns in "The Laughter of the Wapishanas", the issue of environmental plunder and its effects upon other Indigenous communities of the Amazon rainforest are also depicted in "The Age of Kaie" (Harris 2014). The protagonist, Kaie, is both the heroic ancestor as well as his contemporary descendent. He plays the part of the charismatic native leader who sacrificially drowns himself to conquer the enemy of drought, which exposes his community to social and cultural vulnerabilities. In this allegory, Harris portrays the historical specificity of capitalistic machinations that repositioned the centre of the world economy towards the Amazonian hinterlands. Moreover, by focusing on the rainforest artery of the Amazon, which supports global life, Harris not only links North and South America, but asserts his global environmental concerns.

The consciousness of the landscape becomes a method for Harris, which he concretizes in the tensions and national catastrophe of the Rupununi rebellion. Evoked in the metaphor of the insurgency is the larger framework of territorial invasion. He provides therapeutic interventions to the social and environmental upheaval through the creative use of the Macusi myth of Kaie. Seated at the edge of the Central Highlands plateau in Guyana, Kaieteur is the site of transcendence and healing against the background of the Rupununi uprising in Harris' fiction. By entering into the myth of Kaieteur, Harris changes the "discovery" of European conquest into a recovery of space and events. Importantly, Kaie derives his interiority and strength from an intimate connection with the land. As the society plummets into civil war, the Indigenous communities suffer spiritual distress and loss of morale. The elders' roles are threatened and the unavailability of low water reserves induces dislocation and communal fragmentation. Contextually, the causes and events of the 1969 Rupununi uprising were fuelled by the greed and uncontrolled ambitions of transplanted European cattle ranchers of the savannahs, and a group of Venezuelan rebels who disputed national borders. The effect was the displacement of Indigenous communities, who were open targets for state violence and modern warfare.

In Harris' tale, the effects of civil unrest erupt into cosmological disorder. The images of the "fire . . . across the landscape" (Harris 2014, 115), "the torn waterfall" (p. 109), "the diffused radiance of . . . leaves" (p. 111) and "the decline in the volume of the river" (p. 113) foreground the ecological collapse. Not only were the forests damaged by planned fires – with the intent to destroy habitats and ecosystems – but there were the subtle ruses of tyrannical governance, which reneged on former peace treaties with tribal communities. The re-territorialization of lands, which were given to Indigenous small-scale farmers, for example, compromised any semblance of trust and mutual respect. The keen narrator observes that the voices of the gods have gone silent and their absence is felt in the prolonged drought. However, from the many lacerations and communal traumas, Harris conceives an aesthetic of rebirth via specific acts of sacrifice and metamorphosis.

Not unlike the role of Wapishana, the writer illustrates the transformational power of human responsibility in the character of Kaie. There is the deep understanding that Kaie's determination to invoke rainfall, which he believes will end the dry spell and famine, is connected to alternative cosmologies of time and space that exceed capitalism's materialistic narrative of modernity. To begin this enterprise, he summons out of the nearly dried-up waterways, "[h]is namesake ghost [and] long-dead ancestor" (p. 117), who possesses the knowledge to produce rain. An essential feature of Harris' organic concept of community is the absence of a fixed boundary between the living and the dead. The coexistence of both the living and the deceased is cognate with an awareness of the double-faced view of reality and the relativity of time. The symbol of the resurrected ancestral presence serves as a retributive counterpoint and agent of justice to the impact of neocolonialism.

Through this ancestral recovery, Harris delineates the sub-stratums of the Caribbean and South American womb of space to make connections with supposedly exterminated peoples, who cannot be erased from the environment, no matter the circumstances present. It is through the cultural practices of remembrance, enactment and cognitive processes, which recall submerged memories, that Kaie can invoke his namesake ancestor. Equally important is the point that these ghostly presences and buried bodies of the Amerindian holocaust allow for the recirculation of the small histories of those who have been marginalized because of their difference. As the deity rises to the surface, he imparts the knowledge that cosmic healing can only be afforded through a full reunification with the landscape. He admonishes Kaie that animal, vegetable, mineral and human life are equally valuable in the circle of life, and divinely connected to the geological balance of the earth. After internalizing this knowledge, Kaie determines to sail his "sacrificial boat" (p. 117) over the waterfall to appease the rainmaking gods.

While making his crossing, he calls upon the power of the cosmos for pardon and healing. It is an act that foregrounds the precipitation of "[t]he rain [which] began to grow . . . until a spectre of flood arose" (p. 117). As Kaie submerges himself in the constellations of water, sky and sunlight, he arises as an everlasting deity. Ingrained in both his sacrificial leap and the lack of distinction between the human (Kaie) and the non-human (water) is the idea of renewal. The ability to sink wholly into the landscape demonstrates patterns of continuity. The concept of continuity is potently epitomized in the title and cascading beauty of the *Kaie*tueur Falls, which sit valiantly today in a section of the Amazon rainforest. Possession of, or integration with, the earth reflects Harris' eco-cultural resistance to exploitative progress and systems of plunder, which are evident in the era of globalization. For Harris, this act of repossessing the environment through reunification with the region's mythical presences produces a vision of reclamation.

Following his crossover into the world of the gods, Kaie enters into a theatre of memory and becomes "aware of two anchors . . . one grey, one green – lodged together. His namesake ghost . . . had sown the grey one" to Kaie's hook (p. 117). It is here that he comes to the understanding that "the two ages – past and present – [were destined to be] intertwined" (p. 117). The image of the entangled anchors – one old, the other new – facilitates ideas of twinship and rebirth, which becomes an important continuation of thought for Harris' eco-critical eye. The interconnected images of colonial and neocolonial resistance convey the significance of rootedness and attunement through conscious acts of re-possession. The anchors are not only agents of psychic and physical forces, but are signifiers of a guiding vision. It is in this instance of ceremonial contact that the spur of creation is achieved, thus setting in motion the turbulent "torrent" (p. 12) that drenches the entirety of the rainforest. There is the profound awareness that while aggressive neo-extractivist enterprises, such as logging, mining, pollution and deforestation may succeed in destroying the topsoil of the land, the luminous spirit of the folk community cannot be eradicated. They are reborn to redress the devastation of habitat and creature perpetuated by invading forces. This is evoked in the narrative of Kaie, who becomes an everlasting rainmaking deity and returns to the earth as water. In relation to the myth, A.J. Seymour avers that as Kaie "feels the impact of the waters [while] plunging to [his] death on the rocks below [. . . he is] resurrected into lovely mist" (Seymour 1965, 37). More specifically, Kaie's immersion in the waters, followed by his rebirth into mist, parallels the process of gestation, where life is nurtured and given new form in the body of the landscape. The landscape thus appears as a factual and fertile co-presence in the text, which provides important support for human communities. In the larger eco-critical context, Kaie's return as water speaks to a plausible maternal reciprocity between humanity and the earth, and an ongoing relationship that defies the destructive forces of (neo)colonialism and modernity.

Both "The Laughter of the Wapishanas" and "The Age of Kaie" influence the shaping of a significant ecological imagination and work to ventilate the utterances, instructions and guidance from the non-human world. As postulated by Harris in *The Mask of the Beggar*: "The world [itself] will be the driver on [wo/mankind's] return to nurture . . . the birds, the snakes, the fish, the whales, the seals, the lambs, the sheep, the tigers, the butterflies [. . . and the list of] interminable series of destroyed and threatened species" (Harris 2003, 111). There is the revelation that the very landscape, with its animist associations and mythic dimensions, will generate its own forces to outmanoeuvre the systems that have vilified and truncated Indigenous cultures and folkways of being. By close observation of the submerged presences lodged within the Caribbean/South American environment, Harris offers a rich repository of insight into the values, priorities and vigorous cultural practices that are grounded in Indigenous praxes for survival. Thinking through these pathways in relation to the contemporary global space of remembrance engages evidentiary strategies of resistance through discovery and responsibility. It delivers a powerful inventory of how people groups make meaning of their lives and catastrophes, which can be utilized for contemporary and future applications, as embodied in the recent poetic collections of Jason Allen-Paisant and Grace Nichols.

chapter 9

Whispers from the Roots

Reclaiming Nature Through Spirit in Caribbean Poetry

> One could sense a range of things, all sorts of faces – angelic, terrifying, daemonic – all sorts of contrasting faces, all sorts of figures. There was a sudden eruption of consciousness, and what is fantastic is that it all came out of a constellation of two ordinary objects, two anchors.
>
> —*Wilson Harris,* A Talk on the Subjective Imagination

THE CURRENT CRISES OF ENVIRONMENTAL DEGRADATION and climate change have certainly become a focus of intense debate for Caribbean creative writers and theorists, who have turned to representational modalities to grapple with its calamitous effects. In the Caribbean, the loss of forest coverage, extinctions of flora and fauna, and the host of other slowly unfolding environmental catastrophes recall a painful history of colonial domination, where human and non-human ecologies were maimed by the forces of empire. Within this broad historic framework is the implicit standpoint that the very foundation of modern Caribbean society is intricately intertwined with rupture and displacement. Long before the institutionalization of the transatlantic slave trade, which marked a most brutal system of exploitation for the transplanted tribal peoples of Africa in the New World, there was the oppression and decimation of Indigenous communities. The trope of territorial dispossession continues to be a core focus of this project. We therefore take as part of our pivotal argument the articulation of new theoretical tools, derived from both African and Indigenous cosmologies, towards an articulation of environmental healing, processes of renewal and birth, and societal recuperation.

As discussed in the previous chapter, the landscape functions as a fertile repository of spirit energies that permeate the region. It is a locus that represents potentialities for transcendence. Grace Nichols' poems in *Passport to Here and There,* and Jason Allen-Paisant's collection, *Thinking with Trees,* deliver a substantial range of cultural legacies in which the colonizer, the colonized and successive generations are constrained to confront, evade and work through belated hauntings of colonial violence that erupt in the present. These colonial intrusions are most potently realized in the processes of economic development, dormant proprietary claims on resources and other accelerating forms of violence that are linked to a capitalistic world-economy. The selected works reveal how the writers have given epistemic saliency to the Caribbean's mytho-poetic traditions, with two parent cultures – the African and the Indigenous – in an effort to illuminate an eco-historical lineage that pivoted on mutual respect, intimacy and reciprocity.

With specific reference to the Guyana hinterlands, Harris contends that the very soil is a spirit-receptacle and engenders memories. He affirms that in the topography of space, one "may discern . . . a sudden upsurge of bush-baby spectres which [rise] out . . . like wraiths or smoke of sparks of life. Certain vestiges of legend – in this context – have come down to us and the bush-baby . . . corresponds to a figure of . . . a host native" (Harris 169). This conception of nature as sentient informs ethical decision-making processes and sustainable resource management practices. In *The Lessons of Nature in Mythology,* Rachel McCoppin similarly contends that in pre-Columbian communities there was the fundamental identification of the self within the whole creation. There was no demarcation between soil, animal and human realms (including the vegetal world). She affirms, "the Earth was . . . a place where the ancestors went . . . As seeds are broken and give use to shoots, so new life came from the underground realm of the dead" (McCoppin 2015, 22).

This statement echoes through Nichols' aesthetic approaches to reading Guyana's syncretized and maternal earth-spaces. Her self-conscious, nature-based methodology is revealed in her use of symbols and metaphors of the living landscape (wielded to perceive nebulous links between realms and species); an extension of linear time to mythic time (retained to invoke and destabilize oppressive imperial orders and to create preconditions for new liberations); and an arrangement of the journey motif through which discoveries of creativity, responsibility and rebirth are gleaned. The objective is to reclaim an elided ontology that has been negated and dismissed within the wreck of colonial history. Moreover, Nichols aspires to unveil a mounting critique about modern, extractivist enterprises, manifested specifically in the timber and mining industries. The poems "Eldorado", "Georgetown" and "Against My Heart" evince this preoccupation. Turning attention to another people group whose interactions with the environment shape self-understanding, we look at Jason Allen-Paisant's retrieval of ancestral memory through a style of poetry that transforms colonial perceptions by engaging with nature as an experiential map or ancient path.

This interlocks with the theoretical project of Margarite Fernandez Olmos and Lizabeth Paravisini-Gerbert in *Creole Religions of the Caribbean: An Introduction from Vodou and Santería to Obeah and Espiritismo,* where they trace sediments of continental African cosmologies and spiritualities that are resident in the body and the topography of the New World. They determine that during the transatlantic slave trade, "the flexibility . . . and malleability of African religions allowed practitioners to adapt to their new environment, drawing [and imparting] spiritual power from wherever it originated" (Olmos and Paravisini-Gerbert 2003, 3). They further underscore the sentience of the environment with specific reference to "Ochosi, the [African] deity of forests and herbs" (p. 1). As such, to read the Caribbean natural world is to read the land (and seascape) as encryptions of ancestral faiths and energies. This process dovetails with Katherine McKittrick's concept of "Plantation Futures", where the plantation is an apt site to procure alternative worldviews of liberation, resistance and survival. One, therefore, finds that while the landscape bears the memory of colonial torture and violence, it is equally sustained as a powerful and fertile repository of ancestral presence that shapes everyday interactions with the environment.

In *Thinking with Trees*, Allen-Paisant engages nature writing to procure new understandings and identification with his native land, Jamaica. More specifically, trees are the embodiment of origin, through which the intersections between race and concerns for the environment are explored. His use of a highly specialized ecological vernacular, shaped by affective historically textured maps that communities have devised over generations – maps replete with names, creeds, routes and habits – suggests a careful attention to how the material landscape of the Caribbean is engaged as shrine, womb and symbol of collective memory. The overall tone of resentment towards empire underscores his unease with modernization processes and the entanglement with the colonial white experience of nature that passes as universal and normative. In this sense, poetry – through its complex assemblage of times, plots, temporalities and action – becomes a form of social activism. His poems, "Logwood", "Climbing Trees" and "Do You Feel Them Looking At You", effectively spatialize these concerns.

It is worth noting that among the unifying factors between Nichols' and Allen-Paisant's works is the rejection of the ruses of capitalism, heteropatriarchy and domination of the more-than-human universe. Through the crafting of what may be called a Caribbean cosmo-ecological poetics, they have turned to ancestral alliances, nature-infused maternal symbols and cosmological networks to build solidarity and to focus on the endurance of Caribbean ecology. Both poets insist on broader movements that are rooted in the collective necessity of constructing a world that is anchored in syncretic and ecological ethics, resilience and environmental justice. Their combined liberative narrative techniques encapsulate a significant uprooting of the weeds of colonialism and the imperial ideas of the human as divorced from the natural world. Their focus is on the soil in which ancestral bodies were buried, fertilized and are growing, with a participatory and reclaiming impulse to instruct on locating alternative pathways to survival and social agency in a highly racialized world.

The poems in *Passport to Here and There*, by the Guyanese-born Nichols, unravel the process by which she drew on memories of a magnificent and mystical South American landscape to conceive a future that is retributive and attentive to the eco-spiritual dimension of life. Implicit in the idea of remembrance is an emphasis on the relationship with the natural world through cultural memory. Nichols refers to poetry as "a radical synthesizing force", where the landscape "isn't separated from the political and spiritual" (Nichols 1989, 298). In other words, the haunting legacies of empire are encoded in images of ecological disembowelment by deforestation and extractivism by new regimes. At the outset of "Eldorado", Nichols critiques the mineralogical exploitation of Guyana through a gendered lens, positioning the female voice as a critical observer of the male-driven pursuit of wealth. She documents the ambitions of the young Guyanese men, whose quest for riches uncannily recalls the impulses of European imperialism. With sharp clarity, the speaker laments that the male youths are caught in the thrall of gold fever, noting: "[t]he young men liming about the street/corners [are . . .] caught in an old familiar dance" (Nichols 2020, 57). It raises the broader question of inhospitable and failing social systems, in which people groups are bound to repetitious cycles of aggression, haunted by spectres of former selves that are now seeking pathways for malevolent creativity. Nichols' purpose is, in part, to illuminate their consciousness through a language that exposes a historical passage of displacement and oppression, which – if pursued – will strangle their youth. She portends: "Eldorado, long-lost city of gold/that drew so many into its feverish fold/ including Raleigh [who] could not . . . quench the fire of its timeless lure" (p. 57). The myth of Eldorado emerges as a present horror for those who dare to traverse the heartlands. A cautioning voice warns that the landscape is not one of promise, but of peril. The very structure of the poem mirrors the cyclical nature of this historical folly, as the speaker (a vigilant female voice) offers a stern admonition. Nichols employs caesuras and alternating rhyming couplets with enjambment to evoke the speaker's sing-song caution and anticipate her argument. The rhyming of corresponding words – such as "dance" with "chance", and "gold" with "folds" – evokes the dance of temptation and the empty promises of wealth ensnaring the young men in their pursuit of illusory treasures. Because the poem rehearses the repetitive nature of history, the tale requires an alternative mode of hearing – a reverent one – as Nichols begins her pronouncements.

As its title suggests, the poem opens with the framework of the gold rush, which South American journalist Eduardo Galeano dates between 1500 and 1558. It was a time when gold ore constituted more than 99 per cent of mineral exports from South America and the Caribbean. The heavy demand for gold was due to the circulation of capital required to stimulate the slave trade. Galeano asserts: "[T]he bourgeoisie took control of the cities and founded banks, produced and exchanged merchandise, conquered new markets. [. . .] The value of [South] and Latin American precious exports was four times greater than the value of all slaves, salt and luxury goods it imported. The resources flowed out so that the emergent European nations across the ocean could accumulate them" (Galeano 1997, 40). In his estimation, Spain and the rest of Europe "stretched out its arms to clasp" the luxury items (gold, silver and sugar), believing the resources to be not only vast, but also exhaustible. In *Imperial Eyes: Travel Writing and Transculturation*, Mary Louise Pratt also contends that during the British mining boom in the seventeenth and eighteenth centuries, descriptions of Guyana's gold beds, which were flowing freely from the mountain streams, led to dozens of "mining investment companies bourgeoning overnight on the London Stock Exchange as investors prepared to get rich quick" (Pratt 2008, 147).

Embedded within this violent trajectory of the competitive gold trade is the grim standpoint that the Guyanese landscapes, which were home to both First Communities and wildlife, were laced with explosive material. These technologies were hastily detonated to convene expeditions. Tree mortality, soil erosion, encroachment, fragmentation and the perilous destruction of forests epitomize the violence wrought upon both human and ecological systems. The earth's groans and moans are embodied in the poet's use of "fire", "fever", "execution" and "breathing" (Pratt 2008, 57), which are palpable corollaries of its altered state. In this sense, the devastated landscape foreshadows the enslavement of bodies under the militia system established by the Spanish in the late 1560s. The continuities of ecological violence have impelled meaningful interventions by Nichols, whose poetic style summons the presences of history into the present to unsettle the hubris of a human-centred universe. This idea of spiritual endurance amidst intrusive, rupturing activities finds fuller representation in Gianluca Delfino's postulations on the cosmovision of Taino groups, who believed themselves to "have sprung from the ground" (Delfino 2001, 134). This integration with nature is certainly enacted when the speaker notices that the forests have begun to repel human intrusion. Nature promises a retributive fate that betides anyone who pursues its path and enters the dark domain. The assertiveness and power of place are realized in the expressive images of the "misty caul [that falls] over the green secretive face/ of forest" (Nichols 2020, 57). Nichols, it seems, is offering the insight that the traumatic history of the New World is materializing in incarnations that embody modalities of justice, while generating spaces in which old traumas may be confronted and archived.

The poetic imagination is, then, a projection of the mythic unconscious, as Nichols is able to construct images from the traces left by those who have peopled the place. In the restaging of these active presences, she is indeed presenting the Guyanese landscape as a metabolic entity. This interlocks with Harris' idea that Caribbean space turns on the axis of cosmic integrity and is moving into a wider syncretic spiritual continent. The Guyanese hinterland is thus functioning as a catalyst of insight, where the descendants of colonial communities may come to know a horrific reality through transgenerational understandings. The female speaker, as agent, delivers these truths and stands as a memory-keeper of a native cultural value system. which shape-shifts with every new post-independent context.

The phenomenon that nature is a shared body with all things and all species is further interrogated in "Against My Heart". The spirit-centred approach to landscape is illuminated when Nichols writes of the dead "who swim with the pilgrimage . . . of blood" and who "have been busy planting all manner/of vegetation . . . /Hibiscus flowers to gladden the eye/Irrepressible grass to cushion the feet . . . palm trees/to guard their everlasting sleep" (Nichols 2020, 59). Ancestral blood and bones refuse to remain buried and resist permanent erasure. In other words, their refusal to remain buried underscores the interface between the past and present, and emphasizes the persistence of ancestral influence in the natural world. The specific images of the human "eyes" and "feet" in this burial ground engender a historical consciousness that the landscape itself is permeated with the traces of human bodies; each fragment of the earth is a repository for stories of those who have come before. In this way, Nichols weaves together a diversity of histories, making the burial ground a site not of death, but of transformation and regeneration. Moreover, the transformative quality of the burial ground is essential to repurposing the environment as a space for flourishing, rather than a resource for appropriation. Signs of Guyana's geocultural autonomy are encapsulated in the images of a moving ecosystem. The intellect of an operational and divine natural world that sprawls and spreads itself across the region defies the Eurocentric gaze that dismissed Indigenous spiritualities as primitive.

Nichols skilfully superimposes the content of the poem with a fluid poetic style that meanders. While journeying through "the city cemetery", the persona "see[s] [that] the dead/ . . . have been busy/[and] can hear their epitaph"(Nichols 2020, 59). In a clever negotiation between storytelling and oral mapping, the poet contemplates and calculates mythic topographical ranges by composing a prophetic map for the reader as much as for herself. Thus, apart from its communal associations, the poem is also deeply personal, as embodied in the title of the piece. The movement through the burial ground is perceived as a submergence into the depths of an ancestral self and the poet's task is to provide visibility to those who have hitherto lacked it. The verses point to an idea that the passage through the cemetery is an entrance into potentiating layers of the unconscious and of mythic time. Nichols is, therefore, returning to an idea of spiritual perception based on the need for self-preservation and renewal. This achieves its force through psychic detail and a cross-cultural arc of communication that buttresses the authority of antiquity. The impact is the evincing of an artistic tradition that is founded on the desire for renewal, harmony and healing through an interaction with the dead.

Nichols' dual concern with critiquing the cunning frontiers of new colonialisms and transcending these forces via cosmo-spiritual premises is also negotiated in "Georgetown". At the start of the poem, the reader encounters a fertile, pre-colonial Edenic space, where nature appears tranquil, pristine and effortlessly fecund. Nichols proceeds to systematically index a textual tableau by detailing portraits of Georgetown during the pre-Columbian era. It is resplendent with vivacity and colour: "In the silent blooming of memory/I picture . . . your flame-petalled avenues that once/ deemed you *Garden City of the Caribbean* – [with] the red bells of your hibiscus" (Nichols 2020, 60). The idiom of lushness both rehearses the biota of the region and unravels the principles of nature that prevail in the collection. However, there is a marked shift in tone and rhetorical remarks:

> What can you do now, Georgetown,
> but accept the newly sprung up
> concrete monstrosities beside
> . . . your blocked arteries of canals and alleys?
> What can I do but hold fast, Seawall-city
> to your below-sea-level courage? (Nichols 2020, 60).

The lines signpost a clear and radical departure from a tone of reverence for the garden space as a haven, to one of horror and condemnation aimed at Georgetown's ecological ruin. The quick transition chronicles the impact of both a history of rapid commercial exploitation and a contemporary prioritization of the economy over local communities. The sequence of events spotlights the unsafe living conditions that are part of ongoing genocidal structures contributing to disease and death in Georgetown. Melinda Janki laments in her article, "Water is Everywhere in Georgetown" (2018), the undermining activities of state officials and business operators, whose infrastructural projects and illegal waste-disposing activities assault and affect both human and natural communities. According to Janki, modern infrastructure has aggravated the influx of toxic chemicals, such as mercury from industries, while the dumping of waste directly into watercourses since the early 2000s has become a public health hazard and a water sovereignty problem in Georgetown. Janki's awareness weighs heavily in Nichols' concern with Guyana's despoiled landscapes.

With the threat of climate change and coastal portions of Georgetown sitting below sea level, the city remains vulnerable to high spring tides and flooding. Rob Nixon considers the slow but lethal apocalypse that undergirds climate change:

> Violence is customarily conceived as an event or action that is . . . explosive and spectacular in space [. . .]. We need, I believe, to engage a different kind of violence, a violence that is neither spectacular nor instantaneous, but rather incremental and accretive, its calamitous repercussions playing out across a range of temporal scales. In so doing, we also need to engage the representational, narrative, and strategic challenges posed by the relative invisibility of slow violence. Climate change, the thawing cryosphere . . . acidifying oceans, and a host of other slowly unfolding environmental catastrophes present formidable representational obstacles that can hinder our efforts to mobilize and act decisively. The long dyings – the staggered and staggeringly discounted casualties, both human and ecological, that result from . . . climate change – are underrepresented in strategic planning as well as in human memory (Nixon 2011, 2–3).

"Georgetown" divulges this incremental history of ecological violence hidden under images of so-called civilization. The poem engenders an awareness of the ways in which ideas of progress conceal bigotry. Completely at odds with the evil hidden beneath economic progress, Nichols envisions environmental sustainability that is rooted in a knowledge system of mutual respect. She inverses this pain of denigration through a vivid memory that conjures agency and empowerment. Her references to the flamboyant hibiscus and mellow, red-belled gardens sustain a vision of organic growth and transformation. In principle, she is redefining alternative ways of being, based on nuanced understandings of agrarian history, and ethical positions to the land and the coast, while creating plans for a distinct future. This connection feeds her national pride and voice, which become more effectively spatialized in her literary practice that affords activism and intervention.

This idea of transformation bourgeoning out of an engagement with history is similarly echoed in Allen-Paisant's collection, *Thinking with Trees*. His work addresses the intersections of race, class and the environmental conditions that affect people groups of the Caribbean. He responds to the landscape (both Caribbean and English) as extensions of his sense of belonging, exile and ancestral connections. Not unlike Nichols,[1] the memories of the Caribbean's – particularly Jamaica's – tropical rainforests, tree canopies, starry skies, animist settings and diverse fauna provide a creative space through which he contemplates Afro-Caribbean subjectivity, syncretic wisdom systems and the sense in which history shapes new understandings of Caribbean metaphysics.

He expands on the hinterland of Caribbean ontologies by recuperating nature as the vehicle through which to effect his philosophical explorations of Afro-Caribbean freedom. This revitalization of the black self via the natural world rehearses the theoretical postulations of Sylvia Wynter, who critiques the mechanisms of colonialism that divorced man/woman from other lifeforms. Wynter describes coloniality as the creation of the white man at the expense of most of humanity, since the overrepresentation of the colonizer was consolidated through epistemological developments that legitimized his claims of superiority and universality. The effect was the discrediting of non-European populations and forms of knowledge. This hierarchy had its consequences in the manifest structuring of centre-periphery inequalities, the imaging and division of the world in terms of occidental, Eurocentric and imperial/colonial cultural and other racialized categories (McKittrick 2015).

According to Wynter, the forced transplanting of Africans in the colonies is coupled with a reparatory awareness of how the natural world provided sustaining alternative worldviews that effectively challenge practices of dehumanization and imperial control. She imagines that the seeds of a black radical tradition, which thrive on underground projects of emancipation, can be found in ecological knowledges, black diasporic spirituality, folk-based practices and collective memory. Wynter expands on these ideas in "Jonkonnu in Jamaica" (1970) and "Novel and History, Plot and Plantation", where she excavates the "provision grounds" as sites of "secretive history" and "plot culture" (Wynter 1971, 100). These plots and systems of sharecropping reveal the agency and resilience of enslaved communities, whose intimate interactions with the land facilitated creativity and the exchange of values. What colonial powers perceived as simple communal mannerisms were, in fact, deeply embedded ways of knowing and being, a recognition of the earth as both a maternal force and a site of memory, healing and resistance. This sensibility underscores an ecological consciousness that frames the land not merely as property, but as a living, spiritual entity.

This is epitomized in the poem, "Climbing Trees", where Allen-Paisant reminisces about climbing trees as a child in Coffee Grove, Jamaica. He declares:

> Lost inside the guinep branches
> I felt close to God
> and I was hidden in a place before birth
> a womb . . .
> For hours I would
> turn into something else
> one of those brown or green lizards
> living up there
> . . . you travel with your belly
> with your thighs with all your feelings (Allen-Paisant 2021, 74).

The associated images and references to womb, God and birth disclose the poet's conceptualizing of the guinep tree as an extension of Mother Earth, or as a hallowed presence that is further determined by the poet's instinctive crawling activity. This intimate connection and child-like motion signify forms of initiation into self-knowledge and new awakening linked to an idea of place and community. The spatializing of the wood as a powerful maternal force, which empowers the speaker to imaginatively metamorphose into other species – as in "the green lizard" – is an extension of Indigenous totemic traditions. While the image of the lizard signifies an ancestral presence, it equally draws upon Edouard Glissant's theories of relationality. In *Poetics of Relation* (1997), Glissant castigates Western essentialisms that discounted the existence of other conceptions of the world, including the Caribbean's First Communities, together with their cosmogonies and autochthonous forms. For Glissant, the paradigm of relationality engenders an instrumental, cross-cultural, cross-species interrelatedness that coincides with the intuitive insights of creative writers such as Allen-Paisant and Nichols. What emerges is a collision and subsequent production of global networks of entangled histories, cultures and subjectivities. This collision of cultures is realized in Allen-Paisant's expression of the relational matrix of Caribbean being through the image of a womb that is a vehicle of the residual traces of traditions, while simultaneously exuding potential and newness.

Allen-Paisant remembers this newness and unending potential of the Jamaican landscape, since in Manchester, the "beeches are unclimbable, no furrows for feet" (74). Migration exposes an internalized loneliness and estrangement within metropolitan spaces. The featureless landscape signifies an immutability, where the self, in need of nurturing and affirmation, is nullified by a landscape of stiffness and estrangement. From a Caribbean – as well as ecological – perspective, interrelatedness with the landscape is necessary for survival. The poet, it seems, is addressing a recalibration of the conceptions of ontological discovery via the mobilizing framework of memory that recognizes a non-hierarchized principle of relationality. By entering into the mind and heart of the Caribbean landscape, the poet emphasizes a psychic approach to recovering self-affirmation, which eschews the assumption that such knowledge is derived only from monuments and embodied structures of supremacy.

The haunting framework of imperial control is also sustained in the poem "Logwood". Beyond the geometrics of exclusion and entrenched divisions, the poet provides an interesting argument on the ways in which colonial constellations of power operate in contemporary times. The main thesis is that the continuous political and territorial domination of the Caribbean within the hierarchies of world wealth, reveal coloniality as a key attribute in modern regimes. In "Logwood", Allen-Paisant documents the logging concessions that fuel Britain's infrastructure and conceives a hermeneutics of capitalist modernity within this matrix of power. He notes:

> It is an autumn day in 2019. . . . . Today each of the building's three triangular gables carries . . . logwood . . . from Central and South America . . .
> I was again . . . surrounded by . . . the trees[s] of memory . . . I'm trying to remember
> trying to retrieve the meanings of logwood
> . . . this dead wood on the façade of
> the Clothworker's Hall at
> Leeds University . . .
> something stirred in me
> the haunting of place by place
> . . . . The colonizer is . . . everywhere (Allen-Paisant 2021, 101–5).

Several interesting ideas emerge at this point. The slow, surreal process of uprooting trees trigger multiple sensations and ambivalent feelings. The poet's deliberate use of "chiseled . . . logwood" that "comes from . . . the West Indies" (p. 101), the violated "red paths" into the jungle (p. 102), the "dead wood" (p. 103) and "the blood-wood" (p. 106), "the depletion of forests" (p. 106), the "logs of dying", "logs of erasure", "trees [that] have been killed" (p. 108) are moving examples of both the languishing of nature within England's economic boom and a deliberate mapping of Caribbean dendrology in metropolitan spaces.

The mood of excess and greed is embodied in Britain's commercial enterprises in an age of global trade and industrial progress. The scenario directly places the past in a constellation with the present to reflect the extent to which the black experience in the diasporic world continues to be aggravated by recurring patterns of slaughter, death, violation and cultural subjection. Teasing apart the historical layers and entanglements of colonial violence, the poet opines:

> Logwood – prime dyewood and staple of the
> dyestuffs industry
> comes mainly . . . from the West Indies
> Indigo and dyewood were important to the textile industry,
> a primary activity in Leeds
> during the
> Industrial Revolution &
> up until the late 20th century.
> In the eighteenth century, in the West Indies, the most robust importation of slaves and
> expansion of the sugar plantations
> was taking place. The Transatlantic Slave
> Trade was at its apogee.
> Plantations also provided
> indigo and logwood,
> two essential raw materials for
> Britain's textile industries. Profits from sugar provided precious capital for their growth. (Allen-Paisant 2021, 101–2).

This excerpt, positively interpreted by implication, divulges that the Columbian exchange was not simply an Atlantic operation, but was a system engineered to proliferate into lucrative global relationships. The exchanges of people, plants, disease and ecosystems; and the dispersal of indigo cultivation and manufacturing were all components of a demanding empire that spread itself over a decidedly global terrain. This memory of subjugation is exacerbated when the poet witnesses the "bare-backed men struggling with a log, their faces exhausted from carrying the weight and from the heat" in modern England (p. 102). The scene rehashes a historical colonial ontology that was grounded in relation to Europe's rise as a global power. The idea of 'seeing' the entire experience of transatlantic slavery as a whole compels the poet to create an ontology of time that can assert a call for a reawakening of Afro-Caribbean consciousness.

These alternative modalities are spatialized in the strong ideological beliefs in mutual respect for the earth. The history of the Jamaican peasantry suggests a careful attention to how each moving and breathing organism relates to another. The work of Mart A. Stewart reveals how violence against the African enslaved populations in colonial plantations and other green spaces translate into contemporary understandings of environmental interactions (Stewart 2006, 10–20). Stewart observes that working the land under the threat of the whip and sun underscored an integral part of how the enslaved populations combatted the ruthless hegemonies at work. The majority of their time was spent on intimately cultivating the earth and garnering roots, which induced a reclamation impulse to imbue "social and sacred meanings of the things . . . procured in the wild" (p. 14). The implication is that an ancestral cultural practice defined by closeness to the earth – for which thousands of enslaved humans were flogged, killed, hanged and buried – was repurposed to fuel ideas of marronage and the formation of maroon communities in the nineteenth century.[2] It heralded a metaphysical conflation with the human and the natural world, which foregrounds an obligation to the plotting of alternative history via the language of the landscape.

This mutual relationship between the human and the soil is not unlike Wilson Harris' postulations, which similarly render the earth as "the living fossil of buried cultures" (Harris 1981, 90). This process of knowledge production that is encoded in a phenomenological rooting of the self in an active landscape and dialogue with nature across space and time is realized in "Logwood", when the poet declares that:

> in this dead wood on the façade of the Clothworker's Hall at Leeds University
> . . . I can hear them
> . . . in the crowd their breathing
> grows clearer
> . . . how they haunt the façade of this building
> how I came to meet their spirit here
> in the stone . . . down in the wood is their breathing
> the noises are in the crowd
> . . . their breathing grows clearer
> in the spirits of the wood (Allen-Paisant 2021, 104–5).

Spectral presences, tenuously confined beneath the surface of material reality, have created an intrusive, persistent impulse to try and understand and re-member a history that is scattered across the globe. Through his polemic, Allen-Paisant is affirming his right to ritual remembrance and endorses the instrumentality of forces in crafting a socio-cultural order that is retributive and beneficial.

This is carefully located in the spectral whisperings that emerge from the wood and which invoke the reality of a psychic connection that is necessary for working out the centuries-long collective struggle for emancipation. The poet's extrasensory encounter delineates his process of coming to his own metaphysical and ontological liberation, through the instructive cohort of voices that he hears, among which is his "Mama/[who] in this dead wood" (p. 105). This encounter impels him to write and document a new archive of his grandmother's healing remedies, grounded in her forest-dwelling, root-worker disposition that is situated outside of Western conventions (p. 107). This spatialization encourages an active engagement and intellectualizing of how nature, twinned to the human world, must be accompanied by multigenerational responsibility. Allen-Paisant is, in this regard, contributing to the corpus on black ecologies and insurgent knowledges, which are re-imaged to conceive futures outside of permanent destruction and to cultivate alternative worldviews that challenge the practices of dehumanization.

In "Do You Feel Them Looking At You", the tone shifts slightly, as there seems to be an avoidance of nature, perhaps because of the trappings of civilization and self-imposed exile. Despite this physical distancing – which the poet interprets as a deadening experience – he permits various echoes from the woodland to reverberate in his imagination and begins to hear again the language of the ancestors in the cosmos. This reflects an elemental self that finally shrieks with despair and a sense of loss. His instinctive return to the forest allows for contemplation, which generates its own energy. As he moves into the woods, the vestiges and traces of myth rise to the surface and he receives an ancestral admonition:

> I hear the ancestors saying we have avoided the woods [. . .]
> They are writing with us [. . .]
> I hear the ancestors say we have used the woods we have needed the woods [. . .]
> They enter our space again [. . .]
> And know we are with them
> reclaiming time (Allen-Paisant 2021, 174).

The woodland, in this context, lies in what Abraham and Torok refer to as the "crypt": "The buried speech of the parent [location] will be a dead gap without a burial place in the child. This unknown phantom returns [to dialogue] with the host" (p. 174). This dynamic of encryption is one that Abraham and Torok explore in the context of mourning, arguing that the survivor of death and intense trauma will seek to psychically swallow that loss, rather than cope with the reality of death. What is swallowed by Allen-Paisant is the partial loss of an ancestral motherland and a disconnectedness from his island birthplace. This break in connection, which remains intact despite physical distance, erupts as both a longing for home and creative immobility that is evident: "Did I tell you I do not come as often anymore/ It becomes overwhelming to be out of place" (p. 174). The impulse to shut the natural world out is the very impulse that generates creative darkness and void. As a Ulysses figure or drifter, he attempts to repair the broken connections of histories – that is, the repetitive witnessing and expressions of transatlantic nightmares, his marooning between worlds, his encounter with unhomely conditions and a consequential creative impotence.

It is only when he reenters the landscape, where boundaries are eroded, that the gods enter and he is here merged with a primordial perception, in which his senses are synthesized. At this point, he becomes a listening poet, seeing what is present and sensing what is absent. It is interesting that he is both clairaudient and clairsentient, which suggests that he has developed a sixth sense and hears spirits. More than this, however, is the point that the voices, which touch the chords of his deep-seated self, beckon him towards a shared responsibility to issue forth a narrative that would reassess what knowledge and memory signify. In this sense, the woods contain a secret, and though he is located in Leeds, his understanding of place is not defined by the locale, but by his relationship to the cosmos.

The verses that follow vividly reveal a vista of the woodlands that have eyes; the warmth of tree cover; the birds that squark and peep; and shadows that rise – all of which illuminate a leap to a new dimension and state of being. The self that is encased in the forest of spirit finds itself being renewed through a oneness with nature: "This world entering your skin/ This yourself as the elements/This becoming woodland/This becoming stream/This becoming river" (p. 174). The landscape is a connective medium or gateway that sets in train expressions of personal transformation and metamorphosis. This movement, forged by a common memory and history, unites the poet and nature in a secret bond that solidifies a unique way of life not available to outsiders.

He imagines his "body as [the] sound as water [and] river" (p. 174), which are aligned to the process of syncretism that privileges the elements and atmospheric world to generate a new assertiveness. That he becomes a living element suggests an active enactment of the process of transformation that accords with the life of the environment. Through the apparatuses of the senses and memory, the contradictions he feels appear as reversals. The landscape offers a fertile environment with many possibilities for metamorphosis and spiritual power. And nature, when inscribed as felt life, moves past its presence as haunted domain and emerges as an entity that demands to be accepted and owned. Perhaps Allen-Paisant is establishing a dialogue between strength and weakness, responsibility and recklessness. Not until he becomes fully aware of the real shape of his individual and communal history, and admits to the immediacy of suppressed communal and individual hurt, is he able to emerge anew. The images of a mythic unconscious, derived through its traces in the landscape, enable a portrayal of the circuit of relations in the cosmos. It should be noted that this perception of nature is not an abstract one, but is grounded in the imperative of altering sensitivities to the earth for its life-giving value, as opposed to its misuse as a commodity and by-product. Allen-Paisant is advocating for a cultivating of this purposeful vision of the world in order to expand on new recalibrations of the senses that have been inhibited by modernity.

The theme is cosmic harmony that cannot be derived from destructive and material systems of dominance, but is aligned to an elemental power in the face of global greed and commercial exploits. The poem, therefore, reflects a precise tilt of the human will so that it becomes transparent and is a channel for this type of spiritual work, which is embodied in the lines: "This world entering your skin/This yourself as elements." The speaker must learn to feel, just as the trees are made to speak. Nature is no longer silent, as suggested in the reference to many forms of communication, such as bird song, babbling brooks and the trickling of the streams, all of which signpost the earth as a reverberating entity. To participate with nature in this way is to participate in the sacred. Himself a pilgrim, Allen-Paisant learns the place on its own terms and provides multiple epistemologies to encapsulate a broader range of perception. This condenses, for example, an engagement with sensory experiences, where histories that have been elided are pulled back into relevance by intuiting the impressions left in the landscape. This graphing of Caribbean psychic reality via nature revokes the estrangement of hegemonic cultures and does so by destroying internalized beliefs that established knowledge-making and agency with whiteness.

Through innovations in poetic forms, both Allen-Paisant and Nichols have expressed a reparatory vision of the cosmos, in which the divine, the animal, the human and the vegetal interlock and provide prophetic contours with liberatory focus and theoretical rigour. Their respective collections move into an expansive terrain of sacred traditions, ancestral pools of reflections and cross-spiritual portals to subvert the stigma and perceptions of soul sickness and cultural impotence. The combined effort to engender respect and inspire individual participation in the care, management and ritual remembrance of nature means embracing the cultural experiences and values of various Caribbean peoples. The ability to name and frame the landscape is partly anchored in collective and individual memories that inform how Caribbean communities procure a poised and collective sense of environmental activism and intervention.

This awareness about environmental changes has become a prime focus of many other Caribbean writers, who have deployed a type of poetics and storying informed by natural disasters, tropical storms, melting glaciers, heat waves and the intricacies involved in climate change.

Conclusion

ORIGINARY VIOLATIONS OFFERS NEW INSIGHT INTO the literary representations of matrifocality by fourteen Caribbean creative workers and demonstrates the importance of an interdisciplinary conversation when considering the role of ancestral homelands in a Caribbean context. We have contended that the selected discourses of Erna Brodber, Olive Senior, Grace Nichols, Dionne Brand, Nalo Hopkinson, Kwynn Johnson, Kei Miller, Jason Allen-Paisant, Wilson Harris, Paul Keens-Douglas, David Dabydeen, Derek Walcott, Lawrence Scott, Marlon James and others are indicative of existing debates about matrifocal communities and their broader world views. We surmise that a correlation exists between the aesthetic patterns of survival and networks of care and connection, as well as the search for individual autonomy and nurturing spaces.

The experience of Caribbean motherhood has historically been misrepresented and distorted by the androcentric critical tradition. In our introduction, we traced the evolution of discourses that challenged patriarchal hegemonic orders, which has defined, among other things, what it means to be a woman by influencing ways of seeing and imagining women, gender relations, social systems, institutions and, ultimately, the world. Susheila Nasta, Giselle Anatol, Andrea O'Reilly, Jane Flax and Nathalie Elvire Gaillot have raised some of the reactions and concerns to motherhood and mother-daughter relationships in Caribbean literature. Their works demonstrate the extent to which the trope of matrifocality remains pervasive in twenty-first-century Caribbean critical thought, not least because it allows them to think through complex gender identities and relations in the region. We have found that fictive representations of motherhood create a space in which female characters thrive. By this articulation, matrifocality is a capacious metaphor through which writers imagine women as having autonomy and power, even within patriarchal environments like the plantation, or colonial society.

Moreover, even though we recognize the currency and the tight focus for a season on female-authored constructions of mothering, we contend that this strand of critical exploration has matured and it is time to reinsert the voices and perspectives of men into parenting and motherland discourses. Our aim, therefore, does not perpetuate separatism nor does it entrench a female bias towards literary criticism and appreciation. Rather, this text is an effort to balance the scales by giving space and voice to the other sex. Our cross-selection of discourses offers a valid experiential perspective and lays the groundwork for meaningful spaces for recuperation and new beginnings. This foundation also allows us to identify main points of similarity and differences in themes and concerns, style and trends. The analytical insights thus aimed to formulate models and theories of matrifocality, ancestral motherlands, gender and gender relations.

Chapter 1 focused on a comparative reading between Kwynn Johnson's artwork and Miller's *The Last Warner Woman* to underscore the ways in which Caribbean fictions are replete with yearnings for mothers, mother cultures, and motherlands. These represent more than an imperative to demythologize an illusory colonial culture and motherland. We've argued that these longings become the sustaining ground for the emergence of radical modes of being that are vigorous and vital enough to withstand the impact of postcolonial anxieties, disillusionment and multiple secondary migrations. The bewildering series of migrations, urbanization and other forms of social dislocation, loss and adaptation of cultural and religious mores are also advanced in our comparative reading of Dionne Brand's *A Map to the Door of No Return* and Erna Brodber's *Nothing's Mat*. In *Map*, the black woman's pivotal role – as subservient worker in metropolitan societies and of Western capitalist systems – has heightened the issue of her identity and has contributed to her being associated with a range of perceptions and stereotypes. Yet, even within these violent and inequitable environments, like the plantation, or colonial society, spirit-based, matrilineal connections offer inextricable ties and power connections to pre-colonial African traditions that facilitate trajectories of negotiation and healing.

The trope of the more-mythic-than-real maternal figures is also inherent in Olive Senior's short story, "The Pain Tree" and Lawrence Scott's "The Wedding Photograph". Both Senior and Scott are invested in acts of intense recovery and representations of haunted memories. Their discourses lend credence to the correlation between trauma and ageing, cosmic loneliness and particularly the resurgence of traumatic memories when ageing persons forget to forget. In both texts, the protagonists are aroused from their forlorn states by constant acts of assessing and surveying their histories. Parallels were drawn between both writers' engagement with complicated shifts of time and narrative perspective to accommodate an in-depth exploration of the lives of women. Their fascination with the dissimulation imposed on surface reality is manifested in the creation of a fictional world, in which there is a seamless comingling between realism and surrealism, which bears a series of guises, some more disquieting than others.

Much the same dichotomy emerges in the fourth and fifth chapters, in which the black female body becomes a site of abuse and rivalry. Focus is on the womb of darkness; a clear association emerges between the peripheral status of the black woman and domestic crimes that ravage families and generate troubled futures. Nalo Hopkinson's complex deployment of the fantasy genre in *Midnight Robber*, and a case-study with a focus on the lived experience of early pregnancies attend to these realities.

A starker contrast emerges in chapter 6 between the trope of journeying and the adverse forces that continue to militate against women and families in the Caribbean. Marlon James' *A Brief History of Seven Killings* questions the political processes that devastate individuals, families, communities and nations, and spread their tentacles transnationally and transgenerationally. Based on an application of trauma theory, we've unearthed connections between criminality and silenced, submerged unresolved traumas on multiple levels in James' text. We argued that effective intervention must therefore excavate and address these rhizomes, while acknowledging more immediate invidious and societal conditions.

A primary pattern of maternal connections similarly emerges through an interaction with Nature, and a movement from the city to the village, and from metropolitan territories to the islands. Nevertheless, the pull of Western opportunities and the vicissitudes attendant to these struggles remains strong and lead to fictional situations that are discordant. This is effectively spatialized in Olive Senior's "Hurricane Story, 1903" (1944, 1951 and 1988), in which the Caribbean islands are framed within the threat of natural disasters. The rains provide the backdrop for intense inner journeys and increasing smallness of economic opportunity, which necessitates the search for a space to flourish. The tropes of escape and flight from social forces, painful dichotomies of race and class, and expelling wombs are similarly negotiated in David Dabydeen's *Turner*, Derek Walcott's *Omeros*, Erna Brodber's *The Rainmaker's Mistake* and Paul Keens-Douglas' "Story of a Storm – Ivan". Correlation between these writings and the chronicles of exile proved a fruitful field of enquiry into notions of painful alienation, denial of heritage, self-abasement, the independent mothers/women who fathered and the ability to resist destructive assimilation.

The intimate regions of the psyche were also probed in the eighth chapter, in which our readings of Wilson Harris' short stories advanced a search for pre-oedipal and pre-colonial innocence – a primal space, where the self is indistinct in form and embraced by maternal images. Nature provides a sustaining ground and sanctuary – a complex repertoire of values and nexus of ancestral, maternal power relations amidst accelerating forms of neocapitalism and dispossession in modern times. This is also a major concern for Jason Allen-Paisant and Grace Nichols, as demonstrated in their eco-poetry insofar that Nature offers an unaccustomed/alternative modality, which signifies new forms of initiation into self-knowledge and awakening.

Originary Violations, therefore, presents a composite critique in which matrifocality and maternal connections take on a multifaced and visceral function. For each protagonist, the affirmation of a sense of place and belonging is rooted in the relationship to the maternal womb – a site of pre-oedipal synthesis. We have also established the necessity of spiritual journeying and the dream of a return to spirit mothers, which come into prominence during seasons of intense psychic and physical distress. Thus, the orientation is towards community and communal values, which testify to abiding changes in attitudes and efforts regarding Caribbean women's capabilities, their roles and consciousness. Matrifocality bears the power to connect and liberate people in and of the African Caribbean diaspora and the world at large. It is, therefore, an essentially humanist brand that campaigns for an all-encompassing wholeness.

APPENDIX

Interview with Cecelia Beharry

Shalom House, 25 March 2014

Q. "Tell me something about your childhood, Cecelia."

Cecelia: "My childhood. . . . my childhood was hard . . . it was hard. Mother died at the age . . . when I was the age of five. Father was an alcoholic. So me and my two sisters and my brother, we were more or less left to fend for ourselves."

Q. "How did your Mom die?"

Cecelia: "From abuse . . . from my father."

Q. "Do you remember anything about it?"

Cecelia: "About the abuse? (musing) Well, at that age the only thing I really remember was running on a Thursday night . . . every Thursday night because that was the day he get pay . . . so he get pay and he would start to drink and it was the same drama every week."

Q. "Where did you run?"

Cecelia: "Ahm . . . back to my grandmother, my mother's mother. It was not too far . . . not too far from there. And then we would stay there until Sunday when he sober up. And then he would come back and beg, and she would take us and go back home again."

Q. "So your mom would take the children and go to your grandmother?"

Cecelia: (Interrupting) "Every single time . . . she would never leave anybody."

Q. "Do you remember your Mom?"

Cecelia: "No. Not even her face."

Q. "You don't remember her face?"

Cecelia: "No."

Q. "Do you have any photographs?"

Cecelia: "No. My father burned all after she died."

Q. "What was your father like (pause) when he wasn't drunk?"

Cecelia: "Nice. He was nice. I remember even after she died, he would drink and ting, but then I would remember hearing him crying in the night. And then he would get up early in the morning and he would cook, wash (losing composure), go to work. (Tears beginning to flow). And then it would be all the same thing on a Thursday (sniffling) . . . Well, there was nobody to beat because by that time my mother was dead. He would stay out all weekend drinking and he would come back sometimes Sunday morning." (Weeping, long pause)

Q. "Humm. You want to go ahead?"

Cecelia: "Um hum. Ahm . . . there was a point in time when it was every weekend he would be out. And then there was a Saturday night when the three of us, me and my two sisters – one older, one younger – ahm, we in the house. It didn't really have windows and doors . . . there was no electricity. Somebody came in the house behind my sister, Karen. Well, we managed . . . after we started to bawl and ting in the middle of the night, the person left. And after that my grandmother took us from there. We went to live with my grandmother."

Q. "How old were you?"

Cecelia: "At that time, I probably was about eight. We went to live with my grandmother. Well, she was old and it was three of us – three extra mouths to feed. So she thought it was too much. (Long pause, weeping and sniffling). So, we would spend every week by somebody different . . . a different aunt . . . a different somebody because by the end of the day they realize it was a lot to take. One day, my big sister say it was too much and we would go back to the same house . . . which we did."

Q. "Your father was still alive?"

Cecelia: "Yeah, he had moved on. He was living with another woman, had somebody else, went to live with another woman and we stayed there for a couple years. Most days it don't have anything to eat. You don't know what the next day would bring."

Q. "How old was Karen when you went back?"

Cecelia: "Karen was about eighteen. She was working in a cloth store."

Q. "So, almost four to five years you went from place to place and when she was eighteen she took you all back."

Cecelia: "Karen ended up meeting somebody and he started financially to help her. He started to give her money so we was able to get little food off and on."

Q. "So when you couldn't buy food, how did you all live?"

Cecelia: "From the cocoa . . . eating cocoa, eating orange, eating mango, eating whatever was around."

Q. "In the yard?"

Cecelia: "It had a small estate everybody used to go to pass through to go to the river and there was plenty oranges. It had citrus and whatever, so most days that's what we had." (long pause)

Q. "You all pulled together, eh?"

Cecelia: "Um hum." (musing)

Q. "Your dad used to come to see you?"

Cecelia: "Ahm, off and on, off and on. And then he end up getting sick. By that time I was thirteen and because there was nobody to take care of me, I end up with husband (voice softer and weeping more intense). So, at the age of thirteen I went to live with somebody and I had my first child at sixteen."

Q. "Was he good to you?"

Cecelia: "At the starting, yes." (Long pause and intense weeping)

Q. "If you want to stop at any time, it's okay, you know."

Cecelia: "No."

Q. "So at thirteen years old . . . umh . . . how old was he?"

Cecelia: "Twenty."

Q. "Tell me about the experience of having your first baby. How did you feel?"

Cecelia: "I guess not knowing much about that kind of life at the age of sixteen, you telling yourself you is a big woman. You proud to be pregnant . . . not even know what to expect when you reach in the hospital . . . all of that was . . . I guess it was like a little girl getting a dolly, you know. Yuh happy, proud to be a mother because that's all you know is you're a mother now."

Q. "You said not knowing the consequences. So if you had a choice you would have done it differently?"

Cecelia: "Uh hum. As I say, it started out well, but he refused to work and you have two hungry babies crying. At the age of sixteen, you didn't really go to school . . . nobody giving you a proper job so it was hard to take care of two babies." (Weeping and sniffling)

Q. "You went to primary school?"

Cecelia nods.

Q. "And you finished primary school?"

Cecelia: "Ahm. But I didn't pass Common Entrance,[1] so I went to post primary. And just before I had to do the exam is when I met those children father."

Q: So, you have your first baby at sixteen. When did you have your second?"

Cecelia: "Seventeen."

Q. "Did you know anything about birth control in those days?"

Cecelia: "Well, after my daughter, yes."

Q. "Before, you didn't know that you could –"

Cecelia (interrupting): "No."

Q. "How did you find out?"

Cecelia: "You had to join the clinic when you got pregnant. At that young age the nurses started talking to you, 'If you keep going like this, you would end up with twelve children. There is free family planning, so come.'"

Q. "So how was it with the children?"

Cecelia: "It was hard until I started to get little one-day jobs here and there, so I was able to get the important things – the milk, the pampers . . . and then I started to get a little more work and I decided that my children was not going to live the way that I live So all my life what I did . . . " (more intense weeping)

Q. "You have a lot of tears to cry . . . Where were you living with your partner at the time?"

Cecelia: "By his mother." (sniffling)

Q. "How did that work out for you?"

Cecelia: "Well, it had ups and it had downs. For one thing, a young woman living in the in-laws' home with a lot of other young women can't work. It doh ever work! One day, somebody is talking to you and the next day, this one, they not talking to you. You not even sure why . . . you know. At the start of it, I was living inside of their house, so that part of it wasn't easy. So I started to work and I started to put a little money together. Then I say, we can put on a little room at the side, a little kitchen, a little this and that, until eventually we got from inside of their house but I was still in the yard."

Q. "But you make it seem it was your work funded all of this. Is that right?"

Cecelia: "Most of it. You see, he never like working. Every time he get a job is because he get sick or something go wrong why he can't go to work the next day. So most times he get a job, it last three days."

Q. "Was he good with the children?"

Cecelia: "Yes, he was."

Q. "So, he would take care of them when you went out to work?"

Cecelia: "By the time I reach home, everybody bathe, everybody clean, homework finish. He was good with them. That was more or less the only help that I got."

Q. "What advice would you give to a young woman in the situation that you were in then?"

Cecelia: "Well, today, the majority of young women, they have parents looking over them, trying to give them advice and whatever. In my day, I did not have that . . . there was nobody. The first mistake that I made, which I would tell them, whatever happens, to stay in school. It's something that I learned, that at whatever age in your life, there will be a man there for you, so don't rush into things like that."

Q. "Uhm . . . Ever thought of going back to school?"

Cecelia: "Yes, but the way I had to work to look after my children, I think it just sink into my system – just work, work, work, work! Never the time and effort to do it."

Q. "How old are you now? Do you think you can go back to school?"

Cecelia: "I am forty-eight . . . well, I guess I could." (voice trails off, eyes averted)

Q. "Tell me how things are today . . . how things worked out for you and your children.

Cecelia: "Eventually, I left. My son was seventeen, my daughter was sixteen. The same age I was when . . . He started to fool around with young girls the same age as my daughter. So I made the decision. I talked to my children. They decided that they wanted to stay. It was the only life that they knew, and he was a good father to them . . . so I left. Now, before I left, I started to pay for a piece of land. I was paying two hundred dollars a month for the land, but I left before I was finished paying for it.

"I started to rent a little house. I ended up meeting somebody. He turned out to be very abusive. [weeping and sniffling] He put me in the hospital with a stab wound in my back. I ended up building a little house on the land, but he burned it down flat. So, I end up by my sisters.

With all of that, I kept a good relationship with my children [weeping and sniffling], kept working . . . and about three years after that, I met my second husband, who, ahm, decided from day one that he was going to help me. So, he helped me to build back a little house. He didn't have much, I didn't have much . . . I had a mattress, I was sleeping on the floor, but we made it. He had his own. I had mines. Five years after that, I went to live with him. After eight years into the relationship, we get married. I have a good life with him – he works hard, takes care of me and I have a good relationship with my children."

Q. "There is a lot of pain. You've cried from the beginning of the interview. From the minute you started, you cried. Why is there so much pain still?"

Cecelia: "Well, I think I am a person that [sniffling] holds on to things. The majority of the times, you tell yourself you're strong, you can handle it, but then off and on . . . there is that little time when it gets to you. The thing is, I don't forget . . . I don't forget."

Q. "Have you forgiven your father for what he did?"

Cecelia: "I think so. Before he died, he had on three occasions three strokes. When I look at him in hospital or wherever to see the way that he suffered, I didn't have a choice."

Q. "And your first husband?"

Cecelia: "Well, I don't know for him. When I look at him, the only thing now all I feel for him is pity."

Q. "Tell me about the good things in your life."

Cecelia: "The good thing in my life it that my two children are able. I put them through school. My son, he is now a supervisor at the *Trinidad Guardian*. My daughter, she is married, and she has a son, good husband. She is not employed out there, but she does her little thing at home to make ends meet. It's good when I see them. They're happy and I know that they did not go through what I had to go through, to suffer as I suffered. I have an extremely good relationship with my two sisters and my brother, and I have a marriage that I am determined to make work. And this time, I have a good husband."

Q. "Lots of blessings." (laughter)

Cecelia: "And I have more work than I can handle at this time."

Q. "You are happy with your home?"

Cecelia: "I was able to build a home with my husband so big there are rooms I don't go into. I have a good home . . . never took a loan, never borrowed . . . the same way I work Sunday to Sunday is the same way that he worked."

Q. "So what are you going to do about the pain, girl?"

(No response. She shakes her head from side to side.)

Q. "I am hoping that you talking about your experience this way will help other young women. Any last words you'd like to say?"

Cecelia: "Young women should not rush into these things . . . Everybody did well. My sisters have all done well. My big sister, she is married. She has three children . . . beautiful . . . but all of this is not possible without God. The same way he took me out, someone else will be able to get out."

Notes

Introduction

1. Simey (1946, 82) observes, "The pattern of family formation in the Caribbean… is characterized by a high level of non-legal unions, the prevalence of 'household' over 'family' units and a high level of households headed by women."

Chapter 1

1. The 2010 Haitian earthquake led to the deaths of some three hundred thousand persons, rendered two million homeless and impacted the lives of more than three million. The drawings were shown both in Trinidad as a dissertation exhibition and in Jacmel, Haiti, in 2013. The latter was intended to garner the response of the Jacmelians to the representation of their environment as a lived ruinscape.

Chapter 2

1. "Mapping Police Violence." *Police Violence Report 2023*. https://mappingpoliceviolence.org.
2. Although Maud is not at the centre of the mat nor the family, her story acts as a point from which the rest of the mat grows and develops.
3. Renu Juneja suggests that in Caribbean women's writing, orality "functions as a counter-discourse to the voicelessness [. . .]. Telling of stories, listening to stories is an important element in the lives of these women for these stories embody the counter-culture and subvert the norms of established culture" (Juneja 1996, 27).

Chapter 3

1. Toni Morrison, *Beloved* (New York: Penguin Books, 1988). Consider, for example, Toni Morrison's elder Baby Suggs, who teaches the damaged and mutilated emancipated enslaved folk to love themselves (*Beloved*). This is a central theme for Paule Marshall, an American writer of Barbadian lineage,

who evokes matriarchs, spiritual mothers and maternal ancestresses in the majority of her fictional representations. Cases in point include Mrs Thompson (*Brown Girls, Brown Stones),* who forms a safety net for the disoriented, culturally adrift young protagonist and the Barbadian grandmother "To Da-duh In Memoriam", who matches wits with her US-born grandchild. Da-duh, who embodies the folk wisdom of the elders and cultural rooting in the Caribbean birthplace, is fearful of machines. She dies during the 1937 air raids. Marshall's spiritual mothers in *Praise Song for the Widow* administer traditional healing practices as they accompany the protagonist on her journey towards spiritual awakening. Healing mothers also take centre stage in the work of Jamaican Erna Brodber. In *Nothing's Mat,* matriarchs are the keepers of an intricately woven mat which represents hitherto masked fractal, as opposed to fragmented, family networks, interconnected memories and healing practices.

2. Morrison, *Black Women Writers,* 339. This stance is not uniform. In Zora Neale Hurston's *Their Eyes are Watching God,* Nanny, the grandmother figure ravaged by slavery, cultural orphanage and unending life crises, survives as a soul-destroying figure whose craving for security leads her to usher her frisky young granddaughter, Janie, into the safe harbour of a loveless marriage to an exploitative older man. Her fragmentation is succinctly expressed in her plea, "Put me down gently Janie. Ah'm a cracked plate" (Hurston 1937, 17).

Chapter 4

1. Jones, Jemmott and Bailey note in their 2009 study that the definition of incest, which has been generally understood as meaning sexual intercourse between biologically related family members, is now being broadened in popular perception to include "sex with non-biological parents such as step-parents and adoptive children". The researchers surmise that this may be related to wider prevalence of these family forms (Jones, Jemmott, and Bailey 2009, 12).
2. In the context of the Caribbean, the early onset of sexual activity has been identified as a contributory factor in the spread of HIV infection in the region. The gravity of the situation was highlighted in a World Health Organization 2000 study, which found that 42.8 per cent of sexually active Caribbean children had their first sexual intercourse before the age of ten. And by the time a young person reached between the ages of sixteen and eighteen, approximately 29.8 per cent had had more than five sexual partners. Many of these were forced sexual encounters.

3. In Trinidad and Tobago, for example, where multiple marriage laws coexisted up until the mid-2010s, Hindu girls could be legally married from age twelve with parental consent. This was at odds with legislation defining statutory rape. However, those marriage laws were amended in 2017 and child marriage is now illegal.
4. Rape and sexual violence in the imperial context were major tools for asserting ethnic dominance. In Lamming's *Water with Berries,* sexual subordination of women was a fundamental facet of the arsenal which men of the dominant race deployed in their conquest of subordinate races. Lamming's fictions testify about the abhorrent revenge outworkings of master/slave antipathies, through rape and bestiality, inscribed on the master's daughter as ethnic boundary marker and repository of racial superiority.
5. The perpetration of violence against the defiling other – ethnic migrants, refugees, strangers – in support of state interest in preserving stereotypical purities was the subtext of 2018 discourses on laws and walls to enhance national border protection, articulated most vociferously by the United States' Trump-led administration.
6. Postcolonial deployment and critique of trauma demonstrate both its usefulness and its limited applicability to social scenarios of the New World nations. The focus on the highly individualized subject of the Oedipal/familial narrative often does not take into account mass social suffering and the attendant collective nature of trauma. Politically motivated acts of violence assault entire racial minorities, classes and even nations when rogue states turn upon and eat their own children. The focus on trauma as inducing psychic incapacitation and loss of the facility for symbolic representation tends to minimize material dimensions of loss. Additionally, focus on the temporal dislocation inflicted by trauma can obscure the spatial outworkings of the traumatizing catalysts.
7. In the *Dictionary of the English/Creole of Trinidad and Tobago,* Lise Winer indicates that Midnight Robbers first appeared in the early twentieth century in this country in bands of thirty to forty members. In the 1950s, robber bands decreased in size to six or seven members only. Today, the Midnight Robber is a solitary masquerade figure.

Chapter 5

1. Under the UN Convention on the Rights of the Child, anyone under age eighteen is considered a child (Williamson 2013, 4).

Chapter 6

1. The notion is related to Toni Morrison's concept of "unspeakable things spoken", which points to silences and absences that constitute loud declarations of origins and continuities. See "Unspeakable Things Unspoken: The Afro-American Presence in American Literature" (The Tanner Lectures on Human Values, University of Michigan, 7 October 1988). https://tannerlectures.utah.edu/_documents/a-to-z/m/morrison90.pdf.
2. This correlation is succinctly expressed in Derek Walcott's poem, "Laventille", as manifesting the dark underbelly of imperialism and its horrendous outgrowth:

   "Something inside is laid wide like a wound,
   some open passage that has cleft the brain,
   some deep, amnesiac blow. We left
   somewhere a life we never found,
   customs and gods that are not born again,
   some crib, some grille of light
   clanged shut on us in bondage, and withheld
   us from that world below us and beyond,
   and in its swaddling cerements we're still bound."
   —*Derek Walcott, Collected Poems, 1948–1984 (1992, 85).*

3. See Ron Eyerman, *Cultural Trauma: Slavery and the Formation of African American Identity* (2001); Stef Craps and Gert Buelens, "Introduction: Postcolonial Trauma Novels" in *Studies in the Novel* (2008, 1–12): Stef Craps, *Postcolonial Witnessing: Trauma Out of Bounds* (2013); Paula Morgan and Valerie Youssef, *Writing Rage: Unmasking Violence in Caribbean Discourse* (2006); and Morgan, *Terror and the Time* (2014).
4. "Already we have a significant cadre of youth who don't seem to me to believe anything, even their own lives, even the value of their own lives. The casual way with which they take lives and in which they seem to surrender their own is a signal that we are already, in that respect, at what I have termed terminality, that is, definitely a worst case – terminality. The question is how do we turn that kind of thing around. I can't say I know,"– Gordon Rohlehr, interview by Paula Morgan, in "From Apocalypse to Awakenings – Interviews with Gordon Rohlehr," *Tout Moun: Caribbean Journal of Cultural Studies* 2, no.1 (October 2013): 4. https://journals.sta.uwi.edu/toutmoun/papers/oct13/Tout_Moun_2_MORGAN_Rohlehr_Interviews.pdf.

Chapter 7

1. The lexical history of the term 'hurricane', derived from archival research is instructive. David Longshore avers that the Mayan civilization referred to hurricanes as Huracán, the deity responsible for the destructive winds that raged through communities. The Guyanese critic, Wilson Harris, also recuperates the Carib myth of "Yurokon", who embodies both the autumnal equinox and the idea of twinship, since Yurokon is both a mortal and immortal being. In Carib lore, Yurokon, who is half-man, half-god, can transmute at will into the wind. The precepts that constitute indigenous meteorology involves the prediction of the monsoons as well as moralistic judgement. These mythological representations were integral to creation stories that include fables of storm figures who punish transgression and wield divine omnipotence over harvest and crop seasons, birth and death cycles, forest usage, warfare and trade. Encoded in the creative works of Harris and other Caribbean writers, these native storm epistemologies have been deployed as symbols of warnings and cultural pathways, where life and daily living practices are altered by irruptive forces that bring change. See Longshore in *Encyclopedia of Hurricanes, Typhoons, and Cycles*, New Edition (New York: Checkmark Books, 2008), 397 and Wilson Harris, "Yurokon," in *The Sleepers of Roraima and the Age of the Rainmakers* (Leeds: Peepal Tree Press, 2017), 94.
2. See http://www.ancient-mythology.com/mayan/huracan.php).
3. *The Rainmaker's Mistake* by Erna Brodber, published in 2008, is an allegory that addresses issues of patriarchy, myth-making, attempting to deal particularly with the myth of origin. The novel begins with a description of the white plantation owner, Mr Charlie, by the narrative voice, Queenie. Mr Charlie is the benevolent master, the originator and sustainer of identity and existence of the enslaved: "We all look alike: only Mr Charlie does not look like us. Because he is our creator . . . We his creations are all yams. Any difference is under the skin Woodville tells us, and is the difference in our personality . . . We began as yams. Mr Charlie's seeds turned into yams, into us" (Brodber 2008, 8). It is ironic that Mr Charlie uses yams, which have traditionally been seen as a symbol of West African fertility, to demystify the myth of origins of his slaves. Mr Charlie, in effect, has recreated his slave children. There is the celebration of Founders Day every year, where their existence is celebrated, although Queenie notes that the yams are only grown in Mr Charlie's backyard, so no one really knows them. Founders Day is a patriarchal myth of origin and the slaves are all products of the slave master, who controls all fertility. There is absolutely no sense of unique selfhood or identity.

4. John Ruskin was an admiring contemporary critic who not only gave a rapturous account of Turner's painting, but also came to own the picture when it was purchased for him by his father in 1872. See "Of Water, as Painted by Turner".
5. "Re-membering our Scattered Skeletons: Inscribing the *Zong* Massacre in Caribbean Literature." *Lucayos Journal of College of the Bahamas* Vol. 1 (2008): 60–77.
6. Scholars such as Charlotte McClure and Víctor Figueroa have long contended that Walcott imbues the character Helen with layers of mythic parallels. The poet's transposing of the Aegean myth to the island environment of the Caribbean conjures a narrative design of a New World epic that displays his artistic wrestle with mimicry and originality. In his reinvention of the Helen (of Troy) archetype into a "fine local woman" (Walcott 1990, 322), whose powerful force of physical beauty seduces the onlooker – native and foreigner – Walcott introduces the idea of neo-enslavement and neo-colonialism, which is demonstrated when she offers refutations of any servile image of both the island and the islanders. Helen protests that the "tourist . . . men/only out to touch local girls; every minute [she] was brushing their hand from her backside so one day/she get fed up with all their nastiness" (Walcott 1990, 33–34).

Chapter 8

1. The first edition of this chapter was originally published by the *American Studies Journal*, vol. 60, nos. 3/4 (2001): 61–75. Appreciation is extended to the journal for authorizing the reprint of this revised version.
2. While the scope of this chapter does not permit an extensive overview of the Caribbean's intellectual history, it is important to note that there are various phases to Caribbean literature. The fighting or early anti-colonial category that emerged in the 1950s gave epistemic and thematic saliency to revolutionary and material social action. Opposed to Europeanized-inflected discourses, which negated the ontologies of Caribbean persons, intellectuals like Frantz Fanon and C.L.R. James deployed political symbolism and naturalist existentialism, which affirmed the self-rule of societies and people-groups. However, beyond the realism of the canonical writers was a cultural awakening that marked a revival of folk culture in order to assert a more inclusive expression of resistance towards neocolonial forces. This community of intellectuals was known as the poeticist voices, which included figures such as Earl Lovelace, Derek Walcott, Kamau Brathwaite, George Lamming, Wilson Harris and

others, whose works championed causes of intercultural reconciliation, ecological preservation, cosmic-human interrelatedness and syncretic spirituality. Discourses of this nature, effectively facilitated modalities of self-autonomy, healing, negotiation and affective bonding. This shift became definitive after independence (1960s onwards) and continue through to the current era. For further insight into the history of Caribbean intellectualism, see Silvio Torres-Saillant's *Caribbean Poetics: Toward an Aesthetic of West Indian Literature* (1997) and Paget Henry's *Caliban's Reason: Introducing Afro-Caribbean Philosophy* (2000).

3. Anthropologist and theoretician Eduardo Viveros de Castro has dedicated the last four decades of his life to assessing the ontologies of the South American and Caribbean First Peoples. His discipline initiates the ontological turn within Amazonia communities, and offers a decolonial method to understanding the group's ideologies, religion, politics, commerce models and cultural pathways. His research addresses the absence of Indigenous cultures in literary criticism and production from the 1970s onwards and seeks to fill the gap. He accomplishes this by assessing the worth of Amazonia ecology and the multiplicity of interactions between natural and social agents – a disposition that has been eschewed by Eurocentric discourses. De Castro's multidisciplinary works include *Cannibal Metaphysics* (2015a), *From the Enemy's Point of View: Humanity and Divinity in an Amazonian Society* (2020), and *The Relative Native: Essays on Indigenous Conceptual Worlds* (2015b).
4. Although the term 'Amerindian' is arguably outdated and has been replaced by Indigenous in contemporary discourses, the phrase is referred to in this chapter by its original appearance in de Castro's and Harris' respective texts. It is also imperative to note that the titles "First Peoples", "Amerindian" and "Indigenous" are used interchangeably within Caribbean criticism. According to the scholarship of Gordon Rohlehr in "Folk Research: Fossil and Living Bone" (2007), Rose-Marie Belle Antoine, in her keynote speech entitled, "Setting the Stage – an overview of race, discrimination, and ESC in North America" (2013), and Jennifer Rahim, in "Issues and Developments in Caribbean Literary Theory and Criticism" (2013), the expressions have been derived from the oral traditions used to depict the communities of the Caribbean's first inhabitants.
5. The myth of Quetzalcoatl, as deployed in this narrative, illustrates Harris' cosmo-political vision and his emphasis on the entanglements between forests and nature-based communities. The multiplicity of relations established between different mythologies and Indigenous communities calls for a

reappreciation of the role of shamans and deities as brokers, mediators and translators among diverse spaces.

Chapter 9

1. By combining the works of Nichols and Allen-Paisant, the aim is in part, to energize a syncretic and eclectic quest in reading Caribbean narratives, and to demonstrate that cultural interlockings indeed combine to produce what Wilson Harris calls a collective Caribbean consciousness. Where Nichols turns to Indigenous cosmologies to recover a liberatory poetics within a decidedly self-referential matrix, Allen-Paisant probes ideas of freedom and the combatting of ontological relegation through the apparatus of Afro-Caribbean cosmological sensibilities. For Allen-Paisant, nature operates as an extended metaphor for exploring issues of black existence and the intricacies of personal histories that move in tandem with ancestral resemblances – thus yielding greater possibilities for unity in his creative imagination.
2. In the context of the formation of maroon communities, it is believed that the mountains, the coast and the forests came to embody a black domain that existed outside state control and was a space where the seeds of guerrilla resistance began to germinate. See Lisabeth Paravisini-Gerbert and Margarite Fernandez Olmos in "Historical Background" to *Creole Religions of the Caribbean: An Introduction from Vodou and Santería to Obeah and Espiritismo*, 26.

Appendix

1. The Common Entrance exam was a competitive test given to pupils at the end of Standard 5 in primary school to attain a place at one of the secondary schools across the country. It has been replaced by the Secondary Entrance Assessment.

References

Abraham, Nicolas, and Maria Torok. 1994. *The Shell and the Kernel: Renewals of Psychoanalysis*, Volume 1. Edited, translated and introduced by Nicholas T. Rand. Chicago and London: Chicago University Press.

Allen-Paisant, Jason. 2021. *Thinking With Trees*. Manchester: Carcanet Press. Kindle.

American Psychiatric Association. 2013. *Diagnostic and Statistical Manual of Mental Disorders, Fifth Edition*. Arlington, VA: American Psychiatric Association.

Anatol, Giselle. 2000. "Maternal Discourses in Nalo Hopkinson's *Midnight Robber*." *African American Review* 40 (1): 111–24.

———. 1998. "Mother Countries, Motherlands, and Mother Love: Representations of Motherhood in Twentieth-Century Caribbean Women's Literature." PhD diss., University of Kansas.

Antoine, Rose-Marie Belle. 2013. "Setting the Stage – an overview of race, discrimination, and ESC in North America." Keynote speech, Special Forum on Race, Discrimination and Economic, Social and Cultural Rights in North America, 23 November. Montreal: McGill University. https://www.oas.org/es/cidh/afrodescendientes/docs/pdf/discursormba-forum-montreal-nov22,2013.pdf.

Ayres, Robert. 2006. *Crime and Violence as Development Issues in Latin America and the Caribbean*. Washington, DC: World Bank.

Azevedo, Joao Pedro, Marta Favara, Sarah E. Haddock, Luis F. Lopez-Calva, Miriam Muller, and Elizaveta Perove. 2012. *Teenage Pregnancy and Opportunity in Latin America and the Caribbean: on Teenage Fertility Decisions, Poverty and Economic Achievement*. Washington, DC: World Bank.

Balaev, Michelle. 2008. "Trends in Literary Trauma." *Mosaic* 41 (2): 149–65. https://doi.org/10.1057/9781137365941_1.

Beckles, Hilary M. 2000. *Natural Rebels: A Social History of Enslaved Black Women in Barbados*. New Brunswick, NJ: Rutgers University Press.

Benitez-Rojo, Antonio. 1998. "Three Words towards Creolization." In *Caribbean Creolization*, edited by Kathleen M. Balutansky and Marie-Agnes Sourieau. Kingston: University of the West Indies Press.

Bennett-Coverley, Louise. 1966. "Colonization in Reverse." https://www.poetrybyheart.org.uk/poems/colonization-in-reverse.

Bergen-Cico, Dessa Kristen, Arnett Haygood-El, Timothy Noble Jennings-Bey, and Sandra D. Lane. 2014. "Street Addiction: A Proposed Theoretical Model for Understanding the Draw of Street Life and Gang Activity." *Addiction Research & Theory* 22 (1): 15–26. https://doi.org/10.3109/16066359.2012.759942.

Birbalsingh, Frank. 1998. "Guyana: A Nation in Transit – Burnham's Role." In *From Pillar to Post: The Indo-Caribbean Diaspora*, 11. Toronto: TSAR Publications.

Bhabha, Homi. 1992. "The World and the Home." *Social Text* nos. 31/32: 141–53. https://doi.org/10.2307/466222.

Blincoe, Nicholas. 2015. "A Brief History of Seven Killings by Marlon James, Review: 'Vivid and Powerful.'" *The Telegraph*, 29 July. https://www.telegraph.co.uk/culture/books/bookreviews/11213049/A-Brief-History-of-Seven-Killings-by-Marlon-James.html.

Boulter, Jonathan. 2011. *Melancholy and the Archive: Trauma, Memory, and History in the Contemporary Novel*. London: Continuum.

Boyle, Elizabeth. 2009. "Vanishing Bodies: 'Race' and Technology in Nalo Hopkinson's *Midnight Robber*." *African Identities* 7 (2): 177–91. https://doi.org/10.1080/14725840902808868.

Brand, Dionne. 2001. *A Map to the Door of No Return*. Toronto: Vintage Canada.

Brathwaite, Kamau. 1992. "Caliban's Guarden." *Wasafiri* 8 (16): 2–6.

———.1983. "Caribbean Culture: Two Paradigms." In *Missile and Capsule*, edited by J. Martani. Bremen: Bremen University Press.

———.1974. *Caribbean Man in Time and Space*, 1–14. Kingston: Savacou.

———. 1985. "Metaphors of Underdevelopment: A Proem for Hernan Cortez." In *New England Review and Bread Loaf Quarterly* 7 (4): 453–76.

———. 1986. *Roots*. Havana: Casa de las Americas.

Brereton, Bridget. 2010. "The Historical Background to the Culture of Violence in Trinidad and Tobago." *Caribbean Review of Gender Studies: The Culture of Violence in Trinidad and Tobago: A Case Study*, edited by Valerie Youssef and Paula Morgan, 4: 1–16. https://sta.uwi.edu/crgs/february2010/journals/BridgetBrereton.pdf.

Brereton, Bridget, and Kevin A. Yelvington. 1999. *The Colonial Caribbean in Transition: Essays on Post-Emancipation Social and Cultural History*. Kingston: University of the West Indies Press.

Brodber, Erna. 2014. *Nothing's Mat: A Novel*. Kingston: University of the West Indies Press.

———.2003. *The Continent of Black Consciousness: On the History of the African Diaspora from Slavery to the Present Day*. London: New Beacon Books.

———. 2007. *The Rainmaker's Mistake*. London: New Beacon Books.

Butler, Judith. 2009. *Frames of War: When is Life Grievable?* London: Verso.

Carby, Hazel V. 1998. *Race Men*. Cambridge, MA: Harvard University Press.

Carew, Jan. 2006. "Heirs of All Time." *Caribbean Literature in a Global Context*, edited by Funso Aiyejina and Paula Morgan, 23. San Juan: Lexicon Press.

Carter, Martin. 2006. *University of Hunger: Collected Poems & Selected Prose*. Hexham: Bloodaxe Books.

Caruth, Cathy. 1966. *Unclaimed Experience: Trauma, Narrative, and History*. Baltimore: Johns Hopkins University Press.

Cobham, Rhonda. 1993. "Revisioning Our Kumblas: Transforming Feminist and Nationalist Agendas in Three Caribbean Women's Texts." *Callaloo* 16 (1): 44–64. https://doi.org/10.2307/2931815.

Cooper, Carolyn. 1994. "Something Ancestral Recaptured': Spirit Possession as Trope in Selected Feminist Fictions of the African Diaspora." In *Motherlands: Black Women's Writing from Africa, the Caribbean and South Asia*, edited by Susheila Nasta, 64–87. New Brunswick, NJ: Rutgers University Press.

Craps, Stef. 2013. *Postcolonial Witnessing: Trauma Out of Bounds*. London: Palgrave Macmillan.

Craps, Stef, and Gert Buelens. 2008. "Introduction: Postcolonial Trauma Novels." *Studies in the Novel* 40 (1–2): 1–12. https://doi.org/10.1353/sdn.0.0008.

Curtis, Shirley. 2011. "A Health Empowerment Theory Approach to Pregnant Adolescents 18 and 19 Years of Age in the Bahamas." PhD diss., University of Miami.

Dabydeen, David. 2002. *Turner: New and Selected Poems*. Leeds: Peepal Tree Press.

D'Aguiar, Fred. 2015. *Feeding the Ghosts*. Long Grove: Waveland Press.

Davin, Anna. 1978. "Imperialism and Motherhood." *History Workshop Journal* 5 (1): 9–66. https://doi.org/10.1093/hwj/5.1.9.

Delfino, Gianluca. 2001. "Pre-Columbian Legacies." In *Time, History, and Philosophy in the Works of Wilson Harris*, 134–74. New York: Columbia University Press.

Derrida, Jacques. 1994. *Specters of Marx: The State of the Debt, the Work of Mourning and the New International*. New York: Routledge.

Dash, J. Michael. 1998. *The Other America: Caribbean Literature in a New World Context*. Virginia: University of Virginia Press.

de Castro, Eduardo Viveiros. 2012. "Cosmological Perspectivism in Amazonia and Elsewhere." *HAU Journal of Ethnographic Theory* 1 (April): 83–117.

———. 2015a. *Cannibal Metaphysics*. Minnesota: University of Minnesota Press.

———. 2015b. *The Relative Native: Essays on Indigenous Conceptual Worlds*. Chicago: Hau Books.

———. 2020. *From the Enemy's Point of View: Humanity and Divinity in an Amazonian Society*. Chicago: University of Chicago Press.

DeLoughrey, Elizabeth M., and George B. Handley, eds. 2011. "Introduction: Towards an Aesthetics of the Earth." In *Postcolonial Ecologies: Literatures of the Environment*, 3–39. New York and Oxford: Oxford University Press.

de Montellano, Bernard Ortiz. 1990. "Aztec Religion Worldview and Medicine." In *Aztec Medicine, Health, and Nutrition*, 46–48. New Brunswick, NJ: Rutgers University Press.

D'haen, Theo. 2015. "Cultural Memory and the Postcolonial." In *Littératures, Poétiques, Mondes: Comparative Literature and Its Many Divergent Paths*, edited by Micéala Symington. Paris: Honoré Champion.

Dirlik, Arif. 2004. "Spectres of the Third World: Global Modernity and the End of the Three Worlds." *Third World Quarterly* 25 (1) (February): 131–48. https://doi.org/10.1080/0143659042000185372.

Doyle, Laura Anne. 1994. *Bordering on the Body: Racial Matrix of Modern Fiction and Culture*. Oxford: Oxford University Press.

Drake, Sandra. 1986. "Language and Revolutionary Hope as Immanent Moment." In *Wilson Harris and the Modern Tradition: A New Architecture of the World*, 177. Westport, CT: Greenwood Press.

Drayton, Vonna Lou Caleb. 2002. "Contraceptive Use Among Jamaican Teenage Mothers." *Revista Panamericana de Salud Pública* 11: 150–57.

Dutton, Daniel G. 1993. *The Abusive Personality: Violence and Control in Intimate Relationships*. New York and London: Guilford Press.

Eglash, Ron. 1999. "Introduction to Fractal Geometry." In *African Fractals: Modern Computing and Indigenous Design*. New Brunswick, NJ: Rutgers University Press.

Eth, Spencer, and Robert S. Phynos. 1985. "Developmental Perspectives on Psychic Trauma in Childhood". In *Trauma and Its Wake: The Study and Treatment of Post-traumatic Stress Disorder*, edited by Charles Figley, 36–55. Bristol, PA: Brunner/Mazel.

Eyerman, Ron. 2001. *Cultural Trauma: Slavery and the Formation of African American Identity*. Cambridge: Cambridge University Press.

Farage, Nádia, and Maria Aparecida de Campos Brando Santilli. 1997. "Flores da fala: praticas retoricas entre os wapishana."

Ferguson, Moira. 1994. *Jamaica Kincaid: Where the Land Meets the Body*. Charlottesville: University Press of Virginia.

Figueroa, Víctor. 2007. "Encomium of Helen: Derek Walcott's Ethical Twist in *Omeros*." *Twentieth Century Literature* 53 (1): 23–39.

Flax, Jane. 2014. *Disputed Subjects: Essays on Psychoanalysis, Politics and Philosophy.* London and New York: Routledge.

Fraser, Rhone. 2017. "Confronting Neocolonialism: An Evaluation of Marlon James' *A Brief History of Seven Killings.*" *Caribbean Quarterly* 63 (1): 67–82. https://doi.org/10.1080/00086495.2017.1302155.

Gaillot, Nathalie Elvire. 2007. "Mothering Nation: Caribbean Women Writers Interrogating National Identity through Works of Fiction." PhD diss., University of Minnesota.

Galeano, Eduardo. 1997. "Lust for Gold, Lust for Silver." In *Open Veins of Latin America: Five Centuries of the Pillage of a Continent,* 11–58. New York: Monthly Review Press.

Gilkes, Michael, ed. 1989. "Introduction." In *The Literate Imagination: Essays on the Novels of Wilson Harris,* 1–10. London: Macmillan.

Gilroy, Paul. 1993. *The Black Atlantic: Modernity and Double Consciousness.* Cambridge, MA: Harvard University Press.

Glissant, Edouard. 1989a. "The Quarrel with History." In *Caribbean Discourse: Selected Essays,* 61–66. Charlottesville: University of Virginia Press.

———. 1989b. "Cross-Cultural Poetics." In *Caribbean Discourse: Selected Essays,* 104–9. Charlottesville: University of Virginia Press.

———. 1997. *Poetics of Relation.* Ann Arbor: University of Michigan Press.

Gomes, Cristina. 2012. "Adolescent fertility in selected countries of Latin America and the Caribbean." *Journal of Public Health and Epidemiology* 4 (5): 133–40. http://www.academicjournals.org/JPHE.

Grant, Damien. (1970) 2019. "Introduction." In *Realism (The Critical Idiom Reissued),* 1–19. Reprint, New York: Routledge.

Hall, Stuart, and Paul Du Gay. 2012. *Questions of Cultural Identity.* London: SAGE Publications.

Harris, Wilson. 1951. *Fetish.* Georgetown: Miniature Poets Series.

———. 1960; 1988. *Palace of the Peacock.* London: Faber and Faber.

———. 1964. "Kanaima." In *West Indian Narrative,* edited by Kenneth Ramchand, 196–205. London: Nelson and Sons.

———. 1967a. "The Question of Form and Realism in the West Indian Artist." In *Tradition, the Writer and Society: Critical Essays,* 19–22. London: New Beacon Books.

———. 1967b. *Tradition, The Writer and Society: Critical Essays.* London: New Beacon Books.

———. 1973. "A Talk on the Subjective Imagination." *New Letters* 40 (October): 40–41.

———. 1978. *Eternity to Season.* Reprint, London: New Beacon Books.

———. 1981a. "The Native Phenomenon." In *Explorations: A Selection of Talks and Articles 1966–1981*, edited by Hena Maes-Jelinek, 54. Aarhus: Dangaroo Press.

———. 1981b. "The Making of Tradition." In *Explorations: A Selection of Talks and Articles, 1966–1981*, edited by Hena Maes-Jelinek, 90. Aarhus: Dangaroo Press.

———. 1999a. "Amerindian Legacy." In *Selected Essays of Wilson Harris: The Unfinished Genesis of the Imagination – Expeditions into Cross-Culturality*, 167–75, edited by Andrew Bundy and Wilson Harris. London: Routledge.

———.1999b. "Profiles of Myth and the New World." In *Selected Essays of Wilson Harris: The Unfinished Genesis of the Imagination – Expeditions into Cross-Culturality*, edited by A.J. Bundy, 201–11. New York: Routledge.

———. 2003. *The Mask of the Beggar.* London: Faber and Faber.

———. 2006. *Ghost of Memory.* London: Faber and Faber.

———. (1974) 2014. *The Sleepers of Roraima & The Age of the Rainmakers.* Leeds: Peepal Tree Press.

Hartman, Saidiya. 2007. "Prologue: The Path of Strangers." In *Lose Your Mother: A Journey Along the Atlantic Slave Route.* New York: Farrar, Strauss and Giroux.

———. 1997. *Scenes of Subjection: Terror, Slavery, and Self-making in Nineteenth-century America.* New York: Oxford University Press.

Heinemann, Alessandra, and Dorte Verner. 2006. *Crime and Violence in Development: A Literature Review of Latin America and the Caribbean.* Washington, DC: World Bank.

Henry, Paget. 2000. *Caliban's Reason: Introducing Afro-Caribbean Philosophy.* New York: Routledge.

Herman, Judith. 2000. *Father-Daughter Incest.* Cambridge, MA: Harvard University Press.

Hirsch, Marianne. 2008. "The Generation of Postmemory." *Poetics Today* 29 (1): 103–28. https://doi.org/10.1215/03335372-2007-019.

Hodge, Merle. 1974. "The Shadow of the Whip." In *Is Massa Day Dead?*, edited by Orde Coombs, 177–81. Garden City: Anchor Doubleday.

Hopkinson, Nalo. 2000. *Midnight Robber.* New York: Warner Aspect.

Ismond, Patricia. 2007. "Woman as Race-Containing Symbol in Walcott's Poetry." *Journal of West Indian Literature* 8 (2) (October): 83–90.

James, Cynthia. 1994. "The Unknown Text." *World Literature Today* 68 (4): 758–64. http://www.jstor.org/stable/40150621.

James, Marlon. 2009. *The Book of Night Women.* New York: Riverhead Books.

———. 2014. *A Brief History of Seven Killings.* New York: Riverhead Books.

Janki, Melinda. 2018. "Water Is Everywhere in Georgetown, Guyana – Our Disrespect for It Will Kill Us." *The Nature of Cities*, 27 May. https://www.

thenatureofcities.com/2018/05/27/watereverywhere-georgetown-guyana-dis-respect-will-kill-us/.

Johnson, Kywnn. 2015. "How the Light Enters: Visualizing Absence and Continuity in the Jacmelian Ruinscape." PhD Diss., The University of the West Indies.

Johnson, Paul. 1999. "The Totalitarian Theocracy." In *The Civilization of Ancient Egypt*. New York: Harper Collins Publishers.

Jones, Adele B., ed. 2013. *Understanding Child Sexual Abuse: Perspectives from the Caribbean.* Palgrave. 2013.

Joes, Adele, Ena Trotman Jemmott, Priya Maharaj, and Hazel Da Breo. 2014. *An Integrated Systems Model for Preventative Child Sexual Abuse: Perspectives from the Caribbean.* London: Palgrave Macmillan.

Josph, Lorita. 2013. "Introduction." In *Understanding Child Sexual Abuse: Perspectives from the Caribbean*, edited by Adele Jones, 1–8. New York: Palgrave Macmillan.

Juneja, Renu. 1996. *Caribbean Transactions: West Indian Culture in Literature.* London: Macmillan Caribbean.

Keens-Douglas, Paul. 2012. "Story of a Storm – Ivan." Posted 10 January 2012, by Bajanbloom Bloom. YouTube 24:51. https://www.youtube.com/watch?v=N-2eS9_bhhc&t=4s.

Kincaid, Jamaica. 1994. "A Lot of Memory – An interview with Jamaica Kincaid." Interview by Moira Ferguson. *The Kenyon Review* 16 (1): 163–88.

King, Tiffany Lethabo. 2019. *The Black Shoals: Offshore Formations of Black and Native Studies.* Durham, NC: Duke University Press.

Knight, Franklin W. 2012. *The Caribbean: The Genesis of a Fragmented Nationalism.* New York: Oxford University Press.

LaCapra, Dominick. 2001. *Writing History, Writing Trauma.* Baltimore: Johns Hopkins University Press.

Lalla, Barbara. 1998. *Arch of Fire.* Kingston: Kingston Publishers.

Ladoo, Harold Sonny. 1972. *No Pain Like this Body.* Toronto: Anansi Press.

Lambert Peterson, Betsy Ann. 2013. "A Legal Perspective of Child Sexual Abuse in the Caribbean." In *Understanding Child Sexual Abuse: Perspectives from the Caribbean,* edited by Adele Jones. New York: Palgrave Macmillan.

Lamming, George. 1992. *Natives of My Person.* Ann Arbor: University of Michigan.

———. 2016. *Water with Berries.* Leeds: Peepal Tree Press.

Longshore, David. 2008. *Encyclopedia of Hurricanes, Typhoons and Cyclones*, new edition. New York: Checkmark Books.

Ludewig, Hermann. "Languages." In *The Literature of American Aboriginal Languages.* Sydney: Wentworth Press.

Maddock, J., and N. Larson. 1995. *Incestuous Families: An Ecological Approach to Understanding and Treatment*. New York: W.W. Norton.

Maes-Jelinek, Hena, and Bénédicte Ledent, eds. 2002. "Introduction: Approaching Wilson Harris's Creativity." In *Theatre of the Arts: Wilson Harris and the Caribbean*, xix. New York: Rodopi.

Maharaj, Rohan G., Paula Nunes, and Shamin Renwick. 2009. "Health risk behaviours among adolescents in the English-speaking Caribbean: A Review." *Child and Adolescent* Psychiatry and Mental Health 3 (1): article 10.

Mandelbrot, Benoit. 1967. "How Long Is the Coast of Britain? Statistical Self-Similarity and Fractional Dimension." *Science* 156 (3775): 636–38. https://doi.org/10.1126/science.156.3775.636.

Marshall, Paule. 1991. "To Da-Duh in Memoriam." In *Reena and Other Tales*. New York: Feminist Press.

Mbiti, John S. 1990. *African Religions & Philosophy*. Oxford: Heinemann.

McClure, Charlotte S. 1993. "Helen of the 'West Indies': History or Poetry of a Caribbean Realm." *Studies in the Literary Imagination* 26 (2): 7–20.

McCoppin, Rachel. 2015. "Emerging from the Earth." In *The Lessons of Nature in Mythology*, 22–43. Jefferson, NC: McFarland.

McKittrick, Katherine. 2013. "Plantation Futures." *Small Axe* 17 (3): 1–15.

———. 2015. *Sylvia Wynter: On Being Human as Praxis*. London and Durham, NC: Duke University Press.

Mohammed, Saira. 2015. "Of Monsters and Men: Perpetrator Trauma and Mass Atrocity." *Columbia Law Review* 115 (5) (June): 1157–216.

Mootoo, Shani. 1999. *Cereus Blooms at Night*. New York: Perennial.

Morgan, Paula. 2008. "Re-membering our Scattered Skeletons: Inscribing the *Zong* Massacre in Caribbean Literature." *Lucayos Journal of College of the Bahamas* no.1: 60–77. https://ufdcimages.uflib.ufl.edu/AA/00/06/67/36/00001/Lucayos%20Vol%201%202008.pdf.

———. 2014. *The Terror and the Time: Banal Violence and Trauma in Caribbean Discourse*. Kingston: University of the West Indies Press.

Morgan, Paula, and Valerie Youssef. 2006. *Writing Rage: Unmasking Violence through Caribbean Discourse*. Kingston: University of West Indies Press.

Morrison, Toni. 1988. *Beloved*. New York: Penguin Books.

———. 1984. "Rootedness: The Ancestor as Foundation." In *Black Women Writers (1950–1980): A Critical Evaluation*, edited by Mari Evans. Garden City: Anchor-Doubleday Press.

———. 1988. "Unspeakable Things Unspoken: The Afro American Presence in American Literature." Presented at the Tanner Lectures on Human Values,

7 October. https://tannerlectures.utah.edu/_resources/documents/a-to-z/m/morrison90.pdf.

———. 1999. "The Site of Memory." In *Inventing the Truth: The Art and Craft of Memoir*, edited by William Knowlton Zinsser. Boston: Houghton Mifflin.

Nagappan, Ramu. 2005. *Speaking Havoc: Social Suffering and the South Asian Narratives*. Seattle and London: University of Washington Press.

Naipaul, V.S. 1996. *The Middle Passage*. New York: Vintage Books.

———. 2001. *A House for Mr. Biswas*. New York: Vintage.

———. 2002 *Miguel Street*. Oxford: Heinemann Educational Books.

Nair, Supriya, 2013. *Pathologies of Paradise: Caribbean Detours*. Charlottesville: University of Virginia Press.

Nasta, Susheila. 1994. *Motherlands: Black Women's Writing from Africa, the Caribbean and South Asia*. New Brunswick, NJ: Rutgers University Press.

Nichols, Grace, 2020. *Passport to Here and There*. London: Bloodaxe Books.

Nixon, Rob. 2011. "Introduction." In *Slow Violence and the Environmentalism of the Poor*, 2–3. Cambridge, MA: Harvard University Press.

Olmos, Margarite Fernández, and Lizabeth Paravisini-Gebert. 2003. "Introduction." In *Creole Religions of the Caribbean: An Introduction from Vodou and Santería to Obeah and Espiritismo*, 1–19. New York: New York University Press.

———. 2022. "Historical Background." In *Creole Religions of the Caribbean: An Introduction from Vodou and Santería to Obeah and Espiritismo, 3rd ed.*, 23–36. New York: New York University Press.

Okunoye, Oyeniyi. 2007. "The Trope of the Ancestor in Contemporary Black Poetry." *Obsidian* 8 (2): 140–61. http://www.jstor.org/stable/44489264.

O'Reilly, Andrea, ed. 2010. *Encyclopedia of Motherhood*. Thousand Oaks: SAGE Publications.

Osotimehin, Babatunde. "Foreword." In *Motherhood in Childhood: Facing the Challenges of Adolescent Pregnancy*, edited by Nancy Williamson. UNFPA State of World Population 2013, (ii–iii). New York: UNFPA.

Pratt, Louise Mary. 2008. "Reinventing America II: The capitalist vanguard and the *exploratrices sociales*." In *Imperial Eyes: Travel Writing and Transculturation*, 2nd ed., 141–68. New York: Routledge.

Patterson, Anita. 2008. "Signifying Modernism in Wilson Harris's *Eternity to Season*." In *Race, American Literature and Transnational Modernisms*, 130–59. Cambridge: Cambridge University Press.

Puri, Shalini. 1999. "Canonized Hybridities, Resistant Hybridities: Chutney Soca, Carnival, and the Politics of Nationalism." In *Caribbean Romances: The Politics of Regional Representation*, edited by Belinda Edmondson, 12–39. Charlottesville: University of Virginia Press.

Rahim, Jennifer. 2011. "Figuring the Father in Contemporary Caribbean Fiction." *In a Fine Castle: Childhood and the Caribbean Imagi/Nation. Tout Moun* 1 (1): 3–17. https://journals.sta.uwi.edu/ojs/index.php/toutmoun/article/view/8638/7097.

———. 2013. "Issues and Developments in Caribbean Literary Theory and Criticism." In *Methods in Caribbean Research: Literature, Discourse, Culture*, edited by Barbara Lalla et al., 15–40. Kingston: University of the West Indies Press.

Rahming, Melvin. 2001. "Towards A Critical Theory of Spirit: The Insistent Demands of Erna Brodber's *Myal*." *Revista/Review Interamericana* 31 (1–4): 321–40.

Reavis, James A., Jan Looman, Kristina A. Franco, and Briana Rojas. 2013. "Adverse Childhood Experiences and Adult Criminality: How Long Must We Live Before We Possess Our Own Lives?" *The Permanente Journal* 17 (2): 44–48. https://doi.org/10.7812/tpp/12-072.

Renaud, Leighan., 2018. "Representations of Matrifocality in Contemporary Anglophone Caribbean Fiction." PhD diss., University of Leicester.

Regis, Hannah. 2021. "Trajectories of Resilience: Indigenous Healing Folkways in the Selected Short Stories of Wilson Harris." *American Studies* 60 (3): 61–75.

Reyes, Angelita. 2002. *Mothering Across Cultures: Postcolonial Representations.* Minneapolis: University of Minnesota Press.

Rhys, Jean. 1966. *Wide Sargasso Sea*. London: Penguin.

Rock, Letnie. 2013. "Research on Child Sexual Abuse: Caribbean and International Perspectives." In *Understanding Child Sexual Abuse: Perspectives from the Caribbean*, edited by Adele Jones, 145–67. New York: Palgrave Macmillan.

Rohlehr, Gordon. 2007. "Folk Research: Fossil or Living Bone?" In *Transgression, Transition, Transformation: Essays in Caribbean Culture*, 374–84. San Juan: Lexicon Press.

———. 2013. "From Apocalypse to Awakening: Interviews with Gordon Rohlehr." Interviews by Paula Morgan. *Tout Moun: Caribbean Journal of Cultural Studies* 2 (1): 1–16.

Ruskin, John. 1903. "Of Water, As Painted by Turner." In *The Works of John Ruskin*, edited by E.T. Cook and Alexander Wedderburn, 537–73. Published online by Cambridge University Press (2015). https://www.cambridge.org/core/books/works-of-john-ruskin/18CD37902BB04AE3B46403991A501A50.

Scott, Lawrence. 2004. *Night Calypso*. London: Allison and Busby.

———. 2015. "The Wedding Photograph." In *The Haunted Tropics: Caribbean Ghost Stories*, edited by Martin Munroe. Kingston: University of the West Indies Press.

Senior, Olive. 1991. *Working Miracles: Women's Lives in the English-speaking Caribbean*. Oxford: James Currey Publishers.

———. 1994. *Gardening in the Tropics*. Toronto: McClelland and Stewart.

———. 2017. *The Pain Tree*. Leeds: Peepal Tree Press.

Stewart, Mart. 2006. "Slavery and the Origins of African American Environmentalism." In *To Love the Wind and the Rain: African Americans and Environmental History*, edited by D. Glave and M. Stoll, 10–20. Pittsburgh: University of Pittsburgh Press.

Seymour, Arthur. 1965. "The Legend of Kaieteur." In *Selected Poems*, 37. Georgetown: BG Lithographic.

Simey, T.S. 1946. *Welfare and Planning in the West Indies*. Oxford: Clarendon Press.

Stitt, Jocelyn Fenton. 2007. "Gendered Legacies of Romantic Nationalism in the Works of Michelle Cliff." *Small Axe: A Caribbean Journal of Criticism* 11 (3): 52–72. https://doi.org/10.1215/-11-3-52.

Thiele, Verena, and Maria Drews. 2009. *Reclaiming Home, Remembering Motherhood, Rewriting History: African American and Afro-Caribbean Women's Literature*. Newcastle upon Tyne: Cambridge Scholars Publishing.

Thomas, Deborah A. 2011. *Exceptional Violence: Embodied Citizenship in Transnational Jamaica*. Durham, NC: Duke University Press.

Torres-Saillant, Silvio. 1997. *Caribbean Poetics: Toward an Aesthetic of West Indian Literature*. Cambridge: Cambridge University Press.

United Nations Children's Fund. 2006. *A Study of Child Vulnerability in Barbados, St Lucia and St Vincent and the Grenadines*. Bridgetown: UNICEF Barbados and the Eastern Caribbean. https://bettercarenetwork.org/sites/default/files/attachments/A%20Study%20of%20Child%20Vulnerability.pdf

———. 2007. *Child Abuse: The Number One Threat to Caribbean Childhood*. Bridgetown: UNICEF Barbados and the Eastern Caribbean. https://www.unicef.org/reports.

———. 2013. *Sexual Violence against Children in the Caribbean: UNICEF Report 2012*. Bridgetown: UNICEF Barbados and Eastern Caribbean Office. https://www.unicef.org/reports.

United Nations Children's Fund, Adele Jones, and Ena Trotman Jemmott. 2009. *A Study on Perceptions of, Attitudes to, and Opinions on Child Sexual Abuse in the Eastern Caribbean*. Bridgetown: UNICEF and University of Huddersfield.

United Nations Population Fund. 2019. *One Pager on Youth Demographics*. New York: UNFPA.

Walcott, Derek. 1992. *Collected Poems 1948–1984*. London: Faber and Faber.

———. 2014. *Omeros*. Farrar, Straus and Giroux.

Warren, Karen J. 1990. "The Power and the Promise of Ecological Feminism." *Environmental Ethics* 12 (2): 125–46.

Watson, Danielle, Lee Michael Johnson, Nathan Pino, and Paula Morgan. 2018.

"The Interface Between Exercise of State Power and Personal Powerlessness: A Study of Police Perceptions of Factors Impacting Professional Practices." *Police Practice and Research* 19 (5): 458–71. https://doi.org/10.1080/15614263.2018.1443270.

———. 2019. "Police Perceptions of Residents in a High-Crime Area in Trinidad and Tobago: Community Framing and Crime Wars." *Criminology & Criminal Justice* 21 (1): 3–20. https://doi.org/10.1177/1748895819858372.

Williamson, Nancy. 2013. *Motherhood in Childhood: Facing the Challenges of Adolescent Pregnancy (UNFPA State of World Population 2013).* New York: United Nations Population Fund.

Winer, Lise, ed. 2008. *Dictionary of the English / Creole of Trinidad and Tobago.* Montreal: McGill-Queens University Press.

Wynter, Sylvia. 1970. "Jonkonnu in Jamaica: Towards the Interpretation of Folk Dance as a Cultural Process." *Jamaica Journal* 4 (2): 34–48.

———. 1971. "Novel and History, Plot and Plantation." *Savacou* 5: 95–102.

———. 1995. "Beyond the Categories of the Master Conception: The Counter-doctrine of the Jamesian Poesies." In *C.L.R. James's Caribbean*, edited by Paget Henry and Paul Buhle, 63–91. Durham, NC: Duke University Press.

Index

www.ingramcontent.com/pod-product-compliance
Lightning Source LLC
LaVergne TN
LVHW091250110826
845146LV00002BA/794

9789766580681